Disclaimer

This novel is a work of fiction. Although the events mentioned in the book are of a real nature, the novel is fictional. Unless otherwise indicated, all the names, characters, businesses, places, events, and incidents in this book are either the product of the author's imagination or used in a fictitious manner. Any resemblance to actual persons, living or dead, or actual events is purely coincidental. To protect the privacy of certain individuals, the names and identifying details have been changed.

THE DEEP STATE GAMES

Tales of the treacherous and inhumane games played by the world's rich and powerful people who control the governments in various countries.

SIGMA TRAMPS

ISBN 979-8-89673-370-6

Contents

Foreword

Chinese general and strategist Sun Tzu had said in 500 BCE, "All warfare is based primarily on deception of an enemy. Fighting on a battlefield is the most primitive way of making a war. There is no art higher than to destroy your enemy without a fight - by subverting anything of value in enemy's country."

Every power that has aspired for global control has always understood this and has worked on perfecting the art of subversion. Marcus Jullius Cicero, a formidable statesman in ancient Rome captured it succinctly when he said, " A nation can survive its fools and even the ambitious. But it cannot survive treason from within… A traitor rots the soul of a nation; he works secretly and unknown in the night to undermine the pillars of the city. He infects the body politic so that it can no longer resist."

The American Deep State that has its roots in the late 19th century secret society that aimed at widening the circle of influence of the trans-Atlantic, Anglo-Saxon power centers, England and America, has today evolved into a massive behemoth with immeasurable power, that brings about major upheavals in the world, almost at will.

They have taken the art of subversion to a new height by engineering regime change operations through movements that are powered by misinformation and subterfuge. They function through a web of organizations and institutions with seemingly angelic aims like promotion of democracy and protection of environment. They work relentlessly and ruthlessly with single minded focus on promoting American interest at any cost.

Unraveling their complex, multilayered structure and methodology is challenging to say the least. In 'The Deep State Games' Sigma Tramps has handled this challenge with aplomb. His authentic research and racy style of storytelling have created a novel that is disturbing but also unputdownable.

His readers know that Sigma Tramps has perfected the art of creating a heady mix of fact and fiction. 'The Deep State Games' will certainly take this reputation a few notches higher.

January 17, 2025,

Abhijit Joag
Author of Best Seller Books:
Asatyamev Jayate; Termites, Brandnama 1 & 2

foreword

Till I read the Book, 'Deep State' for me was, hazy, complex, somewhat abstract, happening in a distant land and importantly peddled by journalists with an agenda.

The Author, Sigma Tramps (AKA Ravi Joshi) lifts the veil, puts the puzzle together and demolishes the perceptions-piece by piece, with solid Facts, micro details, deep insights, relatable evidence and names plus characters who suddenly appear so real. The author uncovers the veil on secretive, deep-rooted plots happening in different parts of the Globe -all directed towards spreading chaos, taking control and quintessentially anti-establishment. It shows the dangers and threats in our backyard

The machinations of people and characters -*Ross, Alexei, Martin, Sergei, Lemur, Carson...... ...and Mehul* ...sends a chill up the spine. The phrases- 'If you can't have it, break it', 'Diffusion is the instrument of statecraft', 'Educate, Organize, agitate' epitomises destruction, and evil. However, the Garb remains the 'Global ' issues of Sustainability, Freedom, LGBT or even topical ones -Palestine, Kashmir....

The author meticulously traces the various events, developments and connects the Global Dots, seamlessly. He helps unfold the real intents of Deep State.

I found the pages on British lies, American interests in Ukraine, The multiple secretive trips of Mehul and his anti-state Agenda, very revealing.

The Author brings the battleground and the theatre to our living rooms. His description and visualisation are like a *Movie in Prose*.

'Deep State' is Anti Humanity, anti-civilization and downright evil.

But this Book on 'The Deep State Games' is very well researched, so relevant, fact based, engrossing and just *Unputdownable*.

January 17, 2025,

Ramachandra Rao
Senior Leadership Role
Automotive Industry

Foreword

This is an **"unprecedented"** time. Middle East has erupted once again. Israel, post Hamas' barbaric attack on 07 Oct 23 (Jewish religious day), has wiped out Hamas and Hezbollah leadership. Gaza has been razed; thousands of Palestinians killed. Israel's missile target are now the Houthis. Shite regime of Iran, patron of all these "H" proxy groups; Hamas (Gaza based Sunni militant group), Hezbollah (Lebanon based Shia militant group), and Houthis (Yemen based Shia militant group), has been subdued. Its key ally, Syrian President has fled to Russia. Assads, the Alawites, regime ruling Syria since 1971 has come to an abrupt end. Sunni revolutionary group HTH has captured power now. Syria's till date staunch supporter Russia is entangled in Ukraine war since Feb 22. Russians have lost their mediterranean Naval base, Tartus, in Syria. Turkey is attacking the Kurds, located near its Syrian border. Sunnis dominated Muslim countries like Saudi Arab, Egypt, UAE are watching from the fence the unfolding scenario in Syria, being directed from behind the scenes by the US **Deep State.**

The present global scenario is **"unprecedented"**. The fast-shifting geopolitical dynamics in the Middle East and prolonged ongoing Russia-Ukraine war, are reshaping international relations, security, and economics. The Ukraine war has disrupted Russian energy supplies especially of Europe.

It has impacted the global food security as Ukraine is one of the world's largest grain exporters. The war has pushed energy and food prices high and have sent the inflation soaring in Europe. Apart from gloomy economic scenario, there is political instability in France and Germany, the EU's two biggest and most influential players. It spells trouble for an already ailing European economy. But the biggest headache for Europe is the President-elect Trump, whose campaign pledge is to impose 10% tariffs on European goods and proportionately increase their share and resources for NATO. Till now, Europe was enjoying the benefits of being aligned with the Democrats favoured US **Deep State**.

Yes, the current global era is historically **"unprecedented"**. In aftermath of Corona epidemic and zero-COVID policy, China's economy has nosedived, its world supply chain got disrupted. The debt predator, intended to spread its tentacles using BRI world over, is suffering debt crisis of worst kind back home. *Karma* has hit back. High corporate and local government debt, coupled with real estate crisis, low foreign investment, sluggish exports, weak currency, record youth unemployment, shrinking labor force and rapidly aging population, are risking its economic stability. It's expansionist agenda of land / island grabbing has been halted. It's sweeping purge of high-ranking PLA officers in military is going on unabated. And all these have ruined China's dream of becoming *numero-uno* Superpower. Incidentally, whether it is Democrat's supported Deep State or Republican's, both today converge on the idea to restrain and constrain China in realizing the Chinese plan of becoming Global leader. The present Chinese super economic status is courtesy US help and support provided some four decades before. An attempt to undo its *Karma* by the US **Deep State** is now on.

Ongoing multiple military war, terror conflicts, economic turbulences, and the emerging climate changes threat are reshaping the dynamically shifting world order. However, amidst this global gloomy picture, **India** remains a bright spot, with GDP projected to be around 6% to 7%, as one of the fastest-growing world's economies. Young population, largest digital economy, booming IT and service sectors, large infrastructure projects, including roads, ports, & railways, along with a focus on renewable energy, are expected to boost its long-term growth. Even India's foreign policy has been commendable. Maintaining a delicate balancing act, it has managed to preserve its "Strategic Autonomy" along with historically cherished foreign policy core principles like Neighborhood First, Look East / Act East, and Multilateralism. India successfully employed its soft power initiatives like vaccine diplomacy, multi trade agreements and various cultural exchanges all over the globe. G20 summit theme under its Presidency was "One Earth, One Family, One Future", based upon its age-old belief of *"Vasudhaiva Kutumbakam"*. India championed voice of Global South and inducted African Union as a G-20 Member. However, India's advocacy for multi-civilizational, plural ideologies based international system was viewed by few as voice of emerging futuristic superpower and is not being liked by the **Deep States**.

In the **'Deep State Games'** the master storyteller Mr. Ravi Joshi, has forged his raw ideas after tempering them with factual facts and has then masterly crafted, with his anvil & hammer, this absorbing novel. How **"Deep State"**; the shadowy, secretive proxy group within a government operate independently, exercising power without accountability to elected officials or the public, has been very vividly explained. The novel starts on the backdrop of Hamas attack of October 7th and the massacre in Israel.

The US Deep States in the name of saving democracy, human rights, and social justice went on implementing *'project regime change'*, famously known as *'color revolution'*. Former US Presidents George Bush and Obama embracing *'neoconservatives'* ethos, gave the Deep State virtual *carte blanche* to carry out color revolutions around the world. The template based on **"Dictatorship to Democracy"** of Gene Sharp, which is a practical guide to nonviolent resistance, detailing strategies and methods for overthrowing totalitarian regimes were liberally used. These techniques were successfully used against the former Soviet Union republics, for example, ***Rose Revolution*** in Georgia (2003) & ***Orange Revolution*** in Ukraine (2005). If the local populace couldn't be organized effectively to overthrow the targeted authoritarian leaders of the country, as the fallback option, armed radical groups to seize power by violence, using emotive narratives were mustered, as recently seen in Bangladesh. Even, unhesitatingly these templates and toolkit are deployed to derail democratically elected government in the largest democratic country of world, **India**, and instances like Shaheen Bagh etc. are well nuanced in the novel. Pertinent to note that these techniques would eventually be used in ***#BlackLivesMatter*** agitation to target Donald Trump during his previous presidency.

In **'The Deep State Games'**, Ravi has outlined how Deep States project are funded. It is interesting to note that generally funding for *'project regime change'* is distributed through third-party NGOs and is often coordinated through USAID (a component of the State Department that works closely with both the DoD and the CIA). 'National Endowment for

Democracy', a curious entity that is funded through USAID, and plays vital role in channelizing the funds. As explained in the novel, the **Open Society Foundations,** tax-exempt organizations of George Soros orchestrate such activities and pump money into various similar organizations that are enlisted all across the globe, in the name of supporting democracy, human rights, and social justice. They indulge in activism for reasons that are often more commercial than strictly political. But since these entities on paper operate within legal boundary of the host nation, it is difficult for a democratic nation to bar them, until and unless they are caught for illegal methods of funding and for anti-national activities.

'The Deep State Games', is in fact the third novel in series of trilogy. In the first novel of the sequel **'The Inevitable',** Ravi has narrated that China using troika cocktail of: "Technology, Trade and Terrorism" would unhesitatingly use it for the furtherance of its expansionist agenda so to gain superpower status; even at the cost of bringing world on the brink of WW III. In his second absorbing thriller **'The Espionage Games'** keeping the last four decade of Afghanistan geo-political scenario as the backdrop setting, he has sketched Espionage Games played in most deceptive, disguised and dangerous manner by various Intelligence agencies. But one could sense that mastermind lurking behind all these **Games** were the **Deep States** of various countries. It is **they** who plotted the sinister plans, funded it and got it implemented through their specific Int Agencies supported puppets. However, in the final novel **'The Deep State Games',** the **Deep States** are there, out in open. They are here to orchestrate for their three objectives: *Global Geo-Political Control; Global Wealth Control; Generate Proxy Wars.*

Enjoy and get educated by reading the real-life treacherous saga **'The Deep State Games'** characterized through fictional characters coincidentally that may resemble real life characters, sometime.

December 31, 2024,

Air Vice Marshal Pranay Sinha, VSM (Retd)
Ex-Commandant SDI, Indian Air Force
Strategic Advisor, IIT Mandi, HP

Introduction

"Democracy" is essentially a Western concept. It basically boils down to "As long as you behave according to our rules, our regulations, and our dictum, you are Democratic," and the Democracy is "Safe" in your country. If not, Democracy is in "Danger" in your country, and we will adopt all the necessary methods and resources at our disposal to bring "Democracy" to your country... even if it means we have to kill a few thousand people and resort to destruction of property in your country. This "We" consists of not just the Western governments in power but also those who "control" them from behind the curtain.... The Deep State. And then there are of course those "enemy within the country" who are ready to become the puppets of the Deep State to dance to the tunes of their Deep State masters.

A Deep State is a type of governance made up of potentially secret and unauthorized networks of power operating independently of a state's political leadership in pursuit of their own agenda and goals. In popular usage, the term carries overwhelmingly negative connotations. Deep State exists in every country... operating more predominantly in some than others.

According to the Journalist Robert F. Worth, "The expression 'Deep State' had originated in Turkey in the 1990s, where the military colluded with drug traffickers and hit men to wage a dirty war against Kurdish insurgents". Professor Ryan Gingeras

(Professor in the Department of National Security Affairs at the Naval Postgraduate School) wrote that the Turkish term Derin Devlet "colloquially speaking" refers to "'criminal' or 'rogue' element'rogue' elements that have somehow muscled their way into power."

The Deep State refers to the "unelected men" who hold secret power and command over the elected government, who are not accountable and who form a shadowy part of the government to push their secret agendas, at times blackmailing the government. It is something that hides in plain sight... but most common people cannot see and connect the dots.... like the hybrid of wall street, corporate America, and national security (Military Industrial complex). Money, corporate and political control.

As American author Mike Lofgren puts it, "Secret and unaccountable deep state floats freely above the gridlock between both ends of Pennsylvania avenue is the paradox of American government." (Pennsylvania Avenue is a major road in Washington, D.C. that runs through the city's central section, connecting the White House at one end and the US Capitol at the other).

According to an American political conspiracy theory, the Deep State does not consist of the entire government. The deep state is a clandestine hybrid network of members of the federal government, law enforcement agencies... National security + Homeland Security + Pentagon+ State Dept + Treasury + Justice Dept. working in conjunction with high-level financial (Wall Street) and industrial entities (Raytheon, Lockheed Martin etc. Defense Manufacturers) their Contractors, various big private enterprises and Silicon Valley leaders, to exercise power alongside or within the elected United States government. The irony is that all these government agencies are coordinated by the Executive office of the POTUS via the National Security Council. Certain key areas of the judiciary belong specifically to the Deep State such as Foreign Intelligence Surveillance Court.

Washington, D.C. is the most important "Node" of the Deep State... but there are others. The other one is the Wall Street... which one may call as the Ultimate Owner of the Deep State and its strategies. Over the course of the WWII the US built a military industrial machine the world had never conceived before. It could do anything from constructing airfields in Arctic Alaska to building a war winning weapon... the Atomic Bomb which became the conception point of the Deep State. The nuclear weapons were the initiation of the key characteristics the Deep State possesses today... a penchant for secrecy, lack of democratic accountability and extravagant costs. Instilling FEAR became The Tool of choice for the Deep State's prime tactics... what came to be known as Truman Doctrine as President Truman had described "Totalitarian Regime" ... "Scare the hell out of the people!!!"

So, the world is ruled by Organizations, Corporations who have their selfish interest at heart and also by the individuals who own these organizations or corporations... and has his / her own vicious ambition at heart. It is they who control our politicians and our policy makers.

It is not just the US, but several other countries like Russia, UK have their own deep state who call the shots. A classic example is that of Pakistan... where the Military and the ISI control everything and the government is just a puppet dancing to the tunes of the Armed Forces and the ISI. The Chinese Deep State is the Chinese Communist Party- CCP... who runs the show. "Fear" is the key element of their modus operandi. Every Chinese person forms a part of their deep state… willingly or unwillingly.

The International Deep State has been ruling Indian politics even before India's independence. Immediately post-independence, it was the Russians (KGB) who pulled all the strings. The then lady Prime Minister of India even had a code name assigned to her by KGB. Post mid-1991, the US took over the controls and the Western powers held a sway over India.

India is a classic case of literate and illiterate people who always believed in "worshipping" the "White Demigods" from the Western Countries… and never used their "Common Sense" to understand the hidden agenda of these demigods.

As the developed world's population is shrinking, India would be the world's leading source of skilled and disciplined manpower. Therefore, an amenable, malleable, and inexperienced leader in India would be an ideal candidate to further the Western agenda.

The Western Deep State has been unable to digest India's improved relationships with major powers in the West, the Middle East, East, and Southeast Asia. Both China and the Western Deep State see India's rise as a major world power and a promising "world's leading GDP contributor" as a threat to their agendas. Sabotaging the Indian development program is the only way to stop the unstoppable India.

This can be achieved via corrupt Indian politicians, particularly via the one who had Dynastic rule for decades… who at any cost would like to return to power, even if it meant weakening India… and the left liberal Indians (like Sunita Vishwanath or Mukulika Bannerjee or Angana Chatterji etc.) who live overseas and consider themselves as "literate liberals" … supporting these Indian Dynasties via their own vicious networks and condemning India's current "Hindutva" centered ruling party. The US-based "Deep State" sharks like HLF, OSF and other famous "Philanthropists" provide billions of US Dollars to such Indian "Charitable, Socio-Cultural Foundations" to advance their causes in India.

The Europe-based Disinfo Lab had published an 85-page analysis of foreign influence in the Indian general elections 2024 — The Invisible Hand. Among many, the report blamed two organizations and one individual in particular for peddling a specific narrative — the US-based Henry Luce Foundation (HLF), Open State Foundation, and the French Indologist and political scientist Christophe Jaffrelot.

It is no surprise that Christophe Jaffrelot's brainchild 'Caste Census' in India had now become part of the Opposition… Indian National Congress Party's election manifesto. Both the Opposition Party and Christophe Jaffrelot exploited the fault lines in the Indian society and expected Indians to fall for it. Christophe Jaffrelot's other project has been 'Muslims in a Time of Hindu Majoritarianism.' In addition to others, Christophe Jaffrelot was being funded by HLF.

HLF has also funded many other anti-India projects to paint India in a bad light — 'Hindu Nationalism: From Ethnic Identity to Authoritarian Repression,' 'Religion, Citizenship, and Belonging in India,' 'Religion-as-Ethnicity and the Emerging Hindu Vote in India,' are some of their funded "anti-India" projects. Among many "anti-India" writers, California-based activists Angana P. Chatterji and Rutgers academic Audrey Truschke are the prominent ones in spreading the anti-India narrative and are funded by HLF.

George Soros's Open State Foundation has also funded many anti-India foundations and individuals. Prominent among them are Canadian activist Ricken Patel's Namati Foundation and Delhi-based Center for Policy Research (CPR) in addition to the usual culprit Christophe Jaffrelot. Soros uses his Billions to work behind the scenes to manipulate the society at large. He has found a way to influence "how the laws are enforced" in shifting the fabric of the society without ever changing a single law. He has systematically undermined US authority and manipulated the global systems to push his own agenda. Soros manipulated the US's Department of Justice to go against his personal opponents working in US politics. He has backed and boosted so-called "progressive" District Attorneys who were ready to support his ideas and policies which would eventually weaken the society and bring instability. These D.A.s were lenient in enforcing the laws and were soft on the crimes and criminals thereby weakening the effect of the laws.

Not just in the US but globally too, Soros has been pulling strings behind the scenes in various countries meddling in other countries' internal affairs… under the pretext of democracy, equality, and social justice. However, his entire intention has been to weaken the effect of the law and order and create chaotic conditions to gain control.

Indian Parliament's Opposition Leader's frequent international tours are often loaded with "close door meetings" with people (like ISI linked Pakistani, Bangladeshi, Chinese) or organizations (like ISI) which are "anti-India." He often bad mouths India in public during his overseas tours… which is immediately picked up as a divine gospel by the Western Media which is on the payroll of the American Deep State. In the UK, that part is effectively carried out by the BBC and institutions like Oxford University.

The US Deep State and the deep state-owned Western Media is hell-bent on destroying India's image as a democracy and declaring it as an electoral dictatorship. That would give all US companies a moral platform to withdraw all FDI and the Indian economy would plunge, making the current government powerless and put the Dynasty back in the seat of power. However, the world political fabric has become like a noose around the neck of the US political leadership and even the Deep State has started having concerns about it.

The Deep State, whether in the US or in other countries will continue its operations sine-die. New people will join the bandwagon to exercise total control over Global Money… via acquisition of the "Real-World Assets" and total control over all the governments globally.

The basic objectives of the Deep State…or the people who are orchestrating it…is three-fold.

1. *Global Geo-Political Control…. Create and maintain anarchy in various countries in the world and get benefited by driving their own specific agendas.*

2. *Global Wealth Control…. Capture and get ownership of the Real-World Assets…like Agriculture Fields, Mines of minerals and Rare Earth, Sweet Water Bodies, crucial Seaports etc. and*

3. *Generate Proxy Wars…. Initiate wars across the globe and keep them running as long as possible.*

Historically, the Deep States existed but in various forms and shapes. They originated …perhaps prehistorically, then during the era of Greek, the Romans etc. … then came the era of Great Britain, France, Sapin etc. Now it is the age of Deep States of US, China etc.

Efforts have been made while writing this book to try to capture the real-life treacherous functioning of the Deep State via a fictional story and fictional characters. Although the story in this book takes place in the US, the events described could happen in any other country as well… perchance it may already be taking shape somewhere in the world.

Sigma Tramps

November 15, 2024

New York, USA

October 11, 2023; 11.00 AM

The brunette walking past the window with her hair dancing in tune with her rhythmic walk was quite pleasing to the eyes of Jerry, who was physically sitting in the class attending the lecture of Prof. Matthew Chambers but mentally and emotionally was walking alongside the brunette.

"Must find out who the heck she is," Jerry thought to himself as the brunette disappeared around the corner, carrying herself with great aplomb.

"Tomorrow we shall begin discussing the Deep State and its functions and its global effects. The assignment for today's topic is on the board, ensure your submissions by tomorrow morning at Nine Hundred Hours," Jerry's mind jumped back to the class as he heard Prof. Matthew giving his departing instructions in a military fashion.

"Deep State, eh? Must be interesting… let's see what the General has to say," Jerry quipped to himself. He was in awe of Prof. Matthews because not only was he brilliant, highly educated with some exceptional accolades conferred on him, but he was like a military General – sharp, strict, meticulous, to the point. Jerry had received the back end of Prof. Matthew's stick in his very first assignment.

Now outside the class, Jerry wanted to go around searching for the brunette, but he was distracted from his mission as his mobile vibrated inside his hip pocket. Cursing loudly, he looked at the caller… "Dad."

"Now, what the heck does he want?" Jerry muttered to himself as he answered the phone.

"Yes, dad?"

"Nothing, Mr. Jerry Carson. Just wanted to remind you to at least send a message to your mum if you are too busy to call her on her birthday. It is today, by the way." There was a hint of anger and frustration in dad's voice.

"Yes, of course, dad. I was planning to call her later today," Jerry bluffed because he had forgotten about his mum's birthday completely.

"Yeah… whatever!" scoffed dad, and the phone went dead.

Thus far, Jerry had done everything that his parents did not want him to do. Jerry's parents owned a flourishing business – a publishing house – and were well renowned for publishing a range of categories, including promotional titles, instant books, and classic works of literature. Recently, they had diversified into publishing books on boating, sailing, and sea adventures, as well as publishing crime fiction, mysteries, noir, thrillers, and spy novels. The old man had started out from scratch and had built up the business, hoping that his only son would one day take the mantle on his shoulders and run the business.

But Jerry had no such interest. He wanted to tour the world, meet people from different cultures, beliefs, traditions… understand them… Enjoy life.

"Understand them and then what?" Jerry's dad exploded when Jerry was outlining his future plans. "How are you going to earn a living… who the hell is going to pay for your travels?"

"I dunno… but I guess I will find somebody to sponsor me." Jerry's vague answer had angered his dad so much that he stormed out of his room, banging the door behind him.

Jerry was exceptional at studies and had good grades. Peer pressure was something that Jerry could not handle.

"For a guy like you, Journalism is the best field, Jerry, considering your dad's business is not your cup of tea," his friends had told him. "But do you know what, Journalism is like an ocean and unless you have a focus on some subject, you will not be able to excel. So, choose a subject which does not have a death."

"Death?"

"Yeah… like politics. It has no end. As long as human beings are alive, there will be politics. It is global, universal, and eternal. So, do your undergraduate degree in Political Science and then do your master's in Journalism. That is the best combo, Jerry, that you can find."

Jerry was not particularly fond of Political Science, but there were no other interesting subjects that he could find which would gel perfectly with Journalism. He had applied to various universities with the customary "essay," and when he was selected at the prestigious Columbia University for a Major and Concentration in Political Science, he happily accepted. His parents had debated but finally gave up.

"At least he will be graduating from Columbia," his mother had tried to pacify his dad.

"We shall see when he does that," Jerry's dad had very little confidence in his son. "How does that help him in running our publishing business?" Jerry's dad had retorted to Jerry's mother.

"I will. Also, I will do my master's too from the Graduate School of Journalism at Columbia. You will see. I will ensure that I get a scholarship," Jerry had tried to defend his stand.

"We shall see when that happens. Right now, I am shelling out the dough for your education, son. Remember that," dad retorted. "Journalism… my foot… he can't even write one sentence properly. Big talk," he fumed.

"Well, I did write the essay… didn't I?" Jerry tried to retaliate.

"Yeah… I know how you managed it, Mr. Journalist. I keep my eyes open," his dad had retorted.

So far, Jerry had been maintaining his grades and had not given him any chance to complain.

"I dunno, when the old man is going to cool down," Jerry mused to himself as he looked at the cell phone in his hand… It was lunchtime. "Time for a bite before the next sermon," Jerry muttered, shrugged his shoulders, and started walking towards the Blue Jave Café at Everett Library.

"Just enough time to have a panini and a soup. But must find out who the heck that brunette is."

Frankfurt, Germany

October 12, 2023; 06.30 PM

Sitting in his plush office in the Bankenviertel, the central business district in Frankfurt, where many of the largest banks in Germany, like Deutsche Bank, DZ Bank, Commerzbank and Helaba, have their corporate headquarters, Ludolf Hoffmann was looking out of the window lost in his thoughts. Dusk was descending, and the scene from his office on the 35th floor down below on the streets appeared like ants crawling systematically all over.

Ludolf had just finished meeting with the heads of all his companies and had no specific plans for the evening. Although Ludolf had his corporate office in Bankenviertel, close to the financial market, his companies were spread all over Germany and overseas. The total turnover was close to a hundred billion euros.

Germany's main economic hubs were in the large metropolitan regions such as the Ruhr, Munich, Bremen, and Stuttgart metropolitan areas which had been known for high tech and automotive manufacturing. The Rhine-Neckar region was the center of the chemicals and IT industry, while Frankfurt am Main was the financial center.

The first venture LH Raumfahrt, Ludolf had founded in 1981 in Bremen, was a private sector aerospace outfit. The company had eventually become one of the leading manufacturers of satellite radar and space components and, a few years back successfully entered the long-range missiles segment. The missile segment produced a broad portfolio of air & missile defense systems, precision weapons, radars, and command and control systems, which could deliver end-to-end solutions to detect, track, and engage threats. The segment excelled in producing tactical rocket systems for ground forces, air-launched rockets for aerial engagements, and space launch vehicles for satellite deployment and exploration missions. The division also included systems such as air and missile defense systems, tactical missiles, and precision strike weapon systems, Terminal High Altitude Area defense, Multiple Launch Rocket System, Precision Strike missile, Joint Air-to-Surface Standoff missile, Long-Range Anti-Ship missile, and hypersonic strike weapons.

Windenergieanlage was the next venture of Ludolf. Its core business was to operate and maintain wind farms. The company's activities spanned globally, with wind farms and solar farms not only in various European countries like Belgium, Finland, Sweden, France, Italy, Poland, Portugal, Spain, etc., but in Canada, Chile, and Croatia as well. This was established in Mönchengladbach. A few years ago, Ludolf had expanded the unit's outreach into space... as an integration with his LH Raumfahrt company, developing solar panels for the International Space Station and other satellites.

Immuno-Biotronik was Ludolf's third venture... now a leading global biotechnology company that pioneered multiple breakthrough innovations. The company was a provider of biological therapeutics derived from human plasma. The company specialized primarily in the areas of clinical immunology, hematology, and intensive care medicine. It had also developed an advanced pipeline of potential novel therapies across neurology, neuropsychiatry, specialized immunology, and rare diseases.

Ants reminded Ludolf of his grandfather in Villa General Belgrano, Argentina who had often used the term "crush them like ants" when he used to narrate the stories of his youth to Ludolf.

Thought of his grandfather took Ludolf back to Argentina. After all, he was born there. For all practical reasons, Argentina had been his home. Although born in Bariloche, Argentina's other German-dominated town like Villa General Belgrano, Ludolf had gone to live with his grandparents at the tender age of three because of the early demise of his mother. Ludolf's father, unable to take care of the kid, had decided to marry again, and his second wife had refused to take care of Ludolf.

Blue eyes and blonde hair, Ludolf was the typical "Sonnenkinder," literally translated as "child of the sun"... pure Aryan German blood as Ludolf's grandparents would often say. By the age of ten, Ludolf had practically learned by heart his grandfather's life history... virtually lived through the WWII era.

Ludolf's grandfather, Heinz Bauer, General der Waffengattung... SS-Obergruppenführer and General der Waffen-SS... was a Lieutenant General rank officer... a second-in-command of the dreaded Waffen-SS (The Waffen-SS was the combat branch of the Nazi Party's paramilitary Schutzstaffel (SS) organization. Its formations mainly included men from Nazi Germany).

Heinz, who was handpicked due to his pure lineage and trained as a devout SS officer, was also indoctrinated with the idea of the elimination of Jews from the fatherland. He hated Jews and was quite merciless while dealing with them. Heinz rose through the ranks very quickly. By the end of 1943, he had already become the second-in-command of the Waffen-SS. He was just twenty-eight then.

As the war was closing in on Germany and the defeat was evident, Heinz and many German high-ranking militias had escaped Germany and traveled to Argentina with their loot. A Nazi sympathizer Austrian Bishop had helped the German militias to get "Protected Passports" issued by the international committee of the Red Cross. The escaping militias had taken shelter in the Capuchin Monastery and then the Franciscan Monastery before boarding the ships for South America.

Heinz was contacted by the CIC of the US Counter intelligence Corps. The CIC had sought to recruit former Gestapo and SD/SS members as informants to work for US intelligence. Some CIC members looked for a share of the loot. Heinz's CIC contact was more interested in the loot than anything else. In exchange for a part of their loot, the CIC contact allowed Heinz and a couple of German Army officers and their families to escape via a U-Boat.

During the underwater journey of almost 20 days from the southern shore of Italy to Argentina, Heinz, who was unmarried at the time, had fallen in love with the wife of another German officer. The German officer was in his early forties, but his wife was quite young. Heinz and the officer's wife became attracted to each other and decided to get married once ashore.

Undetected by the Allied navy, the U-Boat had finally reached its destination. Within ten days of arrival, the German officer was found dead, apparently poisoned. Since there was no evidence and no inclination to pursue the case, it was dropped without much ado.

Within a month's time, Heinz and Frieda Schafer had married. Frieda also came from a rich and renowned family background with no mixed blood. Heinz was happy. They had settled down in Villa General Belgrano where loads of Germans who had escaped from Germany were settling down. Heinz was keen on keeping his lineage pure… so when his son was born, he was a happy camper. But the son had completely disappointed him in every possible manner. He had chosen to become a farmer rather than taking any other profession. The only saving grace was Heinz had found a Pure-Blooded German girl, Emmeline, for his son Maxim. But unfortunately, Emmeline died after childbirth, and Maxim had married a local Argentinian girl.

Heinz's voice ricocheted in Ludolf's ear… "Never become an emotional fool. Strong men survive, thrive. Emotional fools perish. Become a strong man. Never accept a 'No' from anyone. You are an Aryan with pure blood. You are the supreme race on this planet. Power and Money are the two most important things in life. People can be bought… even your enemies. Every person has a price. You need to find their weak spot and exploit them. Get back to Germany. That is the land of your ancestors. You belong there… not here."

"You know Heinrich Himmler, the 4th Reichsführer of the Schutzstaffel, had all the major German industries in his pocket. On August 10, 1944, a meeting was scheduled and held by Himmler at Maison Rouge Hotel Strasbourg, France where all the representatives of these big German companies were present… Krupp, VW, Rheinmetall, Röchling, Messerschmitt AG, Brown Boveri, Hercules. They were all Honorary SS officers. Why… to transfer all the German wealth outside Germany so that the Brits and the Americans and the Russians cannot lay their dirty hands on that wealth. All those industries are still there and have made a name for themselves in the world. You must also join the rank of these industries. German engineering is the best. That is why I say… you belong there. You can control the world sitting there." Ludolf could almost hear his grandfather's parting words.

"You have a dinner appointment at 7.00 PM, Herr Ludolf," Ludolf's train of thought was broken as his admin assistant had buzzed him on the intercom.

"*Danke Schön, Fräulein,*" Ludolf replied. Momentarily, he had forgotten her name. "Linda *Hecht*!!! Damn it," he muttered to himself as he got up from his chair and collected his jacket.

Moscow, Russia

October 17, 2023; 11.30 AM

Alexei Mikhailovich Zakharov, Alex to his close friends, was a man in a hurry. He was on his way to meet Minister Andrei Petrov at the Ministry of Defense. Alexei did not know the agenda because, as always, it would be confidential.

The main building of the ministry, built in the 1940s, is located on Arbatskaya Square, near Arbat Street. Other buildings of the ministry are located throughout the city of Moscow.

Escorted by his bodyguards, Alexei came to his underground parking space. His bulletproof car had already been waiting for him. "*Arbatskaya, Paydem,*" … (Let us go), Alexei ordered. This meeting was not on Alexei's agenda. He had other plans. He was looking forward to meeting Katya… Ekaterina, his longtime girlfriend. In his business, Alexei did not want a wife or kids… "bloody unwanted nuisance," as he would often say.

He was considered one of the most powerful oligarchs in Russia. Alexei was sixty-two and had reached the most powerful position due to his daredevilish approach and a go-getter attitude. But Alexei was a different kind of oligarch. To a normal person, he was an Oil & Gas Tycoon as well as the owner of various mines in Russia and abroad.

But other than that, his activities included dealing with international arms dealers, drug cartels, mafia bosses, and terrorist group leaders from North Korea to Iran to Guatemala. Many of the ministers were on his payroll. He had his men in the Federal Security Service (FSB) – formerly known as the KGB.

Other than that, he had "special business" ties with his "special friends" in various countries in Europe, Asia, and the Americas. Public opinion was that Alexei was not in the good books of the Russian President. But few knew that in reality Alexei was the President's henchman.

Born in the mining town of Zheleznogorsk, one of the Soviet Union's largest iron-ore-mining basins located in the Kursk oblast region of Western Russia, Alexei ran away at the age of nine to Rostov and started working at a warehouse. At 11, he managed to get himself a job on one of the fishing vessels operating in the Black Sea. There, on the fishing vessel, he learned about illegal trade and its secrets. He understood the basic principle... If you have money, you have the power.

By the age of twenty-two, Alexei had become the Boss Man in the Rostov area. During his "growing up," Alexei understood that the main money-spinner would be oil and gas in the decades to come, with minerals coming in a close second. For that, Alexei needed big bucks. The only sure-shot way to get the big bucks was via illegal arms trading and drug trading. The invasion of Afghanistan by Russia in December 1979 gave that opportunity to Alexei. He shifted his base to Dushanbe. Over the next ten years, Alexei used his skills in arms/ammunition and drug trading to mint money.

When the USSR disintegrated and Russia was formed, Alexei moved to Moscow. He slowly but meticulously worked his way up to the top echelons of the political circle and also society. In the next few years, Alexei had "managed" to get a foot in the Oil and Gas Industry as well as in the Mining Industry. With sheer ruthlessness, he proceeded to acquire what he intended to do. While he was doing his work, Alexei had continued to deal with his team in the arms/ammunition and drugs field. He never abandoned the old contacts and relationships. With money came power. With power came relationships. Relationships in high places are often delicate. One with the Department of Defense was one such relationship that Alexei had to balance. And he hated that because he wanted to be the controller of the relationship. Alexei's net was spread not just through Europe but throughout the globe: the Middle East, Africa, South America, North America, the Far East, and also Central Asia… and he had absolute control over it.

"I hope this is not about Sergei," Alexei muttered to himself.

New York, US

October 18, 2023; 04.30 PM

Cathy Dexter was completely aware of her personal charm, poise, and beauty… and also knew how to use it to her advantage. She also had the gift of the gab and could hold her own in any discussion with anyone of any stature.

A brunette with shoulder-length bouncing hair, long legs, and a full body, she turned the heads of the passersby when she went about doing her rounds through the Columbia University campus. It had been quite a hectic week since the world had learned about the "operation Al-Aqsa Flood" by Hamas, stating it had fired over 5,000 rockets from the Gaza Strip into Israel within a span of 20 minutes.

After the attack, the IDF (Israel Defense Force) had launched Operation Swords of Iron in Gaza and declared a state of emergency for areas within eighty kilometers (50 miles) of the Gaza border. The IDF had proceeded mercilessly to eliminate the Hamas strongholds… of course leading to casualties. But that was a good enough reason for Cathy to get excited because she had found the reason for staging her next act.

Cathy came from a family of steel mill workers. Her father worked as a foreman in a steel plant in Cleveland, Ohio. He always looked overworked. At home, he would always complain to his wife about the unfair treatment meted out to the workers by the management.

"It is always about work and more work… more of this and more of that but never about more bucks." He always used to narrate how harshly the "money-minded rich owners" would treat the "poor working class." He also lectured his wife on "social equality" and how socialism is effective in many other countries.

Growing up, Catherine Terresa Dexter would listen carefully to her dad, whom she admired for his outspoken attitude… but little did she know that her dad was like a mouse in front of his supervisor because he wanted to keep his job intact.

"Honey, you must study hard and attend a well-known university and become a lawyer so that one day you can become the voice of the weak, the poor and the oppressed people," Cathy's dad would always tell her. Cathy took her dad's advice literally and studied hard to gain entry into the prestigious Columbia University.

The first thing Cathy did after coming to Columbia was to find like-minded students who would endorse her views and support her. They had also formed a small group on the campus… "Reformist." Now this war had brought the perfect opportunity to the table… as per Cathy's thoughts… to get Reformist to the forefront. Cathy wanted to do something spectacular for the Palestinians… for the people of Gaza. Cathy hated Israel and its people… because to her mind they were the "oppressors" and needed to be punished. Cathy had already charted her next moves… the big ones!!!

New York, US

October 26, 2023; 12.30 PM

Autumn was almost coming to an end, and the chill of winter could be felt even in the mid-afternoon. Jerry was sitting in the Blue Jave Café at Everett Library, toying with his coffee. The half-eaten croissant was lying on the plate in front of him. He was in no mood to eat it. His mind was still in the classroom attending Prof. Matthew's lecture on the Deep State. Jerry was completely shaken.

"The Deep State is a profligate and incapable method of governance. It exists because of its irrational incentive structure which frequently rewards failures and dresses them up as success. The Deep State does not consist only of government agencies. Private enterprise is an integral part of its operations."

"The origins of the Deep State are Turkish. The Turkish phrase Derin Devlet literally means 'Deep State.' According to historian Ryan Gingeras, the term 'generally refers to a kind of shadow or parallel system of government in which unofficial or publicly unacknowledged individuals play important roles in defining and implementing state policy.' This concept of a Deep State is used to explain why and how agents employed by the state execute policies that directly contravene the letter and spirit of the law. Breaking the law, of course, often means employing criminals. Essentially, dirty work needs dirty workers, so a clandestine force gets recruited from paramilitary and criminal elements."

"The Deep State does not consist of the entire government," Prof. Matthew was drawing a chart on the board as he spoke. "But various important government agencies and departments are part of the Deep State. The Deep State de facto controls the parliament/congress, the likes of NSA/CIA/FBI, Judiciary, Defense lobby, External Affairs, Wall Street and alike, Silicon Valley, Media, Digital Data, Food and Pharma lobby… And through all these, the common people at large."

"It is basically an invisible state. The visible state in the White House is only the tip of the iceberg. The invisible state is operating continuously underneath irrespective of who is in power in the visible state… in the White House."

Prof. Matthew had paused for a minute and looked at the faces of the students in the class. Most of them were dazed with their traps fallen open.

"So, basically Deep State is a shadow government," Jerry had blurted to himself… but he was loud enough to be heard by Prof. Matthew and others in the class.

"Let us not jump to conclusions immediately. We have just started to define the Deep State. It is really quite deep. The deeper you explore, the deeper it gets… as you will see in the next lectures. Right now, let us understand the concept… and the historical perspective first," Prof. Matthew commented on Jerry's remark.

"Various governments across the world have used different methods as part of the Deep State function or operation to get rid of the so-called unwanted, undesired, or disliked governments or rulers or leaders in other countries. The US is no exception. They have used this weapon, calling it a 'Coup.' All these coups had some US government official involved in some form or other… which means these coups were backed up by the US government. The first example is that of Hawaii. Hawaii was an independent country until 1893. It was ruled by queen Liliuokalani. The US government felt that the queen was a threat to US control over sugar… sugar which was grown by the white American Christian Missionaries in Hawaii over the years. So, the US sends ships with thousands of soldiers to Honolulu and overthrows the queen, installing one of the Christian missionaries, Stanford Ballar Dole, as the new President of Hawaii."

Prof. Matthew paused and asked, "Any idea who this Dole was?"

"Dole… Banana guy?" said someone.

"Yes… The unlimited power usurped by Stanford Dole, backed up by the US government, helped Dole to establish the billion-dollar business that you see today. Also, to get Hawaii annexed to the US and become a part of the US."

"Once the US government had a taste of blood, they started using a coup as a tool to create problems in countries where the US government had an interest for strategic reasons like natural resources or a strategic location and started throwing out elected governments or leaders who were disliked by the US government. After Hawaii, the US turned their attention to Spain and Spain's colonies across the world like… Cuba, Puerto Rico, the Philippines, etc., overthrowing the existing leaders and governments and installing a President or a Prime Minister who would be a puppet of the US government."

"Now, let us look at the case of Iran. Mohammed Mosaddegh gets elected as the leader of Iran. The year is 1953. The Cold War is on. Mosaddegh says that the oil should belong to the state and not to the Anglo-Iranian Oil Company (now known as British Petroleum), which was a British company. So, Mosaddegh throws out the British oil company. The British are livid with anger and seek revenge. So, the British government contacts the CIA for help.

"Director of the CIA Allen Dulles was the younger brother of John Foster Dulles, Dwight D. Eisenhower's Secretary of State. The CIA and the Brits devised a plan. They appointed Kermit Roosevelt, who was a CIA Bureau chief in the Middle East, with the ultimate objective of overthrowing Mohammad Mosaddegh. Kermit sneaks into Iran with an amount of USD One million to be used in any way that would bring about the fall of Mosaddegh."

"Kermit starts using the money to bribe politicians, religious clerics and make them say controversial things about Mosaddegh in public. Kermit also uses the money to give to local people to stage attacks on religious leaders, making the attacks look as if they were ordered by Mosaddegh. Thus, within a short time, the CIA was able to create an atmosphere of chaos, hostility, and distrust among the people. The CIA also supplies enough weapons and explosives to support a 10,000-men guerrilla organization for six months… resulting in more chaos and violence in Tehran and surrounding areas. Thousands of paid demonstrators flood the streets… who are beaten up. The country falls into anarchy… All courtesy of CIA money. The end result was Mosaddegh surrendering and the US installing its puppet, Mohd. Reza Shah Pahlavi… who quickly gave all the oil rights to American oil companies. The rest is history. So, as the head of the Central Intelligence Agency (CIA) during the early Cold War, Allen Dulles oversaw the 1953 Iranian coup d'état, the 1954 Guatemalan coup d'état, the Lockheed U-2 aircraft program, the Project MKUltra mind control program, and the Bay of Pigs Invasion in 1961. The coups were the initial versions of the Deep State."

"There were about twenty-odd such coups staged by the CIA and the US administrations at various times. I would strongly suggest that you all should Google all the coups that I had mentioned today and write a short synopsis on the functioning of the Deep State... Of course, this is all external... external to the US. But the Deep State is also operative internally... within the US as well. We will come to that later on. Also, there is a book called Washington Bullets written by Vijay Prashad... If you happen to lay your hands on it, please read."

Prof. Matthew had stopped and looked at the class... which was in a state of daze. Jerry was still in that condition... wondering about the honesty and integrity of the politicians. This was the first relevant class in Political Science he had ever attended. "It is going to be interesting from now on," Jerry muttered to himself. He had no taste left for the coffee... he picked up his unfinished cup and dumped it in the bin and left the café.

Southampton, Long Island, US

October 31, 2023; 07.00 AM

Sitting in his easy chair on the balcony of his bedroom in his sprawling estate in Southampton, Borge Ross was sipping his first coffee while watching the news: the Israel-Hamas war, which was raging in the Middle East.

Ross started seeing Hitler's Nazi soldiers instead of the IDF soldiers on TV. His mind raced back to his growing up days in Poland. He was a Polish Jew, and his family had to go into hiding during the Nazi occupation. Born as Boszke Rosowski to a well-to-do Polish Jewish family, after being targeted, his family survived the war by purchasing documents to say that they were Christians. His family was a prosperous but non-observant Jewish family, who, like many upper-middle-class Jews, were uncomfortable with their roots. His family changed their name from the Polish Jewish "Rosowski" to "Ross" to protect themselves in the increasingly antisemitic Poland during the Nazi occupation... and Boszke was changed to Bjorg, a Norwegian-sounding name... which later became Borge.

Borge had hated the oppressive right-wing attitude of the Germans, although at that time he had no clue about the right wing. He only understood that the Nazis were not liberal. That sort of made him skeptical of any "nationalistic" regimes when he had grown up. Being a Jew, understanding money and making money came easily to him. After the war, the family moved to

Western Europe… where Borge studied and earned his Master of Science Degree. He then joined a Merchant Bank and gained some experience.

He had moved to the US in the mid-1950s and started working as an arbitrage trader at a brokerage house. As time went by, he moved from one firm to another, making money as he went. His aim was to save enough money to start something of his own.

Momentarily, Borge came to the present as his cell phone buzzed. It was his secretary reminding him of his meeting with the President of the Free Society Establishment in the next half hour.

Borge Ross had supported progressive and liberal political causes, to which he distributed donations through his Free Society Establishment, which he had founded in the early nineties, to help countries move away from real socialism in central/Eastern Europe and Russia. He had thus influenced the fall of communism in Eastern Europe in the 1990s and provided one of Europe's largest higher education endowments to the Central European University.

Between 1979 and 2011, he had donated more than $10 billion to various philanthropic causes and by 2017, his donations "on civil initiatives to reduce poverty and increase transparency, and on scholarships and universities around the world" totaled $16 billion. All said and done, this Free Society Establishment was just the front to a much larger initiative that Borge Ross had in mind.

These extensive fundings of political causes had made Ross a "Boogeyman of European Nationalists." Numerous far-right groups had claimed foul play that had characterized Ross as a dangerous "hand puppet master" behind alleged global plots. The

Republican Party had become quite weary of Ross's so-called Liberal and Progressive Political agenda.

Borge got up from his easy chair as it was about time that he got ready to receive Tom Blanchet, the President of his Free Society Establishment. Borge had a plan in mind which he wanted to explain to Tom and make sure that the plan was perfected to the last detail and implemented. There was no time to lose. "The next couple of years are going to be crucial," Borge said aloud.

Niamey, Niger, West Africa

November 2, 2023; 06.00 PM

It was past 6 pm, and the temperatures had started to cool off. It was already early November; the dry season would soon usher in, bringing in the cooler weather.

Sitting on the east bank of the River Niger, Niamey boasted of being the capital of Niger. It had been just over a year since General Abubaker Ouhoumoudou Ubange had taken over as Head of State of Niger. He was sitting in his office smoking his expensive Cohiba Cuban cigar. Tolerating the smell of the cigar was Ibrahim Oumarau, the Prime Minister of Niger… who was just a puppet of General Ubange and Musa Mbumic, the finance minister.

"Alright, you wanted my time. You got it. What is it that you want to tell me?" the General said softly but in a stern voice.

Ibrahim Oumarau cleared his throat and said, "Musa Mbumic was visiting my office this afternoon to discuss various matters, but there is one specific matter that we would like your counsel on. Musa can explain in great detail. We would like to have your point of view and decision as well."

Ibrahim Oumarau looked at Musa and signaled him to go ahead.

"General Sir, we have received a request from a US-based agency, the Free Society Establishment, requesting permission to start their operations in our country. I have done some research on this organization, and I feel that permitting them to open their operations in Niger would be inviting trouble."

"Okay then, don't give them permission. Why come to me if you know the end result?" The General interrupted, blowing out the smoke in Musa's face.

"Well, General Sir, it is not going to be that simple… Please… let me tell you the background of this organization, their real motives and how powerful they are," Musa continued without giving another chance to the General to blow out the smoke in his face.

"The organization is a Borge Ross establishment and is run by his family across the globe," Musa paused to take a look at the papers in his file.

"And who the heck is this Borge Ross guy?" the General barked. He actually wanted to go and immerse himself in his bathtub and enjoy a drink.

"Sir, I am coming to that. He is a US citizen, a Polish Jew by birth. Born and brought up during the Second World War… his family escaped the death camps of Nazis by going underground, changing their names to Christian names and living out the Soviet occupation before moving out to Europe, England, and then to the US. Borge Ross is a graduate of the London School of Economics and is the greatest speculator in financial markets and also very controversial. He has made billions of dollars and donated almost all to so-called social causes. He has a very complex nature, and he is a risk-taker because like his family he has mastered the art of survival. He has said in various interviews that… Money gives him a degree of power and also a degree of freedom to do what he wants to achieve."

"And what the hell does he want to achieve?" The General was getting irritated mainly because he was envious of this American guy who had made billions.

"He wants to build a world with a completely open society and open boundaries. He had a juvenile fantasy of being a God and controlling the entire world. That is his motive and towards that, he has created this organization called Free Society Establishment. The objective of the organization is to "Build an Open World." So, the people from this organization, wherever they have set up their operations, have gone ahead and represented under-represented communities and brought about changes in those countries."

"What countries, what changes… be specific." Suddenly the General became aware of the possible danger.

"Well, Sir, let me start with… they have encouraged dissent behind the iron curtains… that is in the earlier Soviet bloc, fostering open societies… and you know the results. Then there are examples of supporting democracies in Myanmar and Indonesia… advocating for the Rohingya of Myanmar. Supporting democracy in Ukraine, supposedly building a brighter future in Pakistan… where again supposedly these folks were responsible for removing their then Prime Minister Imran Khan from office and putting him in jail."

"Wasn't that the CIA which was responsible for his removal?"

"Well Sir, it is said that the Democratic Party and the likes of the CIA are controlled by or through this organization… or by Borge Ross. He is believed to support all the district attorneys in all the democratic / liberal states in the US and has destroyed the social fabric… like, for example, he believes in gay marriages… supports the LGBTQ community and their church. He believes that in that way, one can control world population growth. He is driven by power and his desire to control the world that way. He has interfered in the politics of Thailand, Malaysia, Indonesia, Japan, and even Russia. He has given $100 million to the Human Rights Campaign ... the HRC organization which gives the scores of or to CEI and DEI."

"And what the hell are CEI and DEI?"

"Sir, there are various bodies like ESG, CEI, DEI... Environmental Social Governance, Corporate Equity Score and Diversity Equity Inclusion... scores of which are decided by HRC for investors to invest in various companies. These are a set of standards for a company's behavior used by socially conscious investors to screen potential investments. That is to say that if a company does not have any LGBT... Gay or Lesbians working in that organization, then that company will not be considered as eligible by the investors to invest in. That is the open and Free Society concept of Ross."

"If they come here, then they will destroy our existing social fabric... and also create issues for the government. Because they will distribute money to all the people and under the pretext of freedom, they will create anarchy in the country... like the CIA and MI6 had done in Iran if you remember."

"What does he get out of this... sarcastic pleasure... what else?"

"Sarcastic pleasure... not sure. Because when he was a child, his sister or mother, I am not sure, was raped by a couple of Soviet soldiers. That had made a deep impact on his mind... mental trauma. So, he basically hates all the so-called oppressive regimes... fundamental regimes... and wants them to be free, chaotic... not disciplined. He had a mentor, Carl Popper, who had written a book called Open Societies and Their Enemies. Ross believes in that book like the Quran."

"And Sir, profit is also the motive. This is a very profitable business. He gets access and control over the tangible assets of that country... like here... in Niger, they will be looking for complete control over uranium. We are the main supplier of uranium to the EU, followed by Kazakhstan and Russia. Now, this organization will try to change all that... by promising our people that the sale money of this uranium will go directly to the people's pocket."

"I see. Then you can tell them to go to hell for all I care." The General was already worried and, in his mind, trying to assess the aftermath of the situation described by Musa.

"Well, Sir, it will create some tension in our relations with the US, and we may not receive the help we need from the World Bank or IMF that we are negotiating." The Prime Minister cleared his throat and took control of the conversation.

"Oh...!!!"

"There is one other way out."

"And that is?"

"We approach the Chinese. They will provide the funds; they will also invest in building our infrastructure. They will not get involved in our politics. They may want to get some special concessions for buying our minerals... which we can consider. We don't have to go to the Americans. And later if we don't want the Chinese, we can ask them to take a walk... they can't and will not be able to do anything... because we are landlocked."

"Good Idea. Let us consider this... Let us meet tomorrow and discuss the plan of action. But we will say a polite NO to this organization of this Ross guy. I don't want them within five hundred kilometers of our border creating problems for us. Thank you for coming and briefing me. I will let you know when to meet tomorrow.... Inshallah." The General stood up, accepted the handshakes of both Musa and Ibrahim, and left. He wanted to get into the bathtub as soon as possible.

New York, US

November 7, 2023; 11.00 AM

Sitting in the spacious boardroom of his office on the 35th floor of Onyx Tower located on the 57th Street in Manhattan, Gregory Brink, Chairman of Cobblestone Inc, was thinking about the follow-up actions decided in the meeting he had just finished.

With over \$10 trillion in assets, Cobblestone exerted control over all major petrochemical corporations, most of the big banks in the US, all the renowned Pharma companies, most of the big tech companies in Silicon Valley, all the big defense companies like Northrop Grumman, Raytheon, etc.; 90% of the mainstream media like CNN, CNBC, etc., and over 10% of all the stocks traded worldwide.

Gregory Brink sat on the board of directors of the most global influential councils, the World Economic Forum, Council of Foreign Relations, and most of the big organizations like Exxon Mobil, Lockheed, etc. Governments relied on Gregory to escape the recessions when the markets collapsed in 2008.

Gregory believed in what Henry Kissinger had said... Whoever controls the money controls the world. Gregory believed that he was almost there. He could feel that the ultimate control of the world was in his hands. He knew exactly what to do and when to do it. He had a master plan and today he had put that master plan in motion.

Although born into a family with modest means, Gregory had a hunger for power from his childhood. He always wanted control and to be in control of everything. After graduating in Political Science, Gregory decided to go into banking and real estate. Being a member of the elite Kappa Beta Phi group, Gregory had come into contact with some influential people from the finance industry. Initial success was followed by some failures, but Gregory had learned quickly from his mistakes and had carefully developed his appetite and understanding of risk management.

Cobblestone's foray into ETFs... Exchange Traded Funds had enabled them to exploit the government. Exchange Traded funds (ETFs) were a type of investment that allowed investors to buy and sell a group of stocks, bonds, or other securities on a stock exchange during market hours. ETFs were similar to mutual funds, but they traded throughout the day like stocks and contained hundreds or thousands of individual securities.

After the 2008 housing crisis, Cobblestone started buying properties in newly built communities mainly in three states, which were rented out and never sold to any individual owner. That move pushed up prices in the housing market, resulting in Cobblestone making more money.

In 2020, Cobblestone entered the Chinese market and made tie-ups with companies blacklisted by the US government. Essentially, this helped Cobblestone generate data on the Chinese people, their spending or buying habits, their preferences, their income... all of which helped Cobblestone perfect its own software, Alibaba. Alibaba was formulating millions of "what if" scenarios of possible failures of various investments and making predictions well in advance as part of risk management.

Cobblestone was now acquiring all the tangible real assets under its wing.

Gregory has now set his eyes on the Bitcoin ETFs... which would be the first step in the Technological Revolution in Finance. The second step would be the Tokenization... Tokenization of the Real-World Assets... RWAs... via Blockchain. That would give Gregory complete control over the real assets across the globe.

He had thought about the plan he wanted to put into action. He would one day soon control the entire world. He smiled smugly to himself.

Washington D.C., US

November 8, 2023; 02.30 PM

"Do you even know how many different lobbies that we have to deal with… These folks not only have money, but they also have power and a massive ego. You touch their ego and then see what happens. Don't try to taste the poison," Martin Kingston was getting angry. "I don't know what the heck you guys in the CIA have to do with this stuff. This is internal… not international… period."

"Look, Martin, we have our instructions… directives, you may say. We need to understand…"

"You need to understand nothing!" Martin cut short Abe Williams… with his voice rising.

"Martin, we have our orders. Please understand. We have other means of getting the information too."

"Then go ahead and get it. Who is stopping you? I am not providing any information. This is out of your jurisdiction," Martin said firmly as he stood up, moving towards the door of his room.

Abe remained seated in his chair with his hands clasped together in a Padma sign. He was an ardent yoga follower. In his job, he needed to have control over his emotions.

"Abe… trust me, I ain't gonna provide you anything even if you remain here for the next 24 hours."

"Okay, so you will give it to me after 24 hours then…"

"Nope. I did not mean that. I am not providing any information on the various lobbies that we deal with. And unless you tell me why you need the information, I can't and will not open my mouth," Martin said firmly.

Martin suspected some sinister play as soon as he received a call from the Secretary of State, Bob Mayers, asking him to meet with Abe Williams, Deputy Director of CIA, and "check if you can provide him with whatever information he needs." He never said, "provide the information."

As the most senior person in the State Department and having worked for various Secretaries over the years, he knew his powers and limitations. But what bugged him was that the CIA was trying to get involved in his jurisdiction. The various lobbies he dealt with were the Pharma people, defense equipment manufacturers, Oil and Gas guys, the Wall Street folks, the Automobile folks, the Silicon Valley guys… who were like the who's who.

All these lobby guys and gals had their wants and paid handsome amounts… "facilitated" that was the right word… to get accomplished what they wanted. The "facilitation" sometimes amounted to billions of dollars. Some of these lobby guys belonged to the "International arena" which was quite discreet in nature. That was managed by a team with only four members… POTUS being one of them.

Most of the lobbyists were young, attractive, smart, and well-educated women who were trained to manipulate the key government officials. They would know the family secrets or personal secrets of the government official they would be dealing with and use it as a weapon… to blackmail them and get their objective accomplished. Monetary and non-monetary benefits were often showered upon the officials… even on Senators.

Today's request from the CIA was somewhat strange. Martin suspected something sinister and was therefore trying to avoid providing any details to Abe. Although Abe had known Martin for a very long time, both had their professional boundaries.

"Unless… I repeat, you tell me why you need the information, I will not give you any info. Period," Martin said, moving back to his chair.

"Okay. Please tell me what the connection or relation between the guys from Pharma or Biotech, Defense manufacturers, Wall Street and Silicon Valley is?" Abe paused… "and where does SecDef come into this?"

"What? That is the stupidest question I have ever heard. Do you even understand what you are asking? And where does SecDef come into all this?"

"I am asking that question. Don't repeat my question… and don't ask me… answer me," Abe said quietly.

"As far as I know, there is no relationship between any of the folks you have mentioned," Martin said, but at the back of his mind, he was thinking fast… "Where do they all connect?" The only possible place in Martin's mind could think of was DARPA because Abe had mentioned SecDef. DARPA came under the authority of US Defense Acquisition, Technology & Logistics… as well as the missile Defense Agency and Nuclear, Chemical & Biological Defense Program. All these three streams reported to USD ATL who in turn reported to SecDef. But the NSA came under USD Intelligence. So, what the heck is happening here… Martin was thinking fast.

"If this involves DARPA, then there must be something really quite big and dangerous," Martin was lost in his thoughts. Abe was watching Martin's face. He knew that he had asked a very poignant question, the answer to which was not an easy one.

Martin's mind was racing… "CIA getting involved… meaning international connection. SecDef meaning defense… most likely DARPA because that is where Biotech and Silicon Valley guys can come together. But what about Wall Street… Borge Ross, Gregory Brink… Carbon Credits… ESG?"

"Unless you provide me with the information we have asked for, neither you nor we will be able to establish the relationship between all these folks. So, it is imperative that you tell me the details," said Abe with a sedate tone.

"Abe, we deal with these folks one on one… not all of them together in one room."

"Oh… come on. Any fool will understand that. But surely, they all are connected in one place… here. You have the information, but you can't see the connection. It is our job to find the links… The connection."

"Where does DARPA come into this?" Martin asked bluntly.

Abe was surprised, and it showed on his face. "What has DARPA got to do with this?" Abe said softly.

Martin knew that the cat was out of the bag. He had hit the nail on the head. "Well, you know that and unless you come clean, I will not give you any information."

"Touché!" replied Abe.

Abe understood that Martin had used the SecDef connection to link DARPA… Defense Advanced Research Projects Agency… the agency famous for its blue Sky Research Technology… the agency that remained 20 years ahead of any other organization in creating innovative weapons systems for defense and national security. Of course, there was also the NRO... the National Reconnaissance Office... the Satellite Technology people. Abe knew that the CIA was not the only intelligence agency... there were 17 different intelligence agencies operating for the US government.

"Alright... what do you want to know?" Abe came around, sort of conceding.

"Why do you need the information? Who wants it?"

"We, the CIA, want the information. Period. Why, at this point in time, we do not know the answer as to what we are looking for, or who we are looking for, we would like to know the possible motives of these people, the Biotech or Pharma, Defense equipment, Silicon Valley, and Wall Street coming together. If they do, their objective, their possible links with countries like Russia, China, Iran, even the EU countries, etc., and the possible end result. If any of our Senators are involved, any possible links to these orgs."

Martin was thinking about ESG and the Carbon Credits because that was something which was hurting quite a few corporate giants... and what if they had used their connections to get to the CIA? But that was the "danger zone" because most of these lobbies were controlled one way or the other by Gregory Brink or Borge Ross. In fact, it was rumored that Borge almost owned the Democratic Party. So, any information given out by the State Department would hurt him as all the fingers would be pointed at Martin.

Carbon Credits were devised as a mechanism to reduce greenhouse gas emissions by creating a market in which companies could trade in emissions permits. Companies received a set number of Carbon Credits under the system that declined over time. They could sell any excess to other companies. Those that could not easily reduce emissions could still operate but at a higher financial cost. This is where the likes of Gregory and Borge made money by providing preferential investments in the companies. Grabbing the fertile land and forests in various poor countries in the Global South under the pretext of Carbon Credits was the prime motive, though no one could openly mention that. The RWAs... the Real-World Assets, the tangible assets were now acquired by companies like Cobblestone.

Martin was scared. But without showing his fear, he simply said, "I do not have the information you need. I can only say that each one of the lobbies has its own demands, mostly around getting permits or preferential treatment in their global positioning and of course, trading... even for any international entity, this holds good... like China would like to reduce the tariff on some specific goods marketed in the US."

"Oh, come on, Martin... let us stop playing games. I know all that stuff. It is basic 101. I need specifics," Abe was losing his patience.

"I don't think I can provide you with anything more than that. If you want, you can approach Bob Mayers and get the information directly from him. He knows all the pieces even better than I do," Martin had sensed that this was going to be a nail in his coffin if he dared to provide information to the CIA. He also knew that Abe would not be able to do anything if Martin did not provide any input. "I am not authorized to give out anything. Period."

Abe got up from his chair. He was frustrated. Before he came to Martin, he was aware that his visit would be futile, but he had his orders. Something was not right. There were whispers in corners of corridors at Langley. Abe could feel that Martin was not hiding anything… he was simply scared of something… or somebody. What and who? Abe walked to the door. He opened the door, stood there, turned his head towards Martin and said, "Someday very soon, I am going to find it out, Martin… and then I will be the one questioning you and your actions… trust me."

"No Abe, you can't, and you will not. You know it too. Good day," Martin said without looking at Abe. The door closed behind Abe.

Martin sat in his chair holding his head in his palms… "Why should Bob Mayers agree to such a request from the CIA? Who is reporting to whom? What is going on? The elections are still a year away." Martin was thinking fast.

"Elections!!! India is going to the polls in March/April… that is another 6 months down the line… but what have DARPA, and the lobbies got to do with the Indian elections." Martin was lost in his thoughts.

New Delhi, India

November 15, 2023; 04.00 PM

Mehul Nandhi had just returned from his road trip across India. He felt that he had accomplished a lot during his road trip... "Awakening the sleeping lower class souls and making them aware of the fact that the current Indian central government and the Prime Minister Rajendra Dodi were supporting only the rich businessmen from his community."

He was at his spacious government-allotted bungalow, where he had lived for almost all his life courtesy of his mother Maria, father Mr. Satjiv Nandhi, who was the ex-Prime Minister, his grandmother Mrs. Mandira Nandhi who was also the ex-Prime Minister... and his great-grandfather (Mandira's father) who was also the ex-Prime Minister of India. His family, he thought, were the owners of India and now, for over a decade, someone else had occupied the Prime Minister's chair. This had hurt the ego of the Nandhi family. Mehul wanted to get back that chair and rule India like a monarch. He was prepared to do anything and go to any extent... even teaming up with the enemies of India... to get the position of the Prime Minister back to his family's fold.

Presently, Mehul was sitting with his sister Riyanka Nandhi, mother Maria, his party's President Nath Kedge, and his father's friend Damodar... Dam Keytruda... who was once a Minister in his father's cabinet but now settled in the US.

"What you have accomplished is great on this tour of yours. But it is the money which gets you the votes, not just this 'awakening.' Also, you must have support from outside India… from enemies of India or enemies of Dodi. If you do not have that support, it will be like fighting a losing war." Dam carefully chose his words as he looked squarely at Mehul and his mum.

"What are you proposing, Dam?" Maria Nandhi asked impatiently. She was in a hurry. She wanted to gain back control of the government. "Once we have control, there will be no more elections… we will rule forever," she thought to herself.

"Well, you need to reach out to your neighbors first… I know you can't travel to Pakistan or Bangladesh… but that does not stop you from meeting these guys in, say, Thailand, Myanmar, Turkey, France, or London… or even in the US. I can arrange these meetings for you." Dam paused and continued…

"You will be able to meet important people like the ISI operatives, heads of different Islamic organizations… Remember you have a big Muslim vote bank and if you want them on your side, you need to keep these people happy. Money plays an important role. Monies can be raised from several sources… Sources like Free Society Establishment… Borge Ross, who can dole out almost a billion dollars to get rid of Dodi. Then you have the Chinese operatives who can provide you with funds. In exchange, they will need a piece of land… which you can always give away when you come to power."

"Yes, this all sounds interesting, but what is the guarantee that people will vote? They will take our money and vote for Dodi and his party," Nath Kedge interrupted Dam.

Dam looked at Kedge as if he were an idiot and said, "Simple… create pandemonium within India. Create issues like the Farmers' protest or something like Shaheenbaag. Khalistanis will support you, ISI will support you in Kashmir, Bangladeshis will help you in West Bengal, and Muslims can help you in various states like Kerala, Karnataka, Andhra, and UP. In addition to that, people like Hindenburg can help you in the stock market crash. Use the media to your advantage with false propaganda. Buy the current opposition MPs… I am sure there would be lots of unsatisfied souls in the government… buy them off. Use the Indian diaspora in various countries to make noise against the present government. Create a Venezuela Model."

"What is the Venezuela Model?" Mehul asked. He was listening to what Dam was saying.

"Promise free stuff… Free electricity, free gas, free grains… cheap petrol… what people want is free stuff. That will help you get elected. Once you get elected, then you can do whatever you want," Dam said, getting up and going to the French window. It was as if the October heat was radiating, and Dam could feel the heat.

"Once this guy comes to power, I will have the control and then I can settle a few scores," Dam thought to himself.

Dan's mind went into the past. He remembered the 60s-70s period. The KGB had complete control of the Indian government. The KGB was running thirty operatives in India, ten of whom were Indian Intelligence officers.

Mehul's grandmother, Mrs. Mandira Nandhi, was on the KGB payroll. Her codename was VINO. KGB head in India, Leonid Shebarshin, was believed to have said… to have personally handed over millions of rupees to Mrs. Mandira Nandhi during 1976. In 1973, the KGB had ten Indian newspapers on their payroll, plus a press agency. During 1975, the KGB had planted 5510 articles in the Indian newspapers. Between 1955 and 1980, the KGB had several union ministers on their payroll. The KGB had run their election campaigns too. The most surprising area of KGB penetration was the defense ministry and those layers of the armed forces which were responsible for military procurement.

KGB operations in India expanded rapidly in the fifties and sixties, and not just within Indian borders. An Indian diplomat, codenamed PROKHOR, in the embassy in Moscow was recruited via the classic honey trap, compromised by a female KGB agent with the delicious code name of NEVEROVA. PROKHOR provided the agency with the embassy codebook and other material and was paid Rs. 4,000 a month. Two other diplomats were also compromised.

Soviet efforts were clearly assisted by India's anti-American policy at the time and the fact that strategically, American dependence on Pakistan as a counterweight to Soviet influence in India pushed Delhi into Moscow's influence. The then Indian defense Minister Krishna Menon, openly anti-American, was backed by the KGB on the assumption that he would succeed Mrs. Mandira Nandhi's father, the then Prime Minister, a prospect that ended with the Chinese invasion in 1962. The KGB then set out to woo Mrs. Mandira Nandhi. Khrushchev presented her with a mink coat on her first solo visit to Moscow (although Mrs. Mandira Nandhi had earlier criticized an ambassador's wife for accepting a similar gift), and the KGB surrounded her with "handsome, attentive male admirers."

Oleg Kalugin, former KGB major General, had mentioned, "It seemed like the entire India was up for sale: the KGB and the CIA had deeply penetrated the Indian government."

Not just the government, the KGB had also recruited one of India's most influential journalists, codenamed NOK. His anti-US articles were considered a major coup in Lubyanka. However, they had other ways of stoking anti-US sentiments. In 1969, Dam remembered, KGB chief Yuri Andropov had informed the Politburo in Moscow that they could "organize a demonstration of up to 20,000 Muslims in front of the US embassy in Delhi and that it would cost Rs. 5,000. I request consideration." Leonid Brezhnev wrote, "Agreed on Andropov's request."

In the early fifties, a KGB "sparrow" (a female seducer) persuaded a cipher clerk in the Indian embassy, ARTUR, to go heavily into debt in order to make it easier to compromise him. He was then recruited as an agent in 1957 after being trapped by a KGB officer. As a result of these and other penetrations of the embassy, Soviet codebreakers were probably able to decrypt substantial numbers of Indian diplomatic communications.

Oleg Kalugin, who became head of The First Main Directorate (First Chief Directorate of the Committee under the KGB, the organization responsible for foreign operations and intelligence activities) Directorate K (Counterintelligence) in 1973, had gone on record saying… 'India is a model of KGB infiltration of a Third World government': 'We had scores of sources throughout the Indian government – in intelligence, counterintelligence, the defense, foreign Ministries, and the police.'

In 1975, 10.6 million Rubles were spent on active measures in India specifically to strengthen support for Mrs. Nandhi and undermine her political opponents.

One of the main aims of KGB active measures in the early 1980s was to manufacture evidence that the CIA and Pakistani intelligence were behind the growth of Sikh separatism in Punjab. In the autumn of 1981, KGB's "Service A" launched operation KONTAKT based on a forged document claiming to contain details of the weapons and money provided by Pakistani Inter-

Services Intelligence (ISI) to the militants seeking the creation of an independent Sikh state of Khalistan.

In November, the forgery was passed to a senior Indian diplomat in Islamabad. Shortly afterward, the Islamabad residency reported to the center (Moscow) that, according to agents' reports, the level of anxiety in the Indian embassy (about Pakistani support for Sikh separatists) showed that KONTAKT had the alarmist effect that the KGB's Service A had hoped for.

In the spring of 1982, the New Delhi residency reported that an agent 'S' had direct access to Mrs. Mandira Nandhi and had personally presented to her another forged ISI document fabricated by the KGB's Service A, which claimed to demonstrate Pakistani involvement in the Khalistan conspiracy.

On 5th May, Moscow congratulated the recently installed main resident, Aleksandr Iosifovich Lysenko (codenamed BOGDAN), on the supposed success of agent 'S' and informed him that the center proposed to use 'S' as a major channel for feeding future disinformation to Mrs. Mandira Nandhi.

Before the agent's meeting with Mrs. Mandira Nandhi, the center (Moscow) sent the following detailed instructions:

"Inform 'S' that, in accordance with the terms laid down by the source (of the document), he must not leave the document with VINO (Mrs. Nandhi). Recommend to the agent that he acts in the following way in order not to arouse a negative reaction in VINO. If VINO insists that the document is left with her, then 'S' should leave a previously prepared copy of the document, without the headings which would indicate its origin. Instruct 'S' to observe VINO's reaction to the document."

'S' had reported that he had shown the document to Mrs. Nandhi on 13 May 1982.

The next stage in the Soviet cultivation of the Nandhi Dynasty was the visit to Moscow in July 1983 by Mrs. Mandira Nandhi's elder son Satjiv, who had reluctantly entered politics at his mother's insistence after the death of his younger brother and was being groomed by her for the succession.

During his visit, Mr. Satjiv Nandhi was plainly persuaded by his hosts that the CIA was engaged in serious subversion in Punjab, where Sikh separatism now posed the most serious challenge to his party's government. He had declared on his return that there was 'definite interference from the USA in the Punjab situation.'

The Central Intelligence Agency (CIA) was no saint either, Dam thought to himself.…The CIA and the German intelligence agency Bundesnachrichtendienst (BND) had run a secret joint operation, codenamed 'Thesaurus' initially and later 'Rubicon,' to spy on India.

Dam could hear Mehul, his sister, mother, and Kedge discussing animatedly the selection of candidates for the parliamentary elections scheduled for March/April 2024.

"Half Christian, half Muslim family with no real aptitude for politics… these guys are here because of their Dynasty. That is their only qualification. Once I get this chum into the PM's chair, I will make sure he damn well listens to me… if not, I can make him fall flat on his face," Dam muttered to himself. "Need to get some meetings arranged for this guy… perhaps London will be a better place than Thailand or Myanmar. There is a lot to accomplish, and the time is short."

New York, US

November 15, 2023; 09.00 AM

"The Deep State has become a big thing of our times," Prof. Matthew was explaining. The entire class sat mesmerized. Jerry was absorbing every word like a sponge.

"It is the ever-expanding circle of non-governmental 'insiders'… the word 'insiders' here is very important…!! It is this ever-expanding circle of the non-governmental insiders from the Banking Industry, Commerce Industry, Armament Industry, High Tech Industry who are not only privy to the classified government information but also have a say… a control over the decision-making of the government."

"It is a sort of connector or wire that runs through the militarization of our foreign policy, de-industrialization of the American economy, the so-called war on terrorism, and the rise of the plutocratic social structure that has led to political dysfunction, which in turn has paralyzed day-to-day governance of the government… whether Federal or State."

"What you are saying is that the government is governed by an outside body of various organizations for their own selfish benefits," someone asked.

"Yes. But that is not the only thing. There is more. The tentacles of this… as you put it… the outside body of organizations… are not just engulfing the US government… but they are engulfing the entire globe. Although, as I mentioned during my last lecture, the coups in the late 1800s or early 1900s were the early versions of the Deep State… but in reality, WWII set the stage for the modern-day Deep State. The US emerged as the global superpower post-WWII… more so after the advent of the Atomic Bomb. The Cold War that followed and the rise of 24/7 politics that emerged post-Eisenhower era helped foster the roots of the 'shadow government.' Prof. Matthew paused.

"The shadow government… the Deep State's earlier version started taking shape during JFK's regime. Allen Dulles… have I told you about him before… if not, do some research on this guy. His elder brother John Foster Dulles… the Dulles Airport is named after him, was Secretary of State in Eisenhower's regime. John Dulles imbibed USSR phobia with constant threats of nuclear annihilation by the Communists. Allen Dulles was the Director of the CIA during Eisenhower's regime and Eisenhower had given him a free rein to police the world against any insurgent threat to the US's dominance."

"Dulles's role during WWII itself was quite debatable; we can look at it later… but as the Director of the CIA, Dulles overthrew nationalist governments in Africa, Latin America, and the Middle East. He also targeted some "troublesome" leaders in allied European countries. Allen Dulles continued as the Director of the CIA when JFK was elected as President. However, after the fiasco of the Bay of Pigs, JFK slowly but systematically eased Allen Dulles out of his role as Director of the CIA. That is when the vicious war began within the camps of Allen Dulles and his loyalists with JFK and his camp."

"Allen Dulles was the most cunning person of secret power ever produced in the history of the US. His ambitious clandestine efforts were not only directed against hostile governments but also against his personal enemies. He had learned to manipulate and subvert people and systems throughout his entire career working with various presidential administrations. The Dulles brothers were always close to Wall Street's accomplished and privileged class, whom they saw as the real seat of power in the US. Their connections to these people in their elite club had firmly established them as members of this exclusive rarefied society." Prof. Matthew paused.

"Alright, in the next lecture, we will see how Allen Dulles was successful in establishing and running the shadow government even after the death of JFK, which would be the real beginning of today's Deep State. So, do your own research on Allen Dulles," Prof. Matthew concluded his class.

All the students were sitting dazed even after Prof. Matthew had left the classroom. Jerry was so overwhelmed that he had almost transported himself to the 1960s. In his mind, he was planning to do some research on Allen Dulles's role in WWII. "That would be interesting," he thought to himself.

New York, US

November 20, 2023; 12.00 PM

Cathy had one too many things on her mind as well as in her hand. She had her sack on her one shoulder, while on the other, she carried her purse… which was almost as big as a grocery bag… in one hand, she was carrying a cup of coffee which she had just picked up and in the other hand she had leaflets that were supposed to be distributed to the students and also stuck on various walls and tree trunks in the campus… for the Society for Civil Rights fighting for the Palestinians who were caught in the war between Hamas and Israel.

Cathy had planned a demonstration on the university campus at 3 o'clock, and she had preparations to do. She had called a meeting of the students who had become members of the Society for Civil Rights… and she would lay out the "plan of attack." She had intended to use the *"Blitzkrieg"* technique. She was sure that there would be a big audience, and she had already invited some press reporters and some freelancers too… who resorted to YouTube, Twitter, and Facebook… the social media in General.

Jerry had seen Cathy while she was buying her coffee and wanted to get introduced to her. He followed her as quickly as he could. Finally, he caught up with her.

"Hi there!" Jerry said as he came by Cathy's side.

"Oh hi…" Cathy said, looking at her side, trying to gauge Jerry.

"Jerry is the name… Jerry Carson."

"Cathy… Cathy Dexter… Nice to meet you, Jerry."

'What's with all those leaflets… just curious,' Jerry had noticed the leaflets and used them as a starting point to continue talking to Cathy.

"Oh… those are for the afternoon demonstration that we are planning for the people of Palestine… we, in the sense, the Society for Civil Rights. I work for them as the chief coordinator."

"Oh, I see. But I fail to understand… what is the point of this demonstration on the university campus… because we ain't got nothing to do with the Palestine war," Jerry remarked.

Cathy stopped and turned to Jerry, facing him. "You see, this is where guys like you need some real dope because you all are like the proverbial ostrich mentality. Of course, we have everything to do with the Palestinians and their plight. Who do you think is supplying weapons and ammunition to Israel to wage the war against the poor Palestinians? It is us, the United States. So, we are involved, you see."

Jerry was quite surprised to see Cathy becoming quite aggressive. Somewhere in his mind, the image of Cathy he had created had started to undergo changes.

"Yes, I understand that, but it wasn't Israel who started the war. It came as a response to the heinous attack carried out by Hamas on the Israeli people. So, why not blame Hamas?" Jerry remarked.

"Yeah, but how did that come about? Palestine has been fighting for their rights… a separate state for themselves… for the last 40-50 years and no one is paying attention to their demands. It is always a "what is good for Israel" policy… Even the UN, which is basically owned by the US, decides in favor of Israel. So, it is not that the war was started now by Hamas… this is an ongoing struggle for the rights of the Palestinians."

"You can't clap it with one hand. Israel had been there since Pharaoh's time… there was no Palestine then. So, this is all modern-day politics…"

"Oh, come off it… that way, we are colonizers here in the US… we conquered the local Indian tribes and captured their land. We are the invaders. Your argument does not hold good in the current era."

By now, Jerry had realized that the brunette he had imagined was like a Medusa… and had started to dislike her.

"But what is the point in staging demos here on the Univ campus in the US? The conflict is in Palestine. I can bet 90% of the people will not be able to tell where Palestine is if I show them the map," Jerry retorted.

"The objective is to educate these guys on the current situation. It is to educate, organize, and agitate. That is the process. If we agitate, protest, we put pressure on the government to take action. We have media to support us… we also have big NGOs to support us… someone like Borge Ross, who himself is a Jew but supports our views. Go figure. Then there is social media… where we broadcast our mission. We run a narrative. That is how the 'Activism' process happens." Cathy paused.

"False Narrative," Jerry quipped.

"Why don't you do one thing, Jerry… come to the demonstration… there will be lots of journalists and reporters from various media houses and also some freelancers. Speak to them and get their views… then you can decide what is right and what is not right. Here… take this… it gives the details of today's meeting. See you there." Cathy handed him a leaflet and walked away in a hurry.

Jerry kept looking at the back of departing Cathy in total disbelief. Her bouncing hair now looked like the head of Medusa. Jerry immediately felt the difference of opinions because he felt that Hamas was a terrorist group which was using Palestinians like a shield and perhaps even Palestinians were also supporting Hamas… there was no way one could find it out. Jerry felt outraged.

"I will definitely seek Prof. Matthew's opinion," Jerry thought to himself. "But let me see what this bitch has to say… I will attend the meeting in the afternoon… perhaps I would rather be a part of the reporters and the media than the students. That might give me a chance to get to know a few of the media guys," Jerry murmured. He then decided to check out more on Borge Ross and all those who supported such ideas… more so on the university campuses.

Jerry sat in the library Googling Borge Ross and his Free Society Establishment. "Jeez… this guy is all over!" Jerry exclaimed. What he had found was really surprising to him.

Ross had many organizations under the name of Free Society… not just Free Society Establishment. There was this Free Society Institute, Free Society University Network, etc.…… and not just that, his "donations" had reached beyond his own foundations… supporting independent organizations like Global Witness, The International Crisis Group, The European Council on Foreign Relations, and The Institute for New Economic Thinking.

His Donor "partners" included the likes of…

- International organizations such as the World Bank,

- The World Health Organization (WHO),

- UNAIDS, UNICEF, UNESCO/International Institute for Education Planning,

- The Organization for Security and Cooperation in Europe (OSCE),

- The United Nations Development Program (UNDP),

- The European Union, the Council of Europe,

- The Global Fund to Fight AIDS, Tuberculosis, and Malaria,

- The European Commission,

- African Commission on Human and Peoples' Rights and the Asian Development Bank.

- The United States Agency for International Development (USAID),

- The United States Department of State's Bureau of Educational and Cultural Affairs,

- The United States Centers for Disease Control and Prevention,

- Britain's Department for International Development & Foreign and Commonwealth Office,

- The French Center National des Oeuvres Universitaires et Scolaires (CNOUS),

- The Swedish International Development Cooperation Agency (SIDA),

- The Canadian International Development Agency (CIDA),

And the list went on and on… Jerry had stopped counting after 100 such agencies. Ross was not only donating to political institutions but to universities as well… such as…

- Bard College ($52.2m),

- Harvard University ($20.4m),

- Central European University ($14.4m),

- American University of Central Asia in Bishkek ($8.5m) and

- Columbia University ($5.7m).

"No wonder!" Jerry exclaimed. "Now I know where Cathy is coming from."

The Foundation had disbursed over $184m in funding to 171 universities and higher education institutions in fifty-one countries between 2014 and 2018. Free Society funding to universities almost doubled from $32m in 2014 to $62m in 2018. The number of beneficiaries has jumped 46% from 65 in 2014 to 95 in 2018.

In Jan 2020, in Davos, Switzerland—Ross announced that he would be creating a new university network to better prepare students for current and future global challenges. He was endowing the network with one billion dollars ($1 billion) and asking other philanthropists to contribute. That was the Free Society University Network. The network's aim would be to reach the students to promote the values of a Free Society—including free expression and diversity of beliefs.

Ross had also created the "Alliance for Free Society International" with the purpose of promoting the values of free, open, democratic societies, both domestically and internationally; and coordinating, administrating, and advising national and regional programs all over the globe on a range of issues, including public health, education and, more generally, the development of civil society.

The AFSI also educated the public about issues concerning societies' attempts to transform from totalitarian or authoritarian rule to democratic market economies. AFSI worked with the US government and was active within the United States to address the specific challenges facing global communities. Ross's son was on the board of directors of the AFSI.

Ross was a heavy donor to political parties… particularly the Democrats. According to the Washington Post and the Center for Responsive Politics, a nonprofit that tracks political spending, Ross spent $125 million on political contributions during the 2022 midterm elections, making him the largest contributor to political action committees (PACs) in the United States at that time.

There was so much information on Ross… that Jerry was finding it hard to believe. Jerry also noted that Ross's Free Society was not the only organization doling out funds. There were others like…

- Bloomberg Philanthropies
- HLF
- Ford Foundation
- The Rockefeller Foundation
- MacArthur Foundation
- Bill & Melinda Gates Foundation
- Obama Foundation
- W. K. Kellogg Foundation
- RWJF

- Skoll Foundation

- William and Flora Hewlett Foundation

- Mastercard Foundation

- IKEA Foundation

Jerry's head had started spinning. He could feel the "Force" of the ghosts running the show from behind the curtain. It was almost 3.00 pm. Jerry closed his laptop and decided to go and check out the demonstration Cathy was holding.

New York, US

November 20, 2023; 03.15 PM

The crowd that had gathered for the on campus demonstration for the Society for Civil Rights was quite sizable. There were lots of students carrying placards, boards displaying various messages… demanding Justice for Palestine, Punishment for Israel, etc. They were shouting slogans too. Jerry could see Cathy on a makeshift dais with some senior students… and some outsiders.

Jerry went around trying to find the media reporters, journalists, and freelancers. Finally, he could spot a small bunch of people with cameras and video shooting equipment. Jerry went up to them and stood quietly next to them, trying to assess who would be willing to have a small talk.

Momentarily, a tall, lean guy came and stood next to Jerry. He looked at Jerry and smiled. Jerry returned his gesture with a brief smile.

"What d'ya think of this circus?" the tall guy asked Jerry.

Jerry smiled. "At least there is someone who thinks like I do," he thought to himself. But openly Jerry replied, "I don't know why this demo is on the campus. This is no place."

"Oh… this is the place… Catch them young… This is where they get the brainy guys who could be mentored and cultivated to be the next-gen leaders."

"And who 'they' might be?" Jerry asked. However, before the tall guy could answer… Cathy's voice boomed over the loudspeakers as she started addressing the gathering.

"They are the guys like Borge Ross… who fund such campaigns. These are all so-called leftists. Even the likes of the CIA use them for running their sinister agenda," the tall guy said.

It was much the same as what she had told Jerry… there were other speakers also repeating the same stuff… with more slogans… more threats.

"What a bloody circus… bunch of assholes. They get the funding and then start barking like dogs," the tall guy commented. The last guy on the dais was speaking… rather yelling at the top of his voice.

"Leo Tracker"… the tall guy extended his hand to Jerry

"Jerry Carson"

"Here is my business card… I am a freelancer. I've worked with a few of the media houses before striking out on my own. How about you?"

"I am still at the university majoring in Political Science… then I will be going for graduation in Journalism."

"Oh, cool. If you have time, we can grab a coffee. It will be on me. I would love to talk to you. What do you say?"

Jerry did not have anything at hand, and free coffee sounded tempting.

"That would be great. Do you want to have it on campus?"

"I would not. Let's take a ride. I have a car… I will drop you back. No worries."

"Thank you, Leo. Appreciated."

"What luck… I always wanted to meet some journo… here is the chance," Jerry thought to himself as they walked towards the parking lot where Leo had parked the car.

New York, US

November 30, 2023; 09.30 AM

Aaron Davis was sitting at his desk sipping his first cup of coffee. The office of the Free Society Establishment was located on 5th Avenue in Midtown Manhattan, the most expensive shopping street in the world. After all, it was Borge Ross's organization. Money was never a problem; it was always plentiful.

Aaron looked after the Southeast Asia segment. The world at Free Society Establishment… FSE, was divided into segments… Africa, Central America, South Americas, Middle East, the Far East, etc., and each region had a controlling chief. These chiefs reported to Tom Blanchet, the President of Free Society Establishment.

A month or so ago, Tom met Borge Ross over breakfast and discussed in detail the expected role of FSE in the upcoming Indian elections. Tom extensively briefed Aaron on how to scheme and strategize FSE's involvement in the upcoming General parliamentary elections in India. Dam Keytruda, an Indian settled in the US, will visit Aaron to discuss this strategy.

Aaron loathed such characters who would act as traitors to their homeland. During his brief career of almost a decade with FSE, he had come across plenty of such characters… unsatisfied souls who were prepared to sell their own mothers for the sake of power and money. With a major in Political Science and

Economics, Aaron had initial stints in some NGOs before shifting to FSE. Initially he liked his job but later started disliking it because he thought that he, even indirectly, was responsible for creating turmoil in various countries. He wanted to leave but now he was married and had a school-going daughter. The money was good, and he moved into elite circles. His family was happy and enjoying the social status. Leaving the job and going elsewhere would be difficult because Aaron knew about Ross's connections… and understood that Ross could make things difficult for him. So, Aaron had no other alternative but to stay on.

Aaron had gone over the dossier of Dam Keytruda as well as the dossiers of the people he was representing… the Nandhi family… rather the Nandhi Dynasty. After reading the dossiers, Aaron had started hating the "cabal." He had thought to himself.

Momentarily, the intercom buzzed. Aaron's admin informed him that Dam Keytruda had arrived, and he was ushered into the special meeting room and served coffee. The special meeting room was equipped with hidden video cameras and microphones. The entire conversation would be videotaped and recorded for the sake of "training purposes." Aaron smirked to himself and got up from his chair.

"Hello Mr. Keytruda… good to see you."

"Oh hi… you can call me Dam… The name is Damodhar, shortened to Dam. Thank you for seeing me at such short notice."

"Oh… it is nothing… we do understand the importance of the situation and also the urgency of the matter that you have on your mind. So, the floor is yours. Pray, tell us what you have on your mind," Aaron tried to sound normal with a fake smile on his face. He had instantly disliked the guy. He looked and sounded so pompous.

"Well, as you might already know, India goes to the polls for the parliamentary elections in March/April 2024... a few months from now. The Nandhi family had been in power for almost six decades before the current party... the religious bigots actually... came to power a decade back, and I can't describe how they have destroyed the country's socio-economic fabric. It has been a disaster. The common man is suffering, and so are the minorities... the Muslims, the Christians, and the backward class people. The Nandhi family and their party... which is over one hundred years old... have been the custodians of Indian democracy. The objective is to remove these religious extremists, these bigots and get the Nandhi family back into the saddle... to bring back democracy to India."

Aaron smiled to himself and thought... "This chum thinks I am an idiot and that I have no clue about what is happening in India. It is just that Ross hates Mr. Dodi, the current Prime Minister of India." Aaron remembered Ross's comments on Indian Prime Minister Dodi and Indian democracy at a conference in Munich, where Ross had specifically questioned the quality of Indian democracy, especially for Muslims, under PM Dodi and the role of "crony" capitalism in its continuity.

Ross's munificence, driven by stock market transactions that triggered financial crises, had characteristically been used by him as a dogmatic reason for his disdain of the right-wingers, and to work on free societies for larger global domination. This was his idea of "free and open societies," with its pursuit for inclusion, and for diluting the dominant groups in political systems. Thus, a range of causes such as minority rights, immigration, and gender diversity, which tend to be driven by progressives, had been favored by Ross and had become the reason to scorn conservative politics. Thus, Ross had been attempting to change the fundamental nature of social and political systems.

Ross's philanthropic organization, FSE, remained a top global donor that consistently funded causes and individuals working on accountability and inclusion in the interest of greater democratization which often equated with support for dissidents and political opposition to power.

Ross had found a legal way to so-called "donate" his money using the mask of charity, education, climate, social justice, preserving democracy, defeating fascism, racism, casteism, LGBTQ rights, Islamophobia, refugees... the list went on. And with billions of pounds at his disposal, he had found it easy to buy that influence... and obtain global control.

It did not matter if Borge Ross believed in all that he preached; it was still Ross's "imperialistic interference" in various countries' politics, including India, to save the "democracy." What an irony... Aaron thought.

The kind of people Ross funded was quite questionable. The radical Islamist hate-monger Khaled Beydoun was funded by Ross. Anurima Bhargava, the "Hindu" member of USCIRF who had recommended sanctions on India and who was always seen on the Islamist organization IAMC's forum, was funded by Ross. Harsh Mander, the guy who authored the infamous Communal Violence Bill for Mrs. Maria Nandhi's NAC, was funded by Ross.

How can such a person, who funded and continued to fund such open Hindu haters, be called a philanthropist? Well, it was simple, those calling him that were also funded by him or the ecosystem he was part of. The US, the Democrats in particular, were perfectly happy to let Borge Ross openly interfere in India's internal matters. Ross funded hundreds of NGOs and media that did control various indices, rankings, reports, and academic research.

"India is an interesting case," Ross had commented. "It's a democracy, but its leader, Rajendra Dodi, is no democrat. Inciting violence against Muslims was an important factor in his meteoric rise. Dodi maintains close relations with both open and closed societies. India is a member of the QUAD, which includes Australia, the US and Japan, but it buys a lot of Russian oil at a steep discount and makes a lot of money out of it," Ross had said.

"Dodi and his Gujarati business tycoons are close allies," and "their fate is intertwined," Ross had said. "One of the business tycoons is accused of stock manipulation," and "Dodi is silent on the subject, but he will have to answer questions from foreign investors and in parliament," Aaron remembered. "What the heck Ross has got to do with India he is not going to go and live there," he had thought to himself.

Aaron also remembered that in spreading negative views about India and Prime Minister Rajendra Dodi, Ross was believed to have sponsored Christophe Jaffrelot, the French writer, and also the Canadian Indian activist Ricken Patel.

Between 2016 and 2022, Patel's Namati Foundation reportedly received millions of dollars from FSE. In early 2023, Patel began chairing the "Friends of Democracy" group, co-chaired by Ross's son, Jeffery Ross. The group's stated goal was to "fight against the ruling party" to save India, and it allegedly spread propaganda on topics such as Russian oil purchases by India, with its views closely mirroring those of the US government. Some of the funds received by Patel's group reportedly reached Indian think tanks, including the New Delhi-based Center for Policy Research (CPR), whose foreign funding license was canceled in 2020!

Christophe Jaffrelot, a prominent French Indologist and political scientist, was a key figure in disseminating anti-India narratives. Jaffrelot's influence was particularly evident in Western Media outlets, with the French daily Le Monde prominently featuring his critiques. His writings extended to Indian media platforms, targeting Indian voters with a particular agenda.

One significant aspect of Jaffrelot's influence involved the promotion of a "caste census." This idea, included in the opposition Nandhi party's manifesto, is attributed to Jaffrelot's research. In 2021, Jaffrelot published a report advocating for a caste census in India and subsequently wrote articles in Indian media, bringing the topic into public discourse, especially during the election season. The report described this as a remarkable feat for an academic, underscoring his ability to shape public opinion on a large scale.

Jaffrelot also spread a false narrative about the increasing "upper-caste dominance" within PM Modi's party. This was part of a deliberate propaganda effort by Jaffrelot to open societal fault lines in India.

The Henry Luce Foundation (HLF) was also identified as a financial supporter of Jaffrelot and other academics involved in India-specific research. Established by Henry Luce, one of the founders of Time Magazine, HLF was said to have provided substantial funding for various projects related to Indian politics and society.

One of the key projects funded by HLF was Jaffrelot's "Muslims in a Time of Hindu Majoritarianism," which reportedly received ~ $350,000 between 2021 and 2023. The Foundation was noted for being staffed by many ex-US government officials and think tank members. HLF's funding extended to other projects as well. It supported the Berkley center for Religion, Peace, and World Affairs at Georgetown University with a project titled "The Hindu Right and India's Religious Diplomacy." Additionally, the Foundation was believed to have provided ~ $125,000 to the Carnegie Endowment for International Peace (CEIP) for articles critical of Hindu nationalism and religious dynamics in India, including titles such as "Hindu Nationalism: From Ethnic Identity to Authoritarian Repression," "Religion, Citizenship, and Belonging in India," and "Religion-as-Ethnicity and the Emerging Hindu Vote in India.".

The Foundation is also believed to have provided Human Rights Watch (HRW) with around $300,000 for a project to document religious violence in Asia, specifically Myanmar, Indonesia, and India. Furthermore, HLF funded research on "anti-PM Dodi's political party" for academicians in the US, including California-based activist Angana P. Chatterji and Audrey Truschke, an academic at Rutgers University. The objective was to use the Indian diaspora… particularly in academics, against Indian right-wingers or, in general, against India… finding faults… by paying handsome amounts in donations to do such research projects and show India in a bad light.

Aaron hated such people. He thought of them as traitors. But as a job, he had to interact with them constantly.

Presently, he turned his attention to Dam Keytruda. "So, tell me how we can be of help to you in achieving your objective?"

"Well, apart from the financial help, which I am sure your organization will be willing to extend in any form or shape, we would like to have your inputs on how we can plan these… well… activities."

"What are your ideas… let us check them out first," Aaron replied.

"Well, it has to be 'divide and conquer'… I mean there are matters such as the Khalistan Issue, like Mr. Pannum, Muslim votes, Kashmir unrest, lower caste votes…" Dam's voice trailed off. He wanted to mention seeking the help of Islamic fundamentalists, China… but kept silent.

"Well, you seem to have worked it all out. Basically, the issues with any government are on financial markets, the Economy, Justice System, etc. In the case of India, you can add armed forces, Farmers, Castes, Minorities, foreign assistance like Russia, etc. You may want to try the Venezuela Model."

"What is the Venezuela Model?"

"Giving everything free to the people to get elected… In the case of India… maybe free electricity, free gas, free water, free groceries… I don't know… I have never been there… You should be an expert. Also, buy out the media and run false narratives… Goebbels' policy… it always works."

"Yes, those are some great suggestions."

"Also, visit the US Dept of State… find a supporter or supporters… Check how the CIA can get involved. They can help create an Iran-like situation… when they removed Mossadegh from power. Find moles in Dodi's cabinet, there would certainly be some unsatisfied souls. Create a Hindenburg-type menace again. Visit US universities and give anti-India lectures. Create or gain control by proxy. There are various ways and means."

"Use people like Greta Thunberg. Approach her. Take her help. Remember protests are for education, Agitation and for organizing people against some serious social causes. You can use any and all means of media that are available at your disposal for this. But then, how to do this is something we can't tell you. You have got to figure it out yourself. False narrative helps because people don't have time to check the facts. Use celebrities, influencers… you can figure it out according to your needs. These are the tools available to you. The toolkit as some people say."

Dan was taking notes on his laptop. He seemed to be quite pleased. Aaron wanted to get up and punch him squarely on his pompous, swarthy face but kept his cool. He wanted to finish the meeting quickly.

"Thank you for all the suggestions. We really appreciate your help. Perhaps in a month or so, I will schedule another meeting with you… a follow-up meeting… if that is fine with you."

"For sure… why not," Aaron replied, getting up from his chair and moving towards the door, indicating that the meeting was over.

"Thank you so much for seeing me. I really appreciate it," Dam said, almost bowed, and then left.

"Traitor… scumbag," Aaron muttered to himself as he went to his room.

Washington D.C., US

December 5, 2023; 10.00 AM

It was the meeting called to discuss the ongoing Ukraine war. The meeting was requested by the SecDef, and it was meant to be a highly classified meeting. POTUS, the VeeP, SecDef and Secretary of State were in attendance in the Oval Office. SecDef had wanted some senior officer… preferably a four-star General from the Pentagon to attend the meeting… but Secretary of State Bob Mayers had turned down the request. "If need be, we can brief him later and take his suggestions if any… as of now we are not having any feet on the ground there in Ukraine," Bob had told SecDef. Although both knew that it was not true. Quite a few US and NATO military personnel were participating directly in the war against the Russians.

"Can we begin?" said POTUS… who wanted to get things over with. As such, his opinions did not matter even if he gave any. The VeeP… the Vice President did not understand much of what was happening… but always pretended to understand everything. Both Bob and Graham Hick, SecDef, resented the VeeP. So, the objective was basically to get the suggested action plan approved.

"Yes, of course," Bob replied and passed around the folders containing specific details. "Graham, the floor is all yours."

"Thank you, Bob," Graham replied.

In his mind, he was clear… he wanted to get the approval of the POTUS to supply more arms and ammunition to Ukraine… including some advanced missile systems, which could possibly reach deep into Russian territory. This war and the one raging in the Middle East… Israel and Hamas were quite profitable wars in Graham's opinion. He was also of the opinion that Bob would also think the same way… as well as the Generals at the Pentagon. After all, the payoff was quite handsome from the defense lobby.

Exploitation… Graham had always avoided the word corruption… in the US armed forces had increased manifold over the years. It was such a big behemoth that no one could get to the bottom of reality. Those who had attempted were no more… they had either met with some accident or died of some weird ailment.

Since all the big defense companies were busy 24x7x365 producing stuff to keep the wars in progress, Wall Street was also quite happy, and the stock prices soared. Happiness was all around.

"Mr. President, the objective of this meeting is to get some specific items approved to be supplied to Ukraine. This has become a must in view of the ground situation in Ukraine. If we are unable to stop the Russians in Ukraine, it will bolster the Russians, and the next aggression will possibly be against any NATO member. You have the list of arms and ammunition in the folder… which is quite exhaustive but self-explanatory. There is nothing that will raise eyebrows."

Ukraine had been pushing for permission from its Western partners to use the long-range missiles they could provide to strike targets deep inside Russia, as Ukrainian forces struggled to hold back Russian advances in eastern Ukraine. Kyiv officials argued that the weapons were vital to weaken Russia's ability to strike Ukraine and force Russia to move its strike capabilities further from the border.

Ukraine wanted long-range missile systems like the US-made Army Tactical Missile System, ATACMS. From NATO... the British-led Storm Shadow and the similar French-made SCALP.

"This list contains the long-range missiles," the VeeP said. "This was not on the cards earlier."

'Yes,' Bob replied, 'but it has become an absolute necessity. Now, the American missile, it's called the ATACM. That, as you might know, stands for Army Tactical Missile System. The long-range version can travel 190 miles. And that's the one the Ukrainians really want. Now, they can use those long-range ones in Crimea, of course, since it's not Russian territory. Ukraine can use some of the American-made missiles to fire into Russia right now - short distances, but only for defensive purposes, let's say Russia is shooting at Ukrainian troops with artillery or missiles.'

Russia had warned that it would consider allowing such long-range strikes an act of war, and Ukraine's Western allies were wary of antagonizing the country with the world's largest nuclear arsenal. But both Bob and Graham did not think that Russia would act on its threats... because up until now, Russia had restrained itself. That had made the US Pentagon Generals think that Russia was a sissy.

"But why should we supply... let NATO members supply their own versions," the POTUS said. Both Bob and Graham were quite surprised to get a pushback from the POTUS. "He must have taken his meds before coming to the meeting," Graham thought to himself.

"Mr. President, the Brits have what's called the Storm Shadow, which can travel about 155 miles and could be used to hit those targets inside Russia. The Brits have already sent a number of them to Ukraine, but that missile has an American component, so they need the US to sign off on those missiles to use inside Russia - the same with the French. They have a similar missile. It's called SCALP. So, if we could give a thumbs up for the use of the British, and also the French, missiles…" Graham trailed off, leaving the sentence halfway.

Both Bob and Graham had discussed what the defense analysts and those pushing for the use of these weapons had said… that they could hurt Russia's ability to launch glide bombs from aircraft deep within Russia. The Institute for the Study of War had mentioned that there were some 250 targets inside Russia that these long-range missiles could strike.

Both Bob and Graham knew that the US really couldn't send a lot more without hurting its own military readiness, which some Pentagon Generals felt was the reality. Because the US had thousands of these long-range missiles, and the allies had hundreds, the long-range missiles would be a way for the Ukrainians to push back against Russia. But of course, most defense analysts at the Pentagon had warned that striking deep inside Russia could "maybe" end the invasion, or at least push Russian President Vladimir Putin to the negotiating table, or alternatively ignite a real brutal retaliation from Russia that the US would not be ready or prepared for. However, the pressure from the defense lobby… and more so from Cobblestone… Gregory Brink, who remained in the shadow but could be felt like Darth Vader, was so high that NO was not an answer.

"Well, apart from the long-range missiles, I am okay to approve the list. I will need to discuss the missile issue with the British PM and also with the French. I would also like to get the opinion of NSA (National Security Agency), NRO

(National Reconnaissance Org) and others at the Pentagon before taking the next step. I have no intention of starting WW3. Next year is the election year, and I have to be realistic," the POTUS replied in a firm tone.

"When can we review this again?" Graham tried to push.

"I will let Bob know. Sometime next year only," POTUS replied as he slowly got up from his chair, indicating that the meeting was over.

"I don't want hassles before the elections. These guys have no brains," POTUS thought to himself.

Graham shrugged his shoulders and collected his files. The VP just made some lame joke, laughed loudly, and left the room… Bob had expected this.

"Patience, my friend," Bob tried to cajole Graham once they were out of the Oval office.

"We are wasting time," retorted Graham.

"Do you really think so?" Bob became serious.

"Well, you know the reasons," said Graham.

"Yes, but the government does not work like this; you know that. It has to be cognizant of reality. You see, we are caught between fire and the frying pan. On paper, we are a force, but you know as well as I do that we are spread thin. Our ammunition stocks are depleted. We have to supply to Israel on priority. Ukraine is not a priority for us. A lot more is at stake in the Middle East."

"I doubt that. Israel can take care of itself," Graham retorted. He always felt that Israel bullied the White House, and the White House could do nothing but yield to Israel's demands.

'You are wrong. If you observe and analyze carefully, no one is supporting the US or Israel, for that matter. The Saudis, The

Emirates, The Kuwaitis, The Qataris, The Jordanians… even the Egyptians… they all have taken a neutral stand… they are supporting neither the US/Israel, nor Hamas. They are just saying "go to the two-state solution." While Hamas has support from the Iranians, Hezbollah, the Houthis, the Syrians, the Iraqis, even the Taliban…. all those where we had messed up thoroughly in the past. It is an uneven battlefield. And that worries me even more. Part of our forces, navy, and air… are in the Mediterranean, part in the Persian Gulf, part in the Indian Ocean, and part near Taiwan. We are already divided.'

"Perhaps. But…" Graham was thinking about the pressure from the defense lobby, which had started to push its agenda. The thought he had in his mind was, "Who really controls the US nukes?" because he was of the opinion that the POTUS was not in his prime mental condition, the VeeP was just a puppet, so if someone from the Pentagon had to decide, then it would be swift… and Graham also was not sure that the US was prepared for any nuclear strikes if they did happen.

Graham suddenly thought about DARPA (Defense Advanced Research Projects Agency), and he turned to Bob, shook hands, and said, "I've got to go… I have another meeting."

Bob kept looking at the back of Graham walking away in the flurries.

Bob knew the real reason for the continuation of the Ukraine war. It benefited US Industries immensely. The Ukraine war started because NATO wanted to add Ukraine to its fold. The objective of adding new countries to NATO was simple… those new countries would have to conform their military purchases to NATO weapon specifications which were controlled by the BIG 6… the US Military Contractors… US defense manufacturers…

Northrup Grumman, Lockheed, General Dynamics, Raytheon, Boeing, etc.

In 2022, the US had already given $113 billion to Ukraine. Furthermore, it had given $24 billion, and most recently, it had given $60 billion. This was considered a "loan" and not aid. When it is termed as a loan, the country had to agree and sign loan conditions and sanctions imposed on them. In the case of Ukraine, it was their agricultural land, the European Breadbasket, the farmland taken over by the big three US companies: Du Pont, Monsanto, and Cargill, which were owned by none other than Cobblestone, a company in the business of owning Real-World Assets (RWAs).

Rebuilding Ukraine would involve major US corporations that would bring prosperity to the US. The main reason for the US's interest in Ukraine was that Ukraine has been sitting on 26 trillion USD worth of rare minerals… important for any industrialized country… like iron ore, cobalt, lithium, uranium, gold, titanium, graphite, coal, and many more. Ukraine already had some mining contracts given to companies in Australia, the UK, and Turkey. The US wanted to take it all… and control it. That was the main reason for the US's interest in keeping the proxy war going on in Ukraine. The US had no interest if Ukrainians died in the war. They would use cheap local labor and exploit them to the US's advantage. That was the real plan.

Bob was completely aware of the various US interest groups involved directly in putting pressure on the US government to get Russia out of Ukraine without the US getting involved directly. But what Bob was not sure about was the real scenario if Russia (and China) decided to retaliate in full force… which he felt… there would be no US left either. He shuddered at the thought.

His opinion of the Ukrainian President was not positive. Bob thought the Ukrainian President was a crook and a corrupt politician who was taking the US for a ride. "Time will tell," Bob muttered to himself and started walking towards his office.

"CIA manages to create anarchy worldwide... in various countries with the help of some individuals like Ross... who are under CIA control, and the Pentagon creates wars under pressure from various big lobbies in the US. So, it is not the US government that runs the country... it is these guys in the dark who do... wow... what a democracy!" Bob thought to himself as he entered his office... completely frustrated.

"Wonder how many skeletons are in the US closet," he said aloud as he sat in his chair.

New York, US

December 6, 2023; 08.30 AM

Gregory Brink, Chairman of Cobblestone Inc, belonged to the "early to bed, early to rise" category. Habituated to getting up at 5 o'clock in the morning, Gregory would spend on average, one hour in his private gym and then half an hour in his swimming pool. By 7.30 am, he would be ready to arrive at his office on the 35th floor of Onyx Tower located on 57th Street in Manhattan and be in his chair by 8.00 am. Unless he was traveling, which was quite seldom, he would follow his routine to the letter.

Between 8.00 am and 8.30 am, Gregory would go over the important matters at hand: reports, actions, decisions… and he would then be ready for the day. With trillions of dollars' worth of assets under his belt – real-world assets – these days, Gregory always thought ten years ahead of the world. Even today, as he sat in his office, having finished his morning routine, his mind was already in the year 2033.

After the BITCOIN ETF approval, Gregory had revealed that soon everything would be ETF'd and tokenized, threatening to fractionalize not just the existing assets and commodities but the entire "natural world," reducing most living things into Wall Street financial products to be traded on a single universal ledger.

His mind hovered over CBDC… the Central Bank Digital Currency, which was a digital version of a country's fiat currency that was to be issued by the central bank. CBDCs were different from cryptocurrencies, which were decentralized and ran on distributed ledger technology. CBDCs were intended to be widely available to the public and could reduce the cost of maintaining a complex financial system, as well as cross-border transaction costs.

"By 2030, I must have absolute global control over food, water, digital media, data, defense, Pharma, environment, RWAs. I must have global governance and dominance. The governments in various countries must yield to my demands. I will have complete control over… the Senators, Wall Street, Silicon Valley, the banks, Pentagon Generals, …."

Pentagon Generals reminded Gregory of his meeting with General Frank Norton… General Frank Norton… a five-star decorated General… later in the afternoon. This meeting was not on his office calendar. For all practical purposes, he was dining privately with his family that afternoon, while in reality he would be meeting General Frank Norton and a special team. The agenda was quite specific… one of the items was "make NATO committed to the Ukraine war." Gregory wanted to pressurize the POTUS and the US lawmakers to send more advanced arms to Ukraine. The other item was still undisclosed.

However, Gregory was skeptical because he had "heard" a certain whisper about CIA leadership asking for information on a "couple of lobbies" their demands and discussions with the State Department. What made Gregory concerned was the mention of the word "DARPA."

"There must be someone who is extremely logical and perhaps a mind reader… and that means I need to be extremely careful," Gregory thought to himself.

Vienna Austria

December 6, 2023; 02.30 PM

While Gregory was thinking about the Ukraine war in his New York office, Alexei Mikhailovich Zakharov was sitting in Restaurant Konstantin Filippou located on Dominikanerbastei in the Wien area of Vienna. It was one of the most expensive restaurants in Vienna, famous for its two Michelin Stars. It had been snowing since morning, and the forecast indicated that the snow would continue into the night as well.

Although inside, it was warm, cozy, and pleasant, Alexei hated the weather… "What is the point of coming here… might as well be in Moscow," he thought to himself. But Alexei was required to visit Vienna to meet Sergei. The meeting was scheduled a few hours ago, requiring Alexei to get on his own aircraft and come to Vienna in a jiffy. Such meetings were never scheduled in advance. Alexei looked at his watch. It was just striking 2.30 PM. "He should be here any minute," Alexei said to himself. He was about to take a sip of his vodka when he saw the Kellner (waiter) directing Sergei to Alexei's table.

"*Grüß Gott, Herr Alex,*" Sergei said, sounding perfectly Austrian. Alexei could not have recognized Sergei if he had met him on the street. He had completely transformed himself into another personality.

"*Grüß Gott,*"… Alexei replied softly.

"It is Christoph Fischer," Sergei whispered.

"*Herr Fischer*," Alexei completed the greetings.

Vienna was considered the Spy Capital of the world. Due to its liberal laws, it allowed the foreign espionage agencies to operate on its ground… including those of China, Iran, and also the Russian Foreign Intelligence Service (SVR) responsible for intelligence and espionage outside of Russia, and the FSB, the Federal Security Service (FSB) responsible for Russian domestic security and counterintelligence.

"It is lousy weather, I would say. Did you have a problem getting in?" Sergei / Christoph inquired. He was referring to Alexei's flight from Moscow to Vienna.

"Not really. It was a reasonably smooth ride," Alexei replied. He could see Kellner (the waiter) approaching.

After taking the order for drinks and the appetizers, the waiter left them.

"Well?" Alexei inquired.

"I have booked a room in HOTEL KAISERHOF on Frankenberggasse in Wien area. My room number is 515. Easy to remember. It is clean. I made sure. You will surely get a room in the same place. Once you are there, you can come to my room at 1700 hours 'cause my room is all cleaned up. We can talk in detail," Sergei whispered.

Alexei was impressed. He liked people who were meticulous and precise. Sergei was someone special. He was a US citizen by birth… born to a couple of Russian descent. Sergei's father was a mechanic in a shipping yard. It was a Greek shipping company and Sergei's father was based in Greece. Sergei's mother worked as a helper at the Soviet Embassy. Both had met at a local event and had fallen in love. As luck would have it, immediately after their marriage, Greece came under German occupation. A rapid German Blitzkrieg campaign followed on 6th April 1941, and by the middle of May, Greece had come under joint occupation by three Axis powers: Germany, Italy, and Bulgaria.

Sergei's parents… just married, decided to flee and were fortunate to board a ship sailing for New York. After landing in New York, both his parents found jobs in their respective fields. Although their first child was born after 15 years of marriage, the next five kids were born over the next 10 years. Sergei was the last child.

Sergei was the smartest of all. He was good at studies. Picked up languages quickly… by fifteen, he could speak English, Russian, Spanish, and Italian fluently. He was a quick learner. He was good with his hands. Just by observing his father, he learned how to repair engines… he could disassemble and reassemble an engine all by himself when he was eighteen. He was very enthusiastic, very amicable and made friends very quickly… mingled with people very quickly. He had an inborn sense of direction and could communicate very well. Another area of expertise, courtesy of his Italian friends, was he could steal anything anytime, anywhere and no one would even know.

His mother was not very happy with his last skill but doted on him because he was their last kid. He was the only one to go to university and earn a degree. He had taken history as his major and had learned German in the process.

After a couple of odd jobs, he got recruited into the CIA… assigned to the Eastern Europe desk. But soon, his boss decided that it was a waste of time to make him work in the office… and that Sergei was meant for the field ops Intelligence and Foreign Affairs, Mission center – Western hemisphere… but in the non-black ops… albeit, laying the ground for the Black Ops teams.

Training followed, and Sergei was first posted in West Germany. A chance meeting with a KGB operative in Spain made Sergei become a double agent. Sergei could never forget the hatred and discrimination he had faced while growing up in New York. That triggered the urge to become a double agent. It was risky… but Sergei had accepted the risk.

Sergei never married… but in every city he went, he had "arrangements." He alone knew the names he used while maintaining these various "arrangements." He was a true chameleon. He could disguise himself very quickly and blend in with the surroundings. The only thing Sergei had not been able to do was to visit Russia.

Sergei and Alexei discussed a few sundry things over drinks and a late lunch. It was time to depart. Sergei eased himself out first. He planned to walk down to the hotel. "It would be quick," he said. Sergei knew every street and every lane in Vienna, like the back of his hand.

Ten minutes after Sergei had gone, Alexei paid for the drinks and lunch, paid a handsome tip, and requested a cab to be ordered.

At exactly 1700 hours, Alexei knocked on room number 515. Sergei carefully opened the door, looked on either side of the corridor, let Alexei in the room, and closed the door quickly but very softly, without any noise.

He indicated Sergei to the chair, went to the side table, poured two large vodkas, brought it to Alexei, gave one to him and said, "*Nahzdah-Rohvyuh*" (Cheers). Alexei softly clinked the glass and took a sip.

"Okay, tell me," Alexei said.

"I guess you all perhaps know this… as to why the US is keen on keeping the Ukraine war going."

"We have a fairly good idea. Is there anything specific?"

"You mean apart from Gregory Brink and the pressure on NATO to get engaged in the direct war?"

"Yes."

"Well, the earlier regime of Democrats… the one before ex-President Trump, is the one who calls the shots even now. It is they… the cabal who are obsessed with Russia. If the Dems come to power again… it is the cabal which will be running their agenda. It could mean the continuation of war… even if Ukraine gets destroyed completely."

"Yes, we understand that."

"Have you explored other ways of inflicting wounds internally on the US and NATO?"

"Such as?"

"Drugs, arms, and viruses… something similar to 9/11… but not 'spectacular' to draw attention. It will be like appendixes bursting… It is terrible."

"What do you have in mind?"

"I asked for you because it is your area of expertise… Drugs, arms, transportation… transportation of humans… human trafficking in a way. Drugs… do you remember Karl Lee… or Li Fang Wei… it happened in 2001. Remember?"

Alexei remembered… Li Fang Wei was a Chinese entrepreneur and international arms dealer. In April 2014, he was indicted by the United States, alleging that he was suspected of violating sanctions and regulations, using shell companies to access the American financial system, and providing Iran with technology related to ballistic missiles.

"What are you suggesting?"

"Iran needs hi-tech stuff for its nukes. There is a guy in Germany who can provide this. In return, you get money. Iran also provides manpower to be utilized by you… I mean Russia… in NATO countries, in the US… there are quite a few unsatisfied souls in the US… homeless, refugees, Muslims… You could use them… via drugs, and you can procure viruses from China… which can be sent inside NATO countries and the US. Then there are other things like cyber-attacks, breaking down critical infrastructure… sabotage."

"I see where you are going with this. Hidden war. Why?"

"Because this is what the US + NATO are alluding to. The regime in the US… the Dems and the regime in the UK… the leftists… are the ones who are jumping with enthusiasm. The Brits are idiots. They still live in their past glory. There is a fire under their butt, but they can't figure out what to do. So, it is something that you, the Russians, can do… destabilize them completely internally."

"Sergei, I suspect that you have something else on your mind that you are not spelling out. You are not here to tell me all these odd things that Russia needs to do… or that I need to do personally for Russia. What is it? Do you have any specific information that the CIA is working on?"

Sergei was quiet for a moment. He was thinking hard. Finally, he said, "Possibly. But I don't know the details and the full extent of what it is. I am just giving you a hint at this stage. I will know more in the coming days. But for now, you have time on your hands. Please take some action. Here is the name and other details of the German guy I spoke to you about. He will soon have your information. Please get connected. This is for your good. I will let you know when something specific develops."

Sergei gave a piece of paper to Alexei. Alexei transferred the information to his cell phone… gave the paper back to Sergei. Sergei took out a lighter, burned the paper in the empty vodka glass and then flushed the ash down the toilet… cleaned the glass and returned.

"Trust me, there might be something sinister going on, and you'd better be prepared. I will let you know once I have the info," Sergei warned.

Alexei was not the kind of person who would be worried… but the way Sergei spoke, Alexei got the hint.

"Neither the UK nor NATO, nor the US is in a position to go to a direct war. So, they will resort to something sinister… which will avoid direct conflict yet inflict severe damage to Russia. So, be careful and work on similar lines," Sergei concluded.

"I will contact the German guy. You please let him know… what is his background?"

"His grandfather was an SS commander in WW2. He was brought up by his grandfather. So, you know his mental setup. Exploit it the way you can."

"*Spokoynoy nochi*" (Good Night), Alexei said… slowly got up. Went up to the door… opened it slowly… looked on either side of the corridor and let himself out. Sergei closed the door softly behind him.

Sergei was feeling sleepy and tired. He had flown in from DC… and he had not been able to make out what he had fleetingly heard in the corridors in Langley. "What the lobbies lobbying in the State Department have to do with DARPA," Abe Williams, Deputy Director of the CIA, was not a guy who would get perturbed over anything… but even he looked perturbed.

As Sergei lay on the bed, he kept thinking… "I need to find out. The US leadership can't touch the Chinese. They are shit scared of the Chinese. Once they have been beaten up by the Vietnamese and then by the Taliban… so the US will think one hundred times before going to war away from its shores…. To save Taiwan."

"Israel is getting beaten up by the 3H… Hamas, Hezbollah and the Houthis, and no Arab nation is willing to support the US. The Egyptian President, Sisi, is hanging by a thread. Even King Abdullah of Jordan has become quite unpopular in his own country. Saudi, Emirates, Kuwait… they are all keeping away from the Israeli conflict. So, the US finds itself isolated in the Middle East."

"The only place the US will decide to go is Ukraine because it has minerals and grains… and there is NATO to fight the war… The US can keep supplying the fodder… the arms and ammunition. And as such, there is no government to run the US. It is run by the Mega Corps like Cobblestone… and of course, the CIA. The CIA has its own agenda and agents like Borge Ross to execute the agenda."

"EU is almost broke. UK will certainly implode one day in the very near future… Germany has realized the mistake it made in dissociating itself from Russia. Same with France… But openly they can't admit it because of NATO. So, it would be in Russia's best interest to break NATO. And people like Alexei can do that effectively. Alexei needs to be coached one of these days."

Sergei had slowly drifted into sleep.

London, England

December 15, 2023; 08.30 AM

Rajan Sharma had been covering all the foreign tours of Mehul Nandhi. Almost 50 now, Rajan had been representing a reputed Indian media house for over 2 decades. His reporting was unbiased and was appreciated by the readers. He was in London covering Mehul's current visit to the UK… which was quite surprising given that the Indian general elections were due from April 2024 till the 1st week of June 2024. Rajan was up at 5.30 am and was in his hotel room typing away his report on his laptop for over 2 hours, giving facts and figures. "Hope I have not missed any point," he said to himself as he looked at the report he had typed. It read….

The Western Deep State has been unable to digest India's improved relationships with major powers in the West, the Middle East, East, and Southeast Asia. Both China and the Western Deep State see India's rise as a major world power and the promise of the world's leading GDP contributor, as a threat to their agendas. Sabotaging the Indian general elections is the only way to stop the unstoppable India."

But the story began back in 2015 when, soon after the colossal loss in the 2014 general elections, Mehul Nandhi, the then Vice President of his party, went away to Southeast Asia for 60 days. While away, the most significant parts of his

stay were spent in two China-friendly countries, Myanmar – 21 days and Cambodia – 11 days.

Myanmar had been completely under the Chinese grip, while in Cambodia, they had thrown out the United States (US) military, proving the mettle of Chinese influence in the region. There was no record of who Mehul Nandhi was meeting and discussing within those countries. Despite being an SPG (Special Protection Group) "protectee," he allowed the SPG to accompany him only to Bangkok. This further proves that Mehul's party didn't want Mehul's schedule and activities to be disclosed through any source.

In June 2015, Mehul visited the United Kingdom (UK), and in September 2015, the US, and the UK. In June 2016, he visited Turkey, and in September 2016, once again, the UK. In March 2017, Mehul visited Italy, and in July 2017, the UK. Between 2015 and 2019, Mehul Nandhi made 257 trips to foreign lands. Even his mother, Mrs. Nandhi, made twenty-seven foreign trips to undisclosed destinations during the same period. The modus operandi was similar; SPG was notified just 5-6 hours before the departure, making it impossible for them to provide cover.

However, finally, the Indian security agencies got alarmed when Mehul Nandhi met with Chinese envoy Luo Zhaohui in July 2017, forcing the ruling party to question his intentions. This meeting took place at the peak of the India-China Doklam standoff. Soon thereafter, Mehul Nandhi met the Bhutanese envoy.

In March 2023, Mehul Nandhi visited the UK and launched a vicious attack on the ruling party. He also urged the US and the UK to intervene in restoring democracy in India. He spoke with students from the University of Cambridge and held meetings at the Grand Committee Room of the House of Commons, painting India in a bad light. This infuriated the ruling party in India. On the contrary, after being thrown out of power, Mehul Nandhi's grandmother and India's former Prime Minister, Mrs. Mandira Nandhi, also visited the UK in November 1978. She was frustrated but remained much more responsible and avoided painting India in a bad light in a foreign land.

In May 2023, Mehul Nandhi had once again visited the US. In September 2023, he had visited the European Union's headquarters in Brussels, followed by France and Norway. In October 2023, he had visited Uzbekistan. Now, in December 2023, just months before the general elections, Mehul Nandhi was planning to visit Brunei, Indonesia, Singapore, Malaysia, and Vietnam.

All these foreign jaunts were not all public gatherings. Rather, most of them were closed-door meetings. Every visit was followed by a barrage of anti-India articles across the world but especially in the West. Articles with a similar agenda:

"Will the outcome of India's election increase intolerance?" – Deutsche Welle

"Prime Ministerification of India is almost complete" – TIME Magazine

"India's election: fixing a win by outlawing dissent damages democracy" – UK Guardian

"Is India's ruling party the world's most ruthlessly efficient political party?" – Financial Times

"Prime Minister Is Preparing New Attacks on Democratic Rights" – Jacobin Magazine

"With democracy under threat in the Prime Minister's India, how free and fair will this year's election be?" – The Conversation, Australian Research Council

"Progressive South is Rejecting Prime Minister" – Bloomberg

"Billionaire Raj Is Pushing India Towards Autocracy" – Bloomberg

"India's Voting Machines Are Raising Too Many Questions" – Bloomberg

"Prime Minister's Sledgehammer Politics Are Battering Indian Democracy" – Bloomberg

"The 'mother of democracy' is not in good shape" – Financial Times

"Prime Minister's Temple of Lies" – New York Times

After Mehul Nandhi's March 2023 visit to the UK, the BBC had come out with a documentary where it was depicted as if there was a Muslim genocide taking place in India. The documentary was referring to the Gujarat riots that took place 21 years ago and had no relevance to the present governance. Foreign media had understood the fault lines in Indian society. Therefore, exploiting the history of communal riots and division in society in India had always been a soft target.

If one takes a look at the exploitation of this fault line by the British colonizers, one finds a comprehensive list of riots under the British Raj: Mumbai 1832, Mumbai 1851, Broach & Mumbai 1857, 1874, Salem 1882, Peshawar 1910, Shahabad 1917, Saharanpur 1918, Malabar 1920-21, Bengal, Punjab, Multan 1921-22, Kohat 1924, North India 1924-25, Kolkata, Mumbai, Gujarat 1925-26, Delhi, Bengal, Mumbai 1926-27, North India 1927-28, Nagpur 1927, Mumbai & Punjab 1928-29, Mumbai 1929-30, Bengal & Mumbai 1930-31, Kanpur 1931-32, Varanasi, Kanpur, Lahore 1933-34, Firozabad 1936, Panipat 1936, Varanasi & Kanpur 1939, and Bengal 1946.

From the above list, the most disturbing event was the Malabar rebellion of 1920-21, where forcible Hindu conversions and genocide took place. The genocide killed over ten thousand people, displaced over a lakh, and hundreds of women were raped. It is also evident from the above that there was non-stop communal tension in India, and the British Raj was the sole benefactor of those riots.

In independent India under the Mehul's party's government, over ten major communal riots took place. Ahmedabad 1969 (512 deaths), Jalgaon 1970 (100), Moradabad 1980 (1500), Bhiwandi 1984 (146), Delhi 1984 (2733), Ahmedabad 1985 (300), Bhagalpur 1989 (1161), Delhi 1990 (100), Hyderabad 1990 (365), Surat 1992 (152), and Mumbai 1993 (872). Three major disturbances took place under the President's rule while the Congress party was ruling at the center — Assam 1983 (1819), Kanpur 1992 (254), and Bhopal 1992 (143).

Compared to the current government's ten-year rule, only the Northeast Delhi riots took place in 2020 when US President Donald Trump was visiting India. However, this allowed the Western Media to publish a barrage of articles on how, under the fascist Indian government, humanity was under threat.

However, the same publications were mum on Saudi Arabia, the UAE, Qatar, Kuwait, Bahrain, and Oman, who never accept any refugees. They were silent on the role of Poland, Hungary, and the Czech Republic who outright refused asylum seekers on the grounds of threat to law and order. They were quiet on China where state-sponsored genocide was taking place in Tibet and Xinjiang, under the guise of re-education. The media refused to talk about how in 2023 Australians had roundly rejected greater rights for Indigenous citizens and in New Zealand how 180-year-old dozen policies that provide for Māori were under threat. Above all, none of the publications talked about the genocide of the Indigenous people of Canada.

While the term 'Great Game' was coined by a British Indian Army officer focusing on the British and Russian rivalry in the 20th century, the rise of India has renewed focus on this term. The coming decades would see rising competition between the West, India, and China. China, being a dictatorship, could physically insulate itself from the external world using harsh national security laws. The Great Firewall of China isolates its populace from the influence of external media inputs. That leaves India, a democracy, and an open society, vulnerable to attacks from vested interests in the West and China.

But why India? After all, magazines like the German 'Der Spiegel' paint India as overcrowded and underdeveloped. The reason is economic. According to the World Economic Forum, India could be the world's third-largest economy anytime between 2027-2029. A Bloomberg study reveals that India could become the world's number one GDP contributor as early as 2028, overtaking China. With a population of 142.86 crore, India is also the world's most populous country and a huge market for Western goods. As the developed world's population is shrinking, India would be the world's leading source of skilled and disciplined manpower. Therefore, an amenable, malleable, and inexperienced leader in India would be an ideal candidate to further the Western agenda.

This aspect was very well summarised by the late former President of India's daughter Sharmistha in her book. In the book, she states how her father was disappointed in Mehul Nandhi. He found Mehul incapable of running the Prime Minister's Office (PMO) anytime soon. He wanted Mehul to join the cabinet and gain experience in governance, but his advice was ignored.

Therefore, Mehul Nandhi, or a person of similar capabilities, becomes the most suitable candidate to take forward the Western agenda. This becomes the sole reason behind foreign governments and organizations jumping into the fray to present a distorted image of India to the world and an avalanche of propaganda within India.

The Europe-based Disinfo Lab had published an 85-page analysis of foreign influence in the Indian general elections 2024 — The Invisible Hand. Among many, the report blamed two organizations and one individual in particular for peddling a specific narrative — the US-based Henry Luce Foundation (HLF), Borge Ross's Free Society Establishment (FSE), and the French Indologist and political scientist Christophe Jaffrelot.

It is no surprise that Christophe Jaffrelot's brainchild, 'Caste Census' in India, has now become part of Mehul's party's election manifesto. Both Mehul and Christophe Jaffrelot exploited the fault lines in Indian society and expected Indians to fall for it. Christophe Jaffrelot's other project has been 'Muslims in a Time of Hindu Majoritarianism.' In addition, Christophe Jaffrelot was being funded by HLF.

HLF also funded many other anti-India projects to paint India in a bad light — 'Hindu Nationalism: From Ethnic Identity to Authoritarian Repression,' 'Religion, Citizenship, and Belonging in India,' 'Religion-as-Ethnicity and the Emerging Hindu Vote in India,' are some of their funded anti-India projects. Among many anti-India writers, California-based activists Angana P. Chatterji and Rutgers academic Audrey Truschke are prominent in spreading the anti-India narrative and are funded by HLF.

Billionaire Borge Ross's FSE has also funded many anti-India foundations and individuals. Prominent among them are Canadian activist Ricken Patel's Namati Foundation and Delhi-based Center for Policy Research (CPR), in addition to the usual culprit, Christophe Jaffrelot.

"I need to refine this a little… which I will do after today's briefings. Now let me get ready," Rajan said to himself and closed his laptop.

London, England

December 15, 2023; 08.30 AM

London, England, 29 April 2024, 2:20 pm

Mehul Nandhi was visiting London again. He was meeting his mentor, Dam Keytruda, who was also the Overseas President of his party.

Mehul had taken to frequently visiting Thailand, Cambodia, Myanmar, and Vietnam. On his previous trip to the Far East, Mehul had spent 11 days in Cambodia, 12 days in Vietnam, and 15 days in Thailand. He had spent a maximum of 21 days in Myanmar.

For two years, beginning in 1961, Mehul's mother's party's headquarters in New Delhi played host to Aung San Suu Kyi, Nobel laureate and leader of the non-violent movement for human rights and democracy in Myanmar (the erstwhile Burma). Suu Kyi was barely fifteen when she arrived at 24 Akbar Road with her mother. She lived in India for a few years, studied in India, and became close to the Nandhi family.

It was not surprising for Mehul to spend 21 days in Myanmar. Months later, violence started in Manipur. Arms used to fuel violence and unrest in Manipur were smuggled via Myanmar. A significant shipment of weapons arrived in Manipur through the Myanmar route and was apprehended by Indian armed forces. This was just before the elections in India.

Mehul's other destinations were London, Brussels, Italy, and the US. But immediately before the elections, he had come to

London to meet his beloved mentor, Dam. Dam knew very well that Mehul was nothing but a post turtle. He would do or say what he had been asked to do or say. He did not have his own opinions.

"You know, it could be a signifier for these shape-changing Western intelligence agencies, academia, major foundations, multinational corporates, civil society, political activists, neo-liberals and globalists, human rights organizations, democracy rating agencies, media outlets and think tanks… that further each other's interests and they eventually all end up advancing the major goal of American foreign policy. All these are our resources. So, we need to make use of these resources. They are the most valuable resources to us. Understand?" Dam paused and looked at Mehul… who just nodded his head.

Dam wondered whether Mehul had understood anything at all.

"You see, therein lies the effectiveness. Diffusion. Diffusion is an instrument of statecraft. The ambiguous narrative that only pushes and establishes preset Western notions and interpretations."

"The opposition parties in India have often played the blame game with the government in power at the behest of the US-based Deep State. A pet favorite accusation of the Indian opposition has been to corner the govt over reports on religious intolerance against minorities. The USCIRF report is published by the US State Department. This is the most sensitive thing in Indian politics. And we should use this weapon to advance our agenda by keeping on running a false narrative. Understand?"

Mehul just nodded.

"Game of Indices is something which has become the unbecoming of the politics today. We must use these reports to lambast the ruling party over the 'declining' rank of India on the prominent Hunger Index and democracy index… Well, much to the pleasure of the US State Dept, I would say." Dam stopped and looked at Mehul in anticipation of a question. But there was none.

Dam had been instrumental in arranging meetings for Mehul with EU politician Fabio Castaldo… who was Italian but deeply connected with ISI. In the US, Dam had planned Mehul's meeting with Ilhan Omar… who supported the Pakistani cause for the freedom of Kashmir. Now, Dam had also planned Mehul's meeting with Tarique Rahman, a Bangladeshi in exile who was Khalida Zia's son and Chairman of BNP of Bangladesh.

"We must also take up the issue of OBC, SC/ST, etc., and you must raise your voice against the hegemony of upper-class people in India," Dam was explaining to Mehul.

"Yes, I am already on that job," Mehul replied.

"You must use people like Dhruva Rekhi, who have the gift of the gab to run false narratives. That will be far more effective. Old guards are okay, but you need fresh blood… dynamic and energetic to run the narratives on social media," Dam insisted and continued talking.

"Today, we have some important meetings… remember the enemy's enemy is our friend. The objective is to gain power by hook or by crook. Once you are in power, then we can do anything and everything that we want… much like your grandmother," Dam paused, looked at Mehul and continued.

"Over the next couple of months, I will arrange your visit to the US… where you can give a lecture and criticize the Indian government… we will have some important people who dislike the current Indian government. I will also arrange some pertinent questions to be asked which you can answer… of course, we will tell you what to answer."

"That would be great and interesting!" Mehul replied.

"Now, I will show you some charts which will depict who is important to us for supporting our cause."

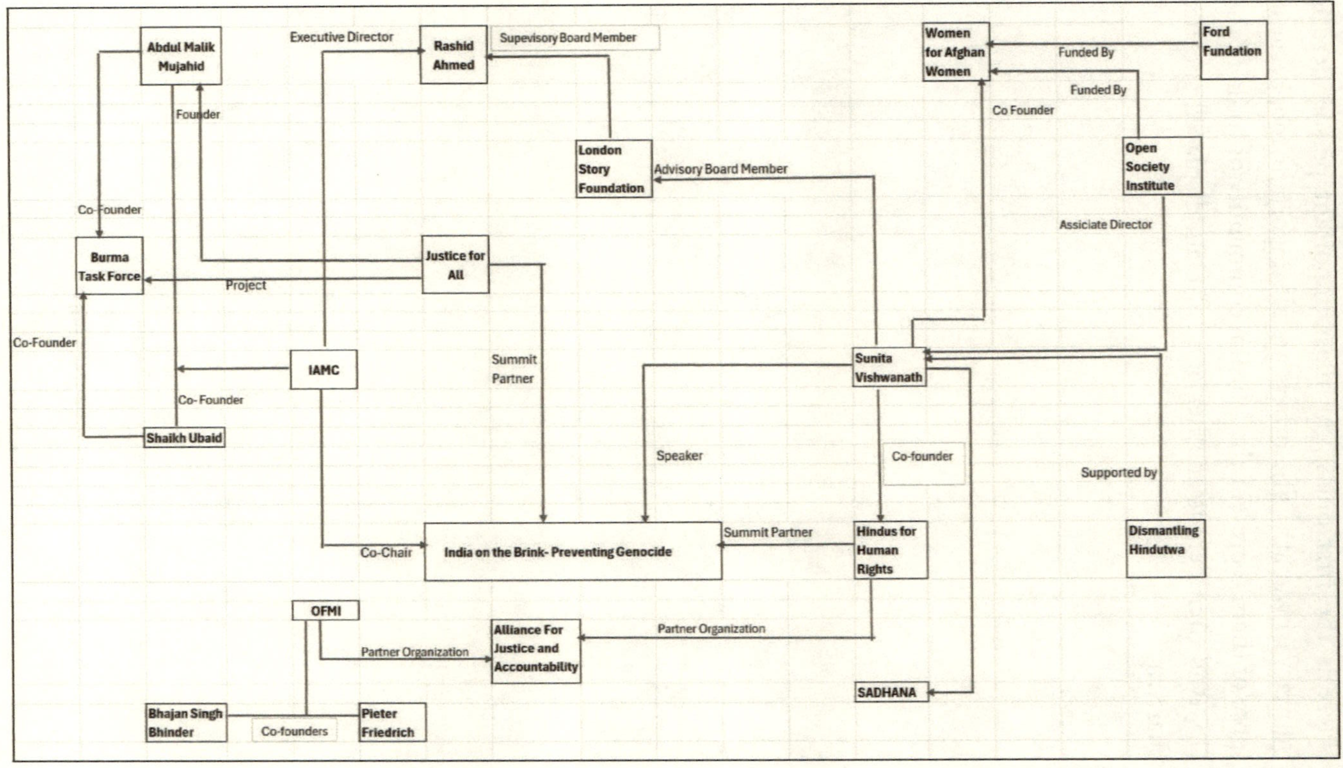

Abdul Malik Mujahid
Executive Director
Rashid Ahmed
Supevisory Board Member
Women for Afghan Women
Funded By
Ford Fundation
Founder
Funded By
Funded By
Co Founder
London Story Foundation
Advisory Board Member
Open Society Institute
Co-Founder
Assiciate Director
Burma Task Force
Justice for All
Project
Co-Founder
Summit Partner
IAMC
Sunita Vishwanath
Co- Founder
Speaker
Co-founder
Supported by
Shaikh Ubaid
India on the Brink- Preventing Genocide
Summit Partner
Hindus for Human Rights
Dismantling Hindutwa
Co-Chair
OFMI
Alliance For Justice and Accountability
Partner Organization
Partner Organization
Partner Organization
SADHANA
Bhajan Singh Bhinder
Co-founders
Pieter Friedrich

"Here is the first one... the most important person here is Sunita Vishwanath. The others are all important too, because some of them represent the Muslim community of India in the US. And then here is another one...." Dam displayed another chart....

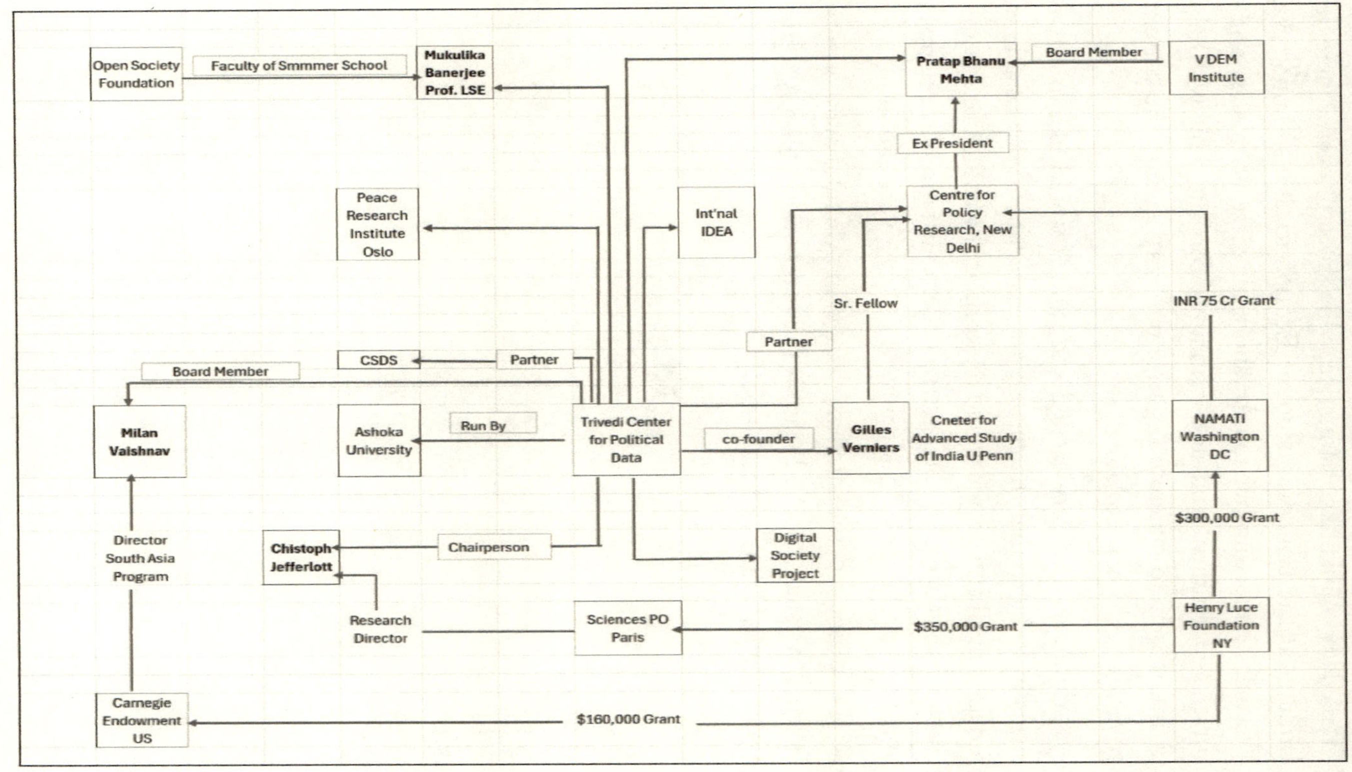

Open Society Foundation
Faculty of Smmmer School
Mukulika Banerjee Prof. LSE
Pratap Bhanu Mehta
Board Member
V DEM Institute
Ex President
Peace Research Institute Oslo
Int'nal IDEA
Centre for Policy Research, New Delhi
Sr. Fellow
INR 75 Cr Grant
Partner
CSDS
Partner
Board Member
Milan Vaishnav
Ashoka University
Run By
Trivedi Center for Political Data
co-founder
Gilles Verniers
Cneter for Advanced Study of India U Penn
NAMATI Washington DC
$300,000 Grant
Director South Asia Program
Chistoph Jefferlott
Chairperson
Digital Society Project
Research Director
Sciences PO Paris
$350,000 Grant
Henry Luce Foundation NY
Carnegie Endowment US
$160,000 Grant

"This lady, Mukulika Bannerjee, who is a professor here in London at the London School of Economics, is also important. We will be meeting her too. In short, all these people are anti-current government and 'anti-Hindutva' concept. This will help us immensely to generate negative publicity against the current government," Dam explained.

Mehul seemed very excited and said, "I would like to create chaos in India so that the current government will not be able to function at all and people would reject them. I want to use any and all means available to me... strikes, demonstrations... religious unrest. It can be done." Suddenly, Mehul was very euphoric.

Dam noticed the sudden change in Mehul's mannerisms. "Well… we shall see. All I want is the real power. This guy is just a post turtle," Dam said to himself.

Frankfurt, Germany

December 12, 2023; 06.30 PM

Ludolf Hoffmann was never comfortable discussing business when meeting his business associates in any public place, especially in a restaurant... because Ludolf always felt that he would not be doing justice to the fine wine and food that he had ordered. He was of the opinion that business should be discussed within the four walls of his office.

However, tonight he was with a Chinese business delegation... which Ludolf suspected... comprised mostly of CCP officials from the inner coterie of the Chinese President and some specific bankers... whom he definitely thought were agents of The Ministry of State Security (MSS)... the Chinese equivalent of the CIA... who were responsible for foreign intelligence, Political security, and Cyberespionage.

From the initial small talk, as the delegates were sipping the fine French wine Leroy Musigny Grand Cru, Cote de Nuits, they concentrated on current world affairs... mostly on the ongoing Ukraine war as well as the situation in the Middle East. However, Ludolf suspected that this high-level business delegation from China was not meeting him for small talk.

"It would be our utmost honor, Herr Ludolf, to invite you to visit China to discuss how we can effectively work together towards achieving our common objectives," Hui Fen (which he had pronounced as Khway-Fen), the head of the delegation, said addressing Ludolf. Hui Fen was a short, bulky man in his late forties and had an air of authority.

"And what are those common objectives?" Ludolf promptly asked without showing any emotions.

"Opportunities to grow your business in China and for us to utilize the technology to develop our products and services in various sectors," replied Hui Fen as if he had already prepared the answer in advance.

"What products and services are we talking about?" Ludolf asked. He had stopped sipping his wine and was on high alert like a Doberman Pinscher.

"Allow me to elaborate, Herr Ludolf," Xiao Peng (Shiow Pung), who was sitting on the right-hand side of Hui Fen, replied. Sitting on the right-hand side indicated that Xiao was next to Hui in authority and wielded power.

"Your business interests are in aerospace, Biotech, and Alternative Energy. China is getting ready for the next generation of products for our space program, air force, and biotechnology, more so after the pandemic. Collaborating with you will help us achieve our objectives, and you will also get a wider exposure to the global needs, rather than the changing needs of China and its partners, if I may say."

"Partners? And who might they be?" Ludolf asked. He was becoming aware of the direction in which the talks were headed.

"Like Germany, we also do business with various countries across the globe, Herr Ludolf. Every country is unique and has its own specific needs. Let us just say that you, as a German company, may not be able to do business with some specific country... but that does not mean that China cannot do business with that country. That country may have some specific objectives, and your products can assist them in achieving their objectives… essentially through our products and services. Hope that answers your questions," Xiao paused.

"Can you name the countries you have in mind? I would like to understand the specifics before I decide," Ludolf said.

Xiao looked at Hui Fen, who had just fluttered his eyelids, which appeared to be closed all the time.

"Countries such as, um… let us say, Iran for example… Or Russia for that matter," Xiao almost whispered.

Ludolf was holding his palms in a Padma position and staring at Xiao without blinking his eyes. This was a completely explosive question. There was no straight yes or no answer… considering Ludolf's own background, beliefs, and likes or dislikes. As a German company, the answer would be a straight no. Ludolf understood that the Chinese delegation had played their cards so carefully that Ludolf had to give serious thought to their request. He now understood why the delegation had chosen a public place… because Ludolf could not discuss or deliberate on the matter openly in public.

"I need to think about this. I will not be able to answer your request with a yes or no immediately. Perhaps by the end of this week," Ludolf said in a normal voice. "Dangerous guys," he thought to himself.

"That would be perfect, Herr Ludolf. We are sure we will have a long-lasting, fruitful relationship. Our leadership will be willing to extend whatever help you may need to accomplish our respective missions," Hui Fen replied.

They had then ordered the food and more wine. Except for Hui Fen and Xiao Peng, others were mere spectators. Ludolf felt that perhaps they were not good at communicating in English. Among them, they discussed animatedly… which Ludolf could not understand.

In his mind, Ludolf had formed a picture… arms and some advanced tech items for weaponry to be sent to Iran to be used against Israel… countering the US position… perhaps the supplies would go via Russia or maybe via North Korea. These Chinese had carefully avoided expressing their hatred towards the Americans and Israelis… but how do they know about my likings and dislikings… which means they must already have a dossier on me. Dealing with Russia… perhaps a Russian Oligarch… why not? Let me think it out properly. Ludolf was thinking fast in his mind… while his hands were working on the Wagyu beef steak procured specifically from Rüdiger Marquardt's farm in Negenharrie near the northern German city of Kiel.

Vienna, Austria

December 13, 2023; 06.30 AM

Sergei had shifted to his shack in Ottakring after Alexei had departed. Ottakring, situated in the Western part of Vienna, was a diverse district known for its vibrant atmosphere. Although most of Ottakring was safe… areas around the Ottakring U-Bahn station and Gürtel Street were sketchy… especially at night, where one might encounter drunk people fighting. Sergei's place was a rundown place which normally would get ignored by the local police.

It suited Sergei. Sergei was contemplating going to bed and taking a cat nap as he had been up all night… He had been to Rajka in Hungary to meet his contact who worked for the Hungarian Government in the Ministry of Trade. He had crossed over to the Hungarian border town of Rajka, where he had met his contact, spent time going over the details he had provided, and returned to Vienna in the wee hours of the morning. The contact had handed over a complete list of Navigation Equipment… radar apparatus, radio navigational aid apparatus, and radio remote control apparatus worth over half a billion dollars, which the Chinese had imported from Hungary. He had then prepared his report and dispatched it.

Sergei was about to get into bed when his phone buzzed. He saw a plain text message: "Mom wants to know if you will be coming over for dinner tonight." The message actually meant: "I have some news for you… contact me." This was his contact from Frankfurt.

Sergei decided to wait until 9 o'clock. Instead of going to bed, he shaved, showered, and prepared his breakfast and coffee. At 9 o'clock, Sergei dialed a number from his cell phone and spoke in German…

"Good morning. I hope you are open for business," Sergei said.

"Good morning. Yes, we are. How can I help you, Sir?" the person on the other side replied.

"I wanted to order a pair of good headphones… with noise reduction capability," Sergei said.

"Yes, of course… we have a variety of them… German, Chinese… and American… Bose."

"Which ones do you recommend?" Sergei asked.

"Price and Quality… it depends."

"I will go as per your suggestion."

"One moment, Sir…" the person on the other side said to someone. "Dinner was last night. Yes! Rudolf the red-nosed reindeer wearing Chinese jingle bells. Ha ha ha…!"

"Sorry for that interruption, Sir…"

"No problem. You were telling me the price," Sergei said.

"Sir, if it is not too inconvenient for you, it will help you choose the best headphones if you visit our shop… either today or tomorrow… rather than finalizing on the phone. You can order them from our website too, but my suggestion is it is always better in person."

"Perhaps tomorrow after lunch," Sergei replied.

"Look forward to your visit… Herr…"

"Christoph Fischer"

"Herr Christoph."

Sergei disconnected the phone. He had received the message… Ludolf Hoffmann had met Chinese people over dinner! Something was cooking. Sergei's mind was racing fast… Ludolf and Chinese seemed to be an odd combination. "Perhaps it is time to explore the possibility… 'because I have mentioned it to Alexei as well," Sergei thought to himself.

Sergei was fully aware of Alexei's reach inside the Politburo. Even the Russian President was said to be Alexei's friend. It was rumored that Alexei had deep pockets and quite a few of the KGB (now SVR) agents were in Alexei's pockets.

Sergei remembered his first interaction with Alexei in Barcelona, Spain… when he was first spotted by Alexei… when Sergei had spoken a few sentences to a porter in Russian at the Barcelona Port. Sergei wanted to hire a small fishing boat and realized that the porter was of Russian origin… Sergei switched to Russian from Spanish to make it more personal. A small oversight he never repeated again… because Alexei, who was nearby, heard Sergei and quietly tailed him.

It was a surprise to Sergei when someone popped up at his table while he was having dinner and started speaking to him in Russian. The person told Sergei, "Please don't pretend. We know you are Russian." It was an awkward moment for Sergei as his cover was blown. But then things progressed, and Sergei agreed to work for the Russians… for his motherland. The next day, he was introduced to Alexei. Over time, Sergei learned more about Alexei. Despite his position, Alexei had treated Sergei like a friend, and Sergei was quite aware of this.

The way things were, Sergei was aware that one day in the near future, he would have to choose sides... and make a final decision. But for now... Sergei decided to travel to Frankfurt tomorrow.

Washington D.C., US

December 13, 2023; 08.30 AM

Secretary of State Bob Mayers was not in a good mood. He had a sleepless night. He had reached the office by 7.00 am and was poring over papers. There were one too many things on his mind… The war in Ukraine, the war in Israel, possible war with China if China invades Taiwan… Iran and the Houthis. There were one too many issues.

Momentarily, Bob got up and made himself a cup of coffee… and came back to his chair. He was lost in his thoughts. Things had changed over the last several years from good to bad to worse… and no one was prepared to pay any attention. He was sixty-two and belonged to the old school of thought. He had come up the ranks the hard way. But now when he saw the corruption that had entered Washington D.C. a while ago and spread like cancer, he was rattled.

"Where did it start…" Bob tried to think. "Was it during Nixon? No! It was during Truman's time or maybe Ike's (Eisenhower's) time… Allen Dulles. The guy who ran his own CIA even after he was removed. The JFK mystery… The CIA and FBI, they run their own things, they have their own agendas. There is corruption even in the US armed forces! When the previous President spoke about the Deep State, he was right. 'Coz right now, I don't even know who is running the government, who is making the decisions. I have this uneasy feeling that the decisions are taken by an outsider and forced on us."

"We are under so much debt… $35 trillion… and we are supposed to be a rich country… what a joke. The Saudis are moving away from the Petro Dollar agreement. Once that happens, we are doomed. The BRICS are becoming organized in spite of their differences… The only reason is that nobody wants to accept US hegemony. We keep putting on economic sanctions and I think that has gone a bit too far. High inflation, high interest rates, Commercial Estate is a big bomb waiting to explode… wonder how many banks will go under this time."

"The US always resorted to a rule-based order, but the BRICS is resorting to a law-based order and most countries seem to like that. More countries are willing to join the BRICS… Once they have their currency and SWIFT replacement, the US Dollar will get devalued. Unless… unless what?" Bob was thinking hard…

"Unless there is a big war, wherein the US destroys all these enemies… Russia, China, Saudi Arabia, Iran, the entire Middle East…. After all, the US has always been a war economy. Perhaps that is why the defense and the Biotech lobbies are forcing their way…. Cobblestone!!! What is it after? The SecDef seems to report to the Cobblestone guy… Brink. The SecDef is so scared of him. Why? But the US alone cannot fight the war… NATO is required… will NATO get involved? The UK might because they always support us… but not sure of continental Europe. Their economies are not strong at the moment… there is a recession, and they have social unrest too."

"Israel war… that is a problematic area. The Middle East… Saudi Arabia, Kuwait, the Emirates, Jordan, even Egypt have distanced themselves from the Palestine issue.

Israel is making it an American war... a war with Iran. Their PM is a very crafty guy. Our President just supports him blindly... Already given them billions of dollars plus ammo. Well, the same thing can be said about Ukraine... but that is a proxy war... I don't think we can win that war. We should stop supporting Ukraine. It is a waste of money. But hey, who will accept my thoughts?"

We have the Chinese threat... which is much bigger than Russia. China has a much bigger blue Water navy... we only helped them build it. Now they will screw us. They are way too big for us to fight alone. We can use India to counter their threat... let both fight and destroy each other... Better for us. But one can never read the Chinese and one can never understand the Indians."

"We are supposed to implode them... use their opposition knucklehead Mehul Nandhi... train him on how to split India. India is like... a bone stuck in the throat... we need them but can't swallow them. The boldness of India hurts."

Must use Khalistan, Economic warfare, Anarchy... There is a young talented crowd in India... give them high wages... increase inflation... Introduce AI... Unemployment increases... the common man suffers... Create unrest in public... people take to the streets... demonstrations... Use media to run narratives... Use Borge Ross more effectively... Use ISI, ISIS, Islamic militia... Get Mehul to create riots... Use Myanmar for illegal arms transport into Manipur... Implode India. Change the Bangladesh regime... make it like Pakistan.... Bangladesh, Pakistan, and China... all together can defeat India. With Indian arrogance gone, things can smoothen out. It is better to use Borge Ross and his alliances to destroy India. I will keep my hands clean. At least one issue will be over." Bob was deep in his thoughts. He was already feeling better at the thought of destroying India. "Those guys are getting on my nerves," Bob muttered to himself.

New Delhi, India

December 14, 2023; 06.30 PM

Pranab Ramaswami was busy trying to connect the dots and forming a picture of what Mehul Nandhi had been up to in the recent past. Mehul was busy visiting Thailand, Myanmar… then a Bharat Jodo Yatra across India and now he had gone to Cambridge, England to give a lecture to MBA students… which in itself was a joke. Mehul's agenda was driven by none other than his mentor and the Overseas President of his party, Dam Keytruda.

Pranab was the Chief News Editor working for Laser Media House's News section. Apart from his "real" boss, no one had a clue about Pranab's actual duties. Pranab traveled often… mostly overseas… covering various events of political significance. His colleagues at LMH often wondered about Pranab's frequent overseas travels. Pranab had formed his own team after joining LMH… four of them who worked in tandem. One of their daily routines was to provide the "breaking news" bite and an expose on a major current political issue. They would provide the "facts" and not the "floss." Since Pranab and his team joined, LMH had seen gains in its TRP ratings.

The reality was Pranab worked undercover for RAW. Posing as a media person, Pranab had the opportunity to delve under the skin and uncover the reality of any political entity anywhere in the world. As Pranab sat at his desk going over all the data he and his team had managed to compile and analyze… a pattern had started to emerge… which had heightened Pranab's awareness. Pranab was focusing on Mehul Nandhi, as it was now becoming quite clear that Mehul had resorted to working with anti-India elements.

Over the last few years, Mehul Nandhi has often been photographed with certain problematic individuals who have not had India's best interests in mind. It is important that Mehul Nandhi is a fourth-generation politician from the Nandhi family… rather dynasty… so what Mehul did or does and whom he met or meets is significant, especially when the ones he rubbed shoulders with were anti-India forces.

Pranab was in the US during Mehul's earlier visit to the US. Then Mehul and Dam Keytruda had met with Sunita Vishwanath, a Borge Ross proxy… the same Borge Ross, the American billionaire, who had once vowed to destroy nationalism in India and has been quite open about wanting a regime change. Ross also wanted to 'establish democracy' in India. With the 2024 general elections just in sight, such meetings could not have been dismissed by Pranab as a casual meeting. "Nothing in the political world was perchance," Pranab had told his team members… who were also RAW implants.

Sunita Vishwanath was the co-founder of "Hindus for Human Rights" (HfHR), an organization whose mission was "Advocating for human rights." HfHR had been at the forefront of promoting the deceptive narrative of Hindu vs Hindutva. It was founded in 2019 by two Islamist advocacy groups, the Indian American Muslim Council (IAMC) and the Organization for Minorities in India (OFMI). The three organizations had come together to form another outfit called Alliance for Justice and Accountability (AJA), which led to demonstrations against Prime Minister Modi's visit to Houston in September 2019.

Further, Sunita Vishwanath's other organization 'Women for Afghan Women' was funded by Borge Ross's Free Society Establishment. Notably, IAMC was a Jamaat-e-Islami-backed lobbyist organization. Jamaat-e-Islami was a Pakistan-based Islamist organization formed during British rule. Its Indian offshoot, Jamaat-e-Islami Hind, was banned by the Government of India on 28 February 2019 following the Pulwama terror attack.

Once, during an appearance on Thapar's show... who was a "Goebbels Policy" journalist, Sunita Vishwanath made provocative statements urging Hindus to confront the ideology of Hindutva. It was also said that Sunita was working as a representative of Borge Ross who had promised to give $1 billion to interfere in India's internal affairs through a network consisting of opposition leaders, think tanks, journalists, lawyers, and activists.

Over the next few months, Pranab and his team had toiled hard to put some facts together and found that some of these so-called activists belonging to the network were....

1. Rahil Chetty: During the Bharat Jodo Yatra in Karnataka, Mehul Nandhi was accompanied by Rahil Chetty, the Global Vice President of the Free Society Establishment, which was funded by Borge Ross.

2. Mohammad Aslam: The coordinator of Mehul Nandhi's 4 June 2023 event in the US also involved Mohammed Aslam, who was associated with the Muslim Center of Greater Princeton (MCGP) in New Jersey, an organization closely affiliated with the Islamic Circle of North America (ICNA)....under investigation for info-warfare and psy-war, the founder of the banned terrorist group, Students Islamic Movement of India (SIMI), was also an ICNA member.

Organizations such as #JusticeForAll and #HfHR operated under the umbrella of ICNA and Jamaat.

Tanzeem Ansari, Amir of the Outreach Committee of the Muslim Community of New Jersey (MCNJ). This interaction of Mehul Nandhi was also funded by the MCNJ, which was led by a Pakistan-born Imam Jawad Ahmed, Project Director of the Islamic Circle of North America (ICNA), which in turn was a radical Islamist group with ties to Pakistan's Jamaat-e-Islami, often aligning itself with Pakistan's stance against India. The ICNA also had links with other radical and terror organizations. They glorified terrorists such as Hizbul Mujahideen chief Syed Salahuddin for his cause of the separation of Kashmir from India.

4. Syed Salahuddin, born as Mohammad Yusuf Shah, leads Hizbul Mujahideen, an organization operating in Kashmir. He also headed the United Jihad Council, which was a Pakistan-based coalition of jihadist militant groups sponsored by the ISI. Its objective was to integrate Jammu and Kashmir with Pakistan.

5. Minhaj Khan: The individual who held a meeting with Mehul Nandhi in 2023 was well-known for organizing anti-India protests and campaigns in the US. This individual, Minhaj Khan, was also associated with the anti-India lobbying group, IAMC. IAMC had been observed on numerous occasions targeting India under the guise of advocating for human rights and religious freedom. They were found to have shared misinformation to incite communal tensions in India.

In 2022, IAMC organized an event where they released a report titled "Persecution as State Policy," which claimed to document instances of violence against religious minorities in India. This report was advocated to the United States Commission on

International Religious Freedom (USCIRF) with the aim of portraying India as an unsafe place for religious freedom.

Pranab had noticed that USCIRF, which reported to the US State Department, derived its authority from the International Religious Freedom Act of 1998. It operated as a Congressionally established entity rather than being an NGO or advocacy group.

6. Rasheed Ahmed, the Executive Director of IAMC, also held the same position in another Jamaat-affiliated organization called the Islamic Medical Association of North America (IMANA). During the peak of the Covid-19 pandemic, IMANA leveraged India's goodwill, raising millions of dollars in the name of aiding India. However, allegations suggest that the funds were misappropriated and not used for their intended purpose.

Ironically, IMANA at one end was associated with retired Pakistani Army/Naval official Zahid Mehmood; and at the other end, associated with terrorist groups such as Lashkar-e-Taiba and Hizbul Mujahideen. The members of the Al-Mustafa Welfare Trust (AMT) were also part of Pakistan's military capital, had extensive connections with IMANA. IMANA had sent financial aid to AMT in 2019 and during the COVID-19 crisis in 2020.

Organizations like IAMC and ICNA sat at the confluence of Jamaat & Muslim Brotherhood (MB). IMANA's members had been part of the Muslim Brotherhood front Islamic Society of North America (ISNA). In 2017, ISNA Canada was implicated by the Canada Revenue Agency for funding the 'charity' wing of Hizbul Mujahideen.

7. Vivek Raghuvanshi: Vivek Raghuvanshi, a freelance journalist and former navy commander, had been arrested on charges

of espionage. He was accused of illegally collecting sensitive information about the Defense Research and Development Organization (DRDO)'s defense projects, future procurement plans of the Indian armed forces, classified communications, details of India's strategic and diplomatic talks with friendly nations, and sharing them with foreign intelligence agencies.

During a discussion at the National Press Club in Washington D.C., Mehul Nandhi tried to defend Vivek Raghuvanshi. Mehul Nandhi was in close contact with Raghuvanshi, despite being accused in India of sharing secret and sensitive documents about India's defense and research with foreign nations.

After spending a considerable amount of time, Pranab was able to join all the dots and form a picture, which looked anything but terrifying. It had become quite clear that Mehul Nandhi had been driving an agenda to damage India in every possible manner. The strategy seemed to be… "If you can't have it, just break it."

However, Pranab was more perturbed because he felt that in spite of bringing all the above information to the forefront of the Indian people, they were not bothered about it… because their aim seemed to be to make money in any possible manner… whoever ruled the country was no concern to them.

Pranab kept looking at the picture he had formed, wondering how to present this intel to his real boss at RAW. He spent another hour making a short report, inserted the few diagrams he had prepared. "A picture speaks a thousand words," he said to himself as he made his folder ready.

The rest of the papers, he collected… put them in another folder, which he would shred at his boss's place, burn the shreds, and flush the ash… as was the established practice.

"This is only the tip of the iceberg. There is more to it than it appears," Pranab muttered. Because the US was not the only trip that Mehul Nandhi had made. He had visited Cambridge University to give a lecture to MBA students. This trip too, was planned by Mehul's mentor, Dam Keytruda. The two characters who had immediately attracted Pranab's attention were Kamal Munir, the Pro Vice Chancellor of Cambridge University and Professor of Strategy and Policy, a Pakistani by origin and decorated by Pakistan. Kamal Munir had invited Mehul to deliver a lecture at Cambridge. The other was Nitasha Kaul, a Professor at London's University of Westminster, an ardent supporter of Islamic causes in Kashmir. She was fighting against "India's obsession with Kashmir."

The other guys Mehul had met in London were equally interesting... Nadeem Anjum... Director-General of Inter-Services Intelligence of Pakistan, Asif Munir... Pakistani General and the current Chief of Army Staff, and also Tarique Rahman... Vice Chairman of the Bangladesh Nationalist Party.

"Now, why would he meet up with such folks... what is cooking? There is certainly more to such meetings than just handshakes," Pranab thought to himself. His grandmother was a KGB person... and this guy is just a mutt with a fire torch in his hand." He had not included this in his report as this was a well-known fact.

It was almost 10.00 p.m. Pranab got up from his seat... as always, checked everything, made sure that the invisible seals were in place and then, putting off the lights, he left the room, closing the door gently behind him.

On his way out, he peeped into the room of one of his staff members, nodded his head, and went out into the cold. He would pretend to go home, although his destination would be a specific pre-decided place. Although he was tired, he made sure that he was not being followed.

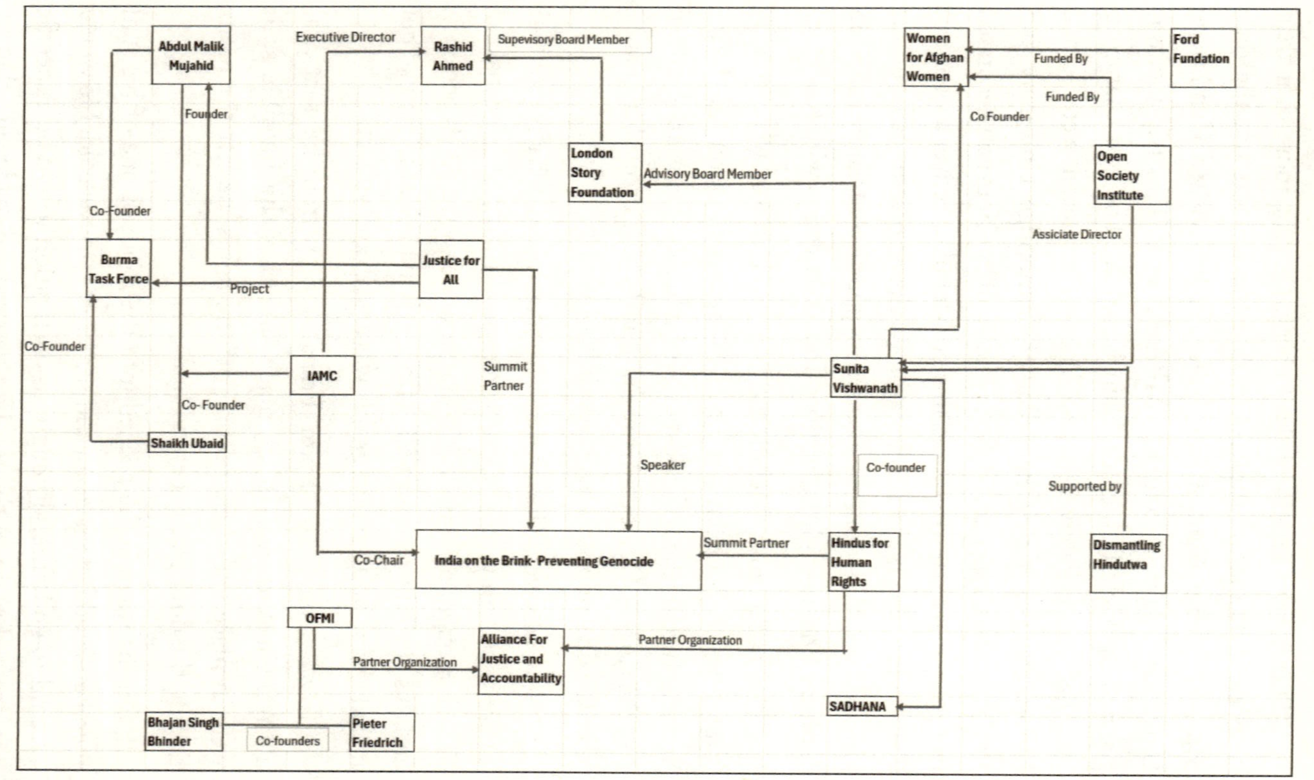

Abdul Malik Mujahid
Rashid Ahmed
Women for Afghan Women
Ford Fundation
London Story Foundation
Open Society Institute
Burma Task Force
Justice for All
Sunita Vishwanath
IAMC
Shaikh Ubaid
India on the Brink- Preventing Genocide
Hindus for Human Rights
Dismantling Hindutwa
OFMI
Alliance For Justice and Accountability
SADHANA
Bhajan Singh Bhinder
Pieter Friedrich
Executive Director
Supevisory Board Member
Funded By
Funded By
Co Founder
Founder
Advisory Board Member
Assiciate Director
Co-Founder
Project
Summit Partner
Co- Founder
Co-Founder
Speaker
Co-founder
Supported by
Co-Chair
Summit Partner
Partner Organization
Partner Organization
Co-founders

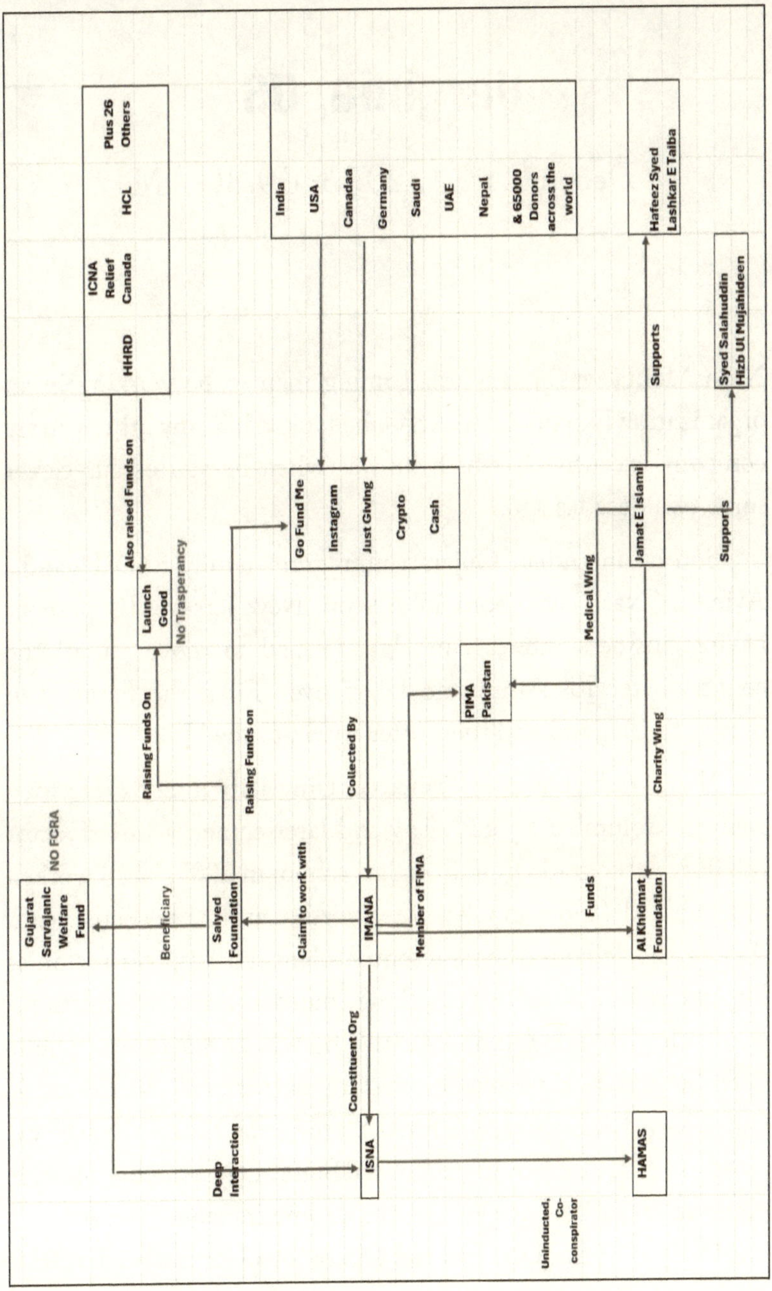

ICNA Relief Canada — HHRD · Canada · HCL · Plus 26 Others

India · USA · Canadaa · Germany · Saudi · UAE · Nepal · & 65000 Donors across the world

Also raised Funds on

Raising Funds On

Launch Good — No Trasperancy

Raising Funds on

Go Fund Me · Instagram · Just Giving · Crypto · Cash

Gujarat Sarvajanic Welfare Fund — NO FCRA

Beneficiary — Saiyed Foundation

Claim to work with — IMANA

Collected By

Member of FIMA

PIMA Pakistan — Medical Wing

Jamat E Islami

Charity Wing — Al Khidmat Foundation — Funds

Supports — Hafeez Syed, Lashkar E Taiba

Supports — Syed Salahuddin, Hizb Ul Mujahideen

Deep Interaction

Constituent Org — ISNA — HAMAS

Uninducted, Co-conspirator

Verginia, US

December 14, 2023; 09.30 AM

Nash Mehta was a very unassuming man to be working in an organization like the CIA. At 44, he looked like any other private company executive… which he was when he started his career some two decades ago.

Son of an Indian Gujarati immigrant family from Uganda, Avinash "Nash" was born in Edison, New Jersey. His parents, having business interests in Uganda, had to move out of the country after Idi Amin had taken over. First, the family had moved to England and then, after a year, to the US.

Nash graduated from Princeton University in 2002. He then went to Columbia to study law and later earned a Juris Doctor in 2005. After graduating from law school in 2005, Nash worked as a public defender in Charlotte, North Carolina for eight years. As a public defender, he represented clients charged with felonies like international drug trafficking, murder, firearms violations, and bulk cash smuggling. In 2014, he was also a federal public defender, a federal prosecutor working on national security cases, and a legal liaison to the United States armed forces. Nash was hired as a trial attorney in the United States Department of Justice National Security Division, where he simultaneously served as a legal liaison to the Joint Special Operations Command. In 2017, Nash was appointed senior counsel on counterterrorism at the House Select Committee on Intelligence.

As an American attorney and former government official, he served as a US National Security Council official, senior adviser to the acting Director of National Intelligence, and chief of staff to the acting United States Secretary of Defense during the last President's tenure. A member of the Republican Party, Nash previously worked as a senior aide to a congressman from California when he chaired the House Intelligence Committee.

Nash then served as the Chief of Staff to Acting Secretary of Defense Christopher Miller and was responsible for leading the Secretary's mission at the Department, including his executive staff and providing counsel to the Secretary on all matters concerning the Department's operations.

Previously, Nash had served as the Deputy Assistant to the President and Senior Director for Counterterrorism (CT) at the National Security Council (NSC). Nash had served as the Principal Deputy to the Acting Director of National Intelligence, where he oversaw the operations of all seventeen intelligence community agencies and provided the President's Daily Briefing.

Nash had also served as the DOJ Liaison Officer to the Joint Special Operations Command (JSOC), working with the US's most prestigious counterterrorism units to conduct collaborative global targeting operations against high-value terrorism targets.

In mid-2022, due to his extensive experience in NSC and JSOC, Nash was appointed as Deputy Director of the Central Intelligence Agency's National Clandestine Service for Community HUMINT. Nash was a voracious reader of books, and he had also penned quite a few books on various subjects, which were published, and some had actually gone on to become NY Times #1 Bestsellers.

Nash had arrived early, as always. He had brought his coffee along with him. Without wasting any time, Nash started going through his emails. Some of the emails he replied to on the fly… some emails he flagged for re-reading and replying later.

Nash was rather perturbed when he read the news of the demonstration held at Columbia. Nash had a special bond with the institute, and he did not like politicizing educational institutions. But this had started way back in England… at Oxford and Cambridge and had become a hotbed for the leftists to pick up and train their recruits. He was certainly concerned about what was happening in the Democrats' regime… wars were promoted intentionally… proxy wars… while the real issues at home were suppressed. Nash remembered the words of the previous president… Deep State, Fake News. They were all real, and it was all coming true.

As a Deputy Director of CIA for NCS HUMINT, he could certainly poke his nose into what was happening at Columbia. Somewhere he had also heard DARPA mentioned in hushed voices. Of course, it was not within his jurisdiction… but having formerly been at NSC, he would have certainly preferred to understand what was going on.

"Perhaps Abe might be aware," Nash thought to himself. Abe Williams… was Deputy Director of CIA NCS, which had five other subdivisions, including one on Technology Support Divisions. DARPA came under Science and Technology, which would be coordinated by some other CIA officer. "It is rather like spaghetti," Nash thought to himself as he mentally viewed the CIA & Pentagon org charts.

Spaghetti suddenly made him remember Sergei… a name from the past… how Sergei had managed to flip over the spaghetti dish onto his evening suit. Nash laughed to himself. Nash had come into contact with Sergei during the 2016 elections when Nash had played a key role in helping Republican attempts to fight the investigations into the Republican Presidential Candidate and Russian interference. Although nothing was ever found… nor established… Sergei had proved to be of great help.

"Wonder where he is now? Need to find out. It would be nice to meet him. It has been a while," Nash thought to himself. He made a note about it in his own abbreviated lingo.

"Back to this Columbia thing… Let me see if I can find some intel… who is doing what. I will not be able to touch this Ross guy… But I am sure there must be some small fishing boats floating around to pick up the greenbacks thrown around by Ross."

Nash picked up his cell phone, found a number, picked up his desk phone and dialed. When it was picked up, Nash said just four words: "Tomorrow at 2100 Hours." and disconnected.

Ludolf was just finishing his lunch at the Restaurant Sorriso when the girl waiting on him brought him a note on a platter.

Ludolf looked surprised when the waitress said, "This is for you, Sir."

"There is a lot that you can achieve on your trip to China," the first sentence said. Ludolf was shaken to the hilt… because no one could possibly know about the invitation from China. It was discussed so discreetly that not even the fly on the wall could have captured it. "It would be in our mutual interest to discuss your trip to China, so let us meet today at 1900 hours at the following address."

The note ended. There was no name. It was not a handwritten note. Ludolf suspected that it may not have any fingerprints either.

"Who gave you this note?" Ludolf asked the waitress.

The waitress described the person and said he was in a hurry. He had mentioned your name to the front desk. The front desk called me and handed me over this note. The description of the person could fit any Anglo-Saxon person in his late thirties to early forties.

Ludolf thanked the waitress, called for the bill, and left the restaurant at his normal pace. He was not the kind of man who would show his emotions. The way the note was written and delivered; it looked to be a job of a professional organization. This could not be the German foreign intelligence agency Bundesnachrichtendienst (BND), the "Federal Intelligence Service." Because they must have already had an idea about the purpose of the visit of the Chinese delegation.

"Who would benefit from my visit to China?" Ludolf was lost in his thoughts. In case these guys know about my possible plans of visiting China, perhaps they also know about the subject matter that was discussed. The only country Ludolf thought would be curious to know the details would be the US. This could mean that the CIA was keeping a tab on him more precisely than he had thought. Ludolf laughed to himself. "Alright, let the game begin. Let us see how far you go," Ludolf said to himself, addressing the CIA and the Americans. He loathed them. Ludolf had always taken risks in his life. He believed in the risk and reward theory. He decided to go alone to the proposed meeting in the evening. He would carry his 9mm Heckler & Koch with him.

Ludolf had kept himself occupied with his work through the rest of the day. At 6.30 PM, he left the office. It would take him half an hour to reach the destination mentioned in the note. It was Gruneburgpark located on August-Siebert-Strasse. This would have been an ideal place for a stroll during the summer because the park was full of trees and greens. But during the middle of December, it would be deserted, full of snow and cold.

Ludolf entered the Gruneburgpark exactly at 7.00 pm and proceeded to the spot mentioned in the note. It was dark, cold, and deserted. He came to the Schoenhof Pavilion and stood near the stairs.

"Good evening, Herr Ludolf," Ludolf heard his name being called out. He saw a dark figure clad in an overcoat and a hat... just like him... approaching him.

"Sorry to have troubled you to come to such a deserted and cold place. I would have certainly preferred some fine dining in a warm place… but the matter that we would like to discuss demanded a place like this. I am sure you will understand," the man said.

"Perhaps. I am not too sure about it. Do you have a name by any chance? I am sure people like you must be carrying passports with different names from different countries," Ludolf retorted.

"Touché!" Replied the person. "You can call me Christoph."

"So, Herr Christoph… here I am. Tell me what it is that you want to discuss that benefits both of us."

"Let me begin with a question, Herr Ludolf… You have been an extremely successful businessman, an entrepreneur… but have you achieved your basic objective with which you left Argentina? Would you not like to achieve it now? Have you changed your mind?"

This was completely unexpected. Ludolf was caught in a conundrum. He could neither say yes nor no. This also meant that his background had already been thoroughly searched, and motives established.

"Before I say anything, I need to understand who I am talking to… CIA?" Although Christoph's accent seemed like that of a normal German guy, Ludolf noticed somewhere that it had a hidden American accent.

"Why CIA? I could be BND or KGB or SIS."

"Tell me what the CIA's interest in my trip to China is. I am going there to increase my footprint. Are you guys… like your Mr. Brink or companies like Apple etc…. not investing in China?"

"Herr Ludolf, I am not here to answer your questions. I am here to suggest how you can successfully achieve your original objectives. Yes, you can increase your footprint, make more money, and yet achieve your goal without ever coming into the picture."

"What do you mean by 'without coming into the picture'?"

"This means we have established the fact that your initial objective is still alive. There would be others who have similar aspirations like yours and would like to get associated with you… who would be fronting your efforts. Whatever the Chinese want, you can safely provide them… Or you can provide them via another agent so that you don't come into the equation," Christoph said.

This was becoming more interesting for Ludolf. Christoph was trying to tell him that instead of Ludolf dealing directly with the Chinese, he should deal through an agent so that Ludolf does not become liable for anything.

"Who would this agent be?"

"Someone of your stature. All that the Chinese demand, you provide to this agent. Ask the Chinese to procure from him. They have no alternative. So, they will go to this agent," Christoph said.

"What is in it for you… the CIA?"

"Come, come, Herr Ludolf… don't pretend as if you know nothing about global politics. Please tell me why the Ukraine war is still going on. Is it that difficult for Russians to get rid of Ukraine… or who in the West is really benefiting from the Ukraine war? You know the answer… right?" Christoph said.

"Defense Contractors and defense manufacturers… Of course," Ludolf thought to himself. But openly he said, "But you did not tell me who this agent is?"

"He will be introduced to you immediately after the start of the new year. We know where and how to reach you. You will be informed," Christoph said.

Ludolf's mind was trying to decipher the situation… was it the Ukraine war or the Israel War that Christoph was really referring to? The Chinese demands suddenly started making sense. But where does the CIA fit into this… then suddenly, it dawned on Ludolf… that the CIA is preparing a case for invasion of Iran or China… like the Iraq war… weapons of mass destruction… Very clever indeed!!! Ludolf remembered the Chinese plans of building massive underground bunkers, putting the missiles into space… another Biotech war like Covid.

Outwardly, Ludolf said… "Okay, I will wait. But this does not stop my trip to China."

"Before you depart for China, you would have had the meeting with our agent. Thank you for coming over tonight, Herr Ludolf. *Gute Nacht*," Christoph said… turned and quickly vanished in the dark.

Ludolf stood there for a minute and then started walking back to his car parked outside the Gruneburgpark. It was 7.40 pm… well past Ludolf's dinner time.

"Well, I am still going to have it anyway," muttered Ludolf to himself. He was elated because his dream might just come true. "CIA seems to be quite cocky… they can't and won't play straight."

Moscow, Russia

December 15, 2023; 08.30 AM

It snowed all night and even in the morning. Late last night, Alexei received a cryptic message saying that the meeting had been arranged for early January.

Alexei enjoyed control and power. But unlike politicians, he never desired to display his power or control in public. He wanted to remain behind the curtains, pulling the strings and making people dance to his tunes. He enjoyed all the fine things in life, including the three Ws, as he used to say: Wealth, Wine, and women, in that order. Never in his life did he get emotionally involved with any woman, and he never carried any liability.

He was a hardcore trader by nature… not a "businessman" per se. KGB agents had used him ever since he was in his teens to get intel on various activities. The rewards would be small or in kind, but they had satisfied Alexei's needs. Then Afghanistan happened, and Alexei almost became a part of the KGB cadre… even the Generals depended on Alexei's intel.

Post USSR's Afghanistan war, Russian businesses of the former Soviet republics rapidly accumulated wealth in the 1990s via Russian privatization after the dissolution of the Soviet Union. The failing Soviet state had decided to leave the ownership of state assets by auctioning, which had allowed people like Alexei to make informal deals with former USSR officials as a means to acquire state property.

The Russian oligarchs like Alexei emerged as business entrepreneurs under Mikhail Gorbachev during his period of market liberalization. Oligarchs like Alexei had become increasingly influential in Russian politics during Boris Yeltsin's presidency; they had, in fact, helped finance his re-election in 1996. Well-connected oligarchs like Alexei acquired key assets at a fraction of the asset value.

The majority of oligarchs had been initially promoted by the Soviet apparatchiks, with strong connections to Soviet power structures and access to the funds of the Communist Party. With the ascent of the current Russian President in the Kremlin, the influence of the Yeltsin oligarchs had dissipated; some were imprisoned, while others had emigrated, sold off their assets, or died under suspicious circumstances.

A second wave of oligarchs emerged in the 2000s, friends and former colleagues of the current President either from his years in the St. Petersburg municipal administration or his Dresden tenure in the KGB. Alexei had survived and had risen quickly as his association with the KGB over the last few decades had paid off. In fact, he had become a close associate of the current President.

After the 2022 Russian invasion of Ukraine, Canada, the US, and European leaders, with the addition of Japan, took unprecedented steps to sanction Russia and the oligarchs directly. Reacting to the sanctions, the targeted oligarchs started to hide wealth in an attempt to prevent the Western nations from freezing their assets. Since the invasion began, nine of the Russian oligarchs' yachts had turned their navigation transponders off as they sailed to ports where they were less likely to be searched and seized. Alexei's yachts were among such yachts.

Alexei's Gas venture RussGazz initially took a hit as the sanctions were imposed… but soon it had managed to sail over the sanctions. RussGazz was a privately owned Russian oil company headquartered in Moscow, specializing in the extraction, production, and sale of petroleum and petroleum products. While a small part of RussGazz's oil earnings was derived from upstream sales within Russia, the company had large-scale operations internationally.

Western sanctions and boycotts targeting Russian oil exports to Europe meant that transparency over their routes had vanished not only for Western watchers, but for the Russian government as well, which was too preoccupied then to see that the state budget was being deprived of a substantial share of oil revenues.

The EU embargo on Russian crude and oil products came into force on December 5, 2022. But energy-starved Europe was keen on getting oil and gas any way it could. There was still a brisk trade of Russian oil in Europe. Cargo changed hands in the North Sea and Mediterranean ports, and prices were kept manageable and meaningful to lure the EU countries.

The gamble had paid off… even countries like Germany had resorted to procuring Russian oil and gas in spite of the sanctions. Then there were countries like China and India who were quick to cash in on the opportunity to get oil and gas at a very reasonable rate. As time went by, the effect of the sanctions had waned. Alexei had managed to stay afloat due to his control of the logistics… which was his childhood forte.

Post USSR's Afghanistan war, the business growth brought him closer to the Politburo members… and now, courtesy of KGB contacts, closer to the current President… who was once a KGB agent himself. The bond had grown stronger over the years.

Although Alexei had slowly taken control in his hands, he had pretended that the control still lay with the President. It was easy for him to get a nod from the President if ever Alexei wanted to do certain things his way. The Politburo members, as well as quite a few KGB bigwigs, were on his payroll. Alexei had not touched the armed forces. That was one area he had kept clear of. Alexei preferred the international arena… where he could enter at will and do whatever business he could that would generate lots of money in a short time… He therefore fancied the drug business and arms business. Since he had complete control over logistics, he never hesitated to take risks.

So, when Sergei had suggested, "Iran needs hi-tech stuff for its nukes. There is this guy in Germany who can provide this," Alexei had thought over… he had reached out to his sources to get some inputs on in what way the German guy can help Iran in achieving their objectives of making the nukes. There were many questions in Alexei's mind like… why Russia can't fulfill the need… why Iran can't buy it from cash-strapped Pakistan or from North Korea? It was just a question of make it or buy it. What is the guarantee that the German guy would provide the required tech support or parts to Iran?

Alexei knew very well how to benefit from any war. He was a pro in that field. He would do it even for Iran… if he were to get tons of money. But in this case, Alexei did not want to undertake this work unless he had spoken to the President. That was what Alexei wanted to accomplish before Christmas… if possible, tonight.

The biggest question was, would the President agree to such a deal? Sergei had already started the stopwatch without waiting for Alexei to confirm. Of course, Alexei knew the answer to that… Sergei would inform his boss at the CIA that Iran is planning to buy xyz from the German guy for their nukes… and that would lead the US to open another war front against Iran… just like they did against Iraq… with Weapons of Mass Destruction. "The buggers are good at spreading fake narratives," Alexei thought to himself.

He toyed with his cell phone for a while before calling someone. He spoke briefly for 2 minutes and hung up. Five minutes later, he received the phone call he was expecting… Alexei's meeting was fixed with the President at 8.30 pm tonight.

"I need to prepare myself properly," Alexei thought to himself.

Virginia,US

Lemur was rather surprised to get the message from Nash… suddenly out of the blue… as he thought to himself. "Must be something special and interesting!"

Lemur was his operating name while at the FBI. It had been a few years since Lemur had taken retirement from the FBI… although he was running his own FBI for a fee as there were people who needed his services. Lemur's contacts in the FBI also helped in providing details where required on a "You did not get it from me" basis.

It did not matter to Lemur as long as the intel was accurate and helped him meet his purpose. His relationship with Nash was quite different. Nash had actually saved his ass when Lemur was on the trail of a senator like a bloodhound trying to solve the rape and murder case of an intern. The senator was well-connected and moved in circles of some extremely powerful people. The President himself had ordered Nash to extinguish the fire and get the FBI off the back of the senator… Otherwise, the consequences would have been dire, especially for Lemur.

Lemur was quite unhappy, but Nash had made him understand the reality… "Sometimes you need to let go of the integrity and look at the reality." It was much later that Lemur had realized the meaning of what Nash had told him.

Lemur had arrived at The Old Fire Station #3 on University Dr. in Fairfax half an hour early. He had gone inside and taken a table in the far corner and ordered a Heineken. Lemur was observing the people in the pub. Being the beginning of the weekend and also the festive season, the pub was crowded. A quick scan of the faces and Lemur was sure that there was not a single familiar face. Momentarily, he saw Nash coming his way... clad in a thick overcoat and a woolly hat, Nash looked more like a fisherman on a fishing boat than a CIA bigshot.

"Good to see ya... old fella!" Lemur rose from his chair and greeted Nash.

"Same here... you haven't changed a wee bit since I saw you last," Nash remarked.

"Remember... we are hounds. We are, and we always have to remain in shape," Lemur said with a smile. "So, chief... what made you remember a small fry like me?"

"Vodka, a slice of lemon and a Sprite," Lemur ordered as the waitress appeared. "Right?" Lemur looked at Nash.

Nash just nodded.

"What do you know about the protests on the university campuses that are taking place all over the US... supporting Palestine?"

"Well... nothing, actually. Why? Which university do you have in mind, chief?"

"Let us start with the Ivy League ones. Columbia. What is happening there... who is behind the protests... that is, who is funding them. I might know the answer, but I need to get some ground reality... because this has to do with the Palestine issue...

it is an external matter. But I need to know more about it because we don't want another 9/11."

Lemur understood what Nash meant. Although the FBI had information about the possible plot, the CIA was kept in the dark.

"Why come to me? You could use the official line," asked Lemur.

"No, I don't want the concerned stakeholders to be aware of being 'observed' or under surveillance. I would rather have someone like you check it out and gather some intel. It may not be a long-term thing, I am guessing… perhaps a month or two. Money is not an issue."

"I don't need money… and certainly not from you, chief. I will do it for you any day. What exactly do you have in mind… well, at Columbia and why?"

"Simple… It is my alma mater. So, I would like to know who is at the forefront, who are the backers, who all are funding and is there a bigger plot that is being hatched? I need to know all. Plus, what is the grapevine in general? Based on the intel, we will decide the next moves. If you find anyone specifically interesting or taking an undue interest, mark him and let me know. Rest is as usual."

"I am guessing you would like me to start as soon as possible."

"Yes. If you can. Please."

"Hmm… let me see because we are now approaching the Christmas holidays. There may not be much activity on the campus. But I can always pick up some titbits."

"That would be great…!" Nash put some bills on the table, stood up, shook hands with Lemur and disappeared into the crowd.

After five minutes, Lemur gulped down his Heineken and walked out into the bitter cold. It had started to snow.

"Wonder, what the heck is he looking for?" Lemur muttered to himself as he entered his car.

frankfurt, Germany

December 16, 2023; 08.30 AM

Even though it was Saturday, Ludolf had woken up as usual at 6.00 am, finished his workout and swimming by 7.30 am, and completed his shave, shower, and breakfast by 8.30 am. He was ready for the day. He would never change his routine, even if he were traveling.

Ludolf was still thinking about the meeting at the Gruneburgpark he had with the CIA guy, if he was a CIA guy indeed. Ludolf hated the leftists and the people of color in General. He, as his grandfather had mentored him, believed in the pure Aryan race… with blue eyes, golden hair, and white complexion, Ludolf hated Jews, Muslims, Chinese, Russians, Americans, Brits… even the Swiss and the Italians. But when it came to business… if Ludolf was getting benefited with a certain leverage of power, then he had no qualms.

In his mind, Ludolf had summarized what that CIA guy was alluding to… in short… let the Chinese buy the required stuff from you, the logistics would be run by a Russian, and the final destination of the stuff would be Iran. Where Iran would use the stuff was a basic 101… but who would be their target was not a simple question. It could be Israel, Saudi, the US, or some countries in the West… including Germany. Ludolf saw no issues with the rest of the targets except Germany.

"I don't want to create my own death trap," he thought to himself. In Germany, he had kept both the leftists and the right-wingers, including the Neo-Nazis, in his pocket. The AfD Party, dubbed as the Neo-Nazi party, was the extreme right party and was gaining popularity. Ludolf was secretly funding AfD and was secretly in contact with Bjorn Hocke, the main leader of the AfD Party. AfD was against all immigrants, Muslims, and people of color, especially black.

There was another party which was secretly funded by Ludolf…The Third Way (III Path) Party. The party described itself as a national revolutionary and partially based itself on the ideology of the Strasser Brothers of the early Nazi party. The III Path had widely been described as an ultra-nationalist and Neo-Nazi party. The party was registered at the Federal Returning Office as "DER DRITTE WEG" short form: "III. Weg." They always carried out a torchlight parade at night in Wunsiedel, a town of 9,000 in the mountains of Bavaria, where Rudolf Hess was buried. The party had supported the Nordic Resistance Movement in the Nordic countries as well. The Neo-Nazi movement was fast spreading throughout northern Europe.

The Neo-Nazi movement had started gaining roots in France as well. The OAS Party had been rejuvenated from ashes.

And then there was a town in Northeastern Germany called Jamel… which was referred to as a Nazi town. All the people living there were Neo-Nazis. Some of Ludolf's "charity" went to these people as well. Ludolf was happy.

"As long as the unwanted elements are eliminated… even if indirectly, it is okay with me," Ludolf thought to himself. Although he supported the left liberals… the ruling Social Democratic Party (SPD) with funds and verbal support, he never asked for any favors from them or from Angela Merkel's Christian Democrats

CDU-CSU. But Ludolf definitely secretly exercised his control over the ruling party.

"You can't demand respect; you have to command respect." Ludolf always remembered the words of his grandfather. "You need not express your actual ambition or objectives to anyone… Just work on them quietly. If people come to understand your real ambition or objectives, then they will create obstacles in your way and make you fail in your quest. Just do everything quietly and achieve your results. There is nothing right or wrong in this world. It depends on one's perception. One man's poison could be another man's elixir. So, don't bother about right or wrong. Clean up the dirt and gain control. Control is the most important aspect of one's life."

Ludolf was still trying to place the CIA guy in his mind. The guy certainly did not appear to be a Bundesnachrichtendienst (BND) employee… neither did he appear to be a British SIS agent. He certainly did not appear to be KGB material. His mannerisms, attitude, accent - everything appeared to be American, yet Ludolf was somewhat reluctant to accept him as a CIA operative. But the only agency that could have known about his Argentinian connection would be the CIA.

"Those guys dig deep. Hope they know nothing about my motives," Ludolf mused to himself. "Let us do it," he said openly, got up from his chair and went to the window… Flurries had started.

Washington, D.C., US

December 18, 2023; 06.30 PM

It was dark and cold outside, and Martin Kingston could feel the chill in his bones sitting inside his warm office. It was less than a year until the 2024 Presidential Elections, and Martin was unsure who would come to power.

He just shrugged his shoulders in exasperation… "What difference does it make anyway?" Martin thought to himself. "The Dems or the Reps, whoever comes to power, their outlook on the real world is quite delusional. Ever since the end of the Cold War, the fundamental thinking of the US administration, the lawmakers, the State Department, the Pentagon, and the CIA has not changed. They think that the US has the right to go around the globe interfering in the internal matters of any country and screwing them if they don't fall in line with US policies. They all tend to live in the past, thinking that the US is the only global superpower."

Martin's thoughts were speeding faster than Voyager 1. "These lobbyists control all the strings, and they goddamn force the policies from various countries… and the lawmakers on both sides, Dems or Reps… to just fall in line." Martin was thinking of Victoria Nuland, who was part of both the Republican and the democratic governments and always had her "views" on the policies of various countries. Martin never liked her because he felt that she was also a puppet controlled by someone outside the government. Otherwise, how could both Reps and the Dems make her a part of their respective teams?

Martin realized that he was a part of the "system." Everybody that belonged to the "system" had been there for over 20-plus years at the least. Everybody thought that it was their birthright to drive their own agenda… have their own views on the policies made by the governments. And everybody had some godfather either within the "system" or outside the "system" or the powerful, influential people outside who ran the "system."

Unfortunately, Martin had no godfather. He had worked hard to get to his current position. He was the senior-most in the State Department and most experienced. But he was a go-getter. He would get the work done. He was the most reliable and knowledgeable in the department. But that is where it ended.

Martin was now sixty-two and still in good shape, but he still had a mortgage, and his youngest daughter had one more year at Med School. So, he had decided to work for one more term of the next government until he turned sixty-seven. He would then take his retirement, get a pension, collect social security and his 401K… since the housing market had been booming, he would get rid of his current house and downsize to his next residence… some place cheaper… with a lower cost of living. "A pension and the social security should be enough for both of us to survive," Martin thought to himself.

"The question is how to survive the next 5 years… because it is becoming increasingly difficult to manage everybody. They all have their own specific agenda, and they will crush you if they can." Martin remembered Abe Williams, Deputy Director of the CIA's visit. "There is something fishy going on and I don't want to be a part of it," Martin's mind went back to the meeting he had with Abe.

In his mind, Martin had gone over all the discussions he had had with various lobbying firms… but could not think of any such "CIA important" incident. He had referred to his scrapbooks, notations, but could not remember anything that could link it to DARPA or to the CIA.

"I don't want to become a scapegoat in this. I need to find out what is going on. Abe will not spell it out. I need to find out. Who can tell me… who can I take into confidence?" Martin was thinking hard. His cell phone rang, and Martin's chain of thoughts was broken. His wife was calling him… it was past 7.00 pm and would Martin be home for dinner on time?

"Yes… I am leaving now," Martin replied and got up from his chair, collected his laptop, backpack, overcoat, cap, and checked for his car keys. While he was about to leave, his eyes fell on one of the books on the shelf; the author's name suddenly brightened Martin's mood. "Nash… of course," he said aloud and smiled to himself, closing the door behind him as he left his room.

"There is someone who can certainly help me," Martin thought to himself as he entered his car.

New York, US

January 4, 2024; 09.00 AM

Christmas vacation was over, and so was the new year. Jerry had been busy completing his assignments. He had gone home to meet his parents over Christmas. His dad had mellowed down a little. He was happy that Jerry had taken to his studies quite seriously and his quest for Journalism could prove to be a good sign for his publishing business… "Another 3-4 years… not a big deal. Time flies. I can manage to wait," Jerry's dad had told Jerry's mum.

Jerry had come back immediately after Christmas and had immersed himself in completing the assignments. He was looking forward to Prof. Matthew's class on the Deep State. He had tried to lay his hands on whatever literature he could find on the Deep State. He was quite intrigued. He was eagerly looking forward to Prof. Matthew's class, and here he was today.

"Beginning in the 1990s," Prof. Matthew had begun… "an increasing number of defense Contractors from Southern California began to relocate their HQ to Washington D.C. so as to be closer to the political action. Even the British contracting giant BAE Systems Inc. had opened its office in Virginia just across Memorial Bridge in Washington. This hobnobbing with a foreign entity like BAE Systems was due to a historical special relationship with the UK government… as part of the deal to engage politically and militarily where the Americans were legally barred from participating… like during 1990 when the Reagan administration wanted to make a military sale of unprecedented size to Saudi Arabia, but the Congress balked, so as a reward for Mrs. Thatcher's unrelenting support of the US nuclear policy in Western Europe, BAE got a GBP 45 billion Saudi deal… of which GBP 6 billion were unauthorized commissions to Saudis. That should explain the UK's unwavering support for US actions anywhere in the world… including that of the Iraq war… the famous WMDs… which were never found, but the British PM had claimed to have had evidence. The people who sat on the Board of Directors of BAE Systems were Lee Hamilton, the Vice Chairman of the 9/11 commission, General Antony Zinni, former commander of US central command, a military authority in charge of Middle East conflicts."

"Washington is in the business of running a global business empire… trying to profit from various wars instigated at various places across the world. The CIA and the Pentagon are located in close proximity not by chance. There is a visible state in Washington D.C… which is like the tip of the iceberg… and there is another invisible state, the subsurface portion of the iceberg, which operates on its own terms irrespective of who is formally in power in the White House. This is a hybrid entity of public and private institutions ruling the country and other countries around the globe, according to their needs to fulfill their specific objectives…"

"The Deep State does not consist of the entire government. It is a hybrid of national security, law enforcement agencies and key parts of other legal branches… like the Dept of Defense, Dept of Homeland Security, CIA, the Justice Dept; Dept of Treasury… hand in hand with Wall Street, defense manufacturers / Contractors, Silicon Valley, and various big private enterprises.

The irony is that all these government agencies are coordinated by the executive office of the POTUS via the National Security Council. Certain key areas of the judiciary belong specifically to the Deep State, such as the Foreign Intelligence Surveillance Court."

"Washington, D.C. is the most important 'node' of the Deep State… but there are others. The other one is Wall Street… which one may call the Ultimate Owner of the Deep State and its strategies. Over the course of WW2, the US built a military-industrial machine the world had never conceived before. It could do anything from constructing airfields in Arctic Alaska to building a war-winning weapon… the Atomic Bomb. The latter became the conception point of the Deep State. The nuclear weapons were the initiation of the key characteristics the Deep State possesses today… a penchant for secrecy, lack of democratic accountability, and extravagant costs. Instilling FEAR became the tool of choice for the Deep State's prime tactics… what came to be known as the Truman Doctrine, as President Truman had described the 'Totalitarian Regime'… 'Scare the hell out of the people!!!'."

"In 1952, the National Security Agency was created with the idea that the US should and would maintain a large, capable military across the globe and a comprehensive intelligence establishment regardless of whether it is in a formal state of war. The Deep State, with the military-industrial complex at its core, fully crystallized by the 1960s. That was the beginning of the formation of the Wall Street-Pentagon Nexus."

"What is the point of having this superb military that we are always talking about if we can't use it?"

"If we have to use force, it is because we are America; we are the indispensable nation. We stand tall and we can see further than other countries into the future… and we see danger here to all of us. Remember… scare the hell out of the people!"

"The focus is on pressurizing CIA to find whatever evidence is necessary to justify NATO and or US Military intervention to start the war… and justify that to the naïve population via the bought-out media… like the WMD case. CIA also runs the "dark side" of the war… that is Kidnapping, Rendition, Torture and Assassinations."

"In 2014, the Pentagon published its Quadrennial Defense Review (QDR). The Pentagon's summary of strategic goals identifies the following regions as 'arenas for potential national security concern' … Europe, Russia, the Middle East, South Asia, China, Northeast and Southeast Asia, Oceania, The Indian Ocean, Latin America, Africa, The Arctic, and Cyberspace… The only thing left out was Canada… otherwise, it covered the entire planet!"

"The QDR's definition of vital interest implies that the US will be in a condition of war, near war or Cold War in perpetuity. The state of perpetual war was and is good for business. The Military-Industrial Complexes and their commercial stakeholders see crises anywhere around the globe as an opportunity to mint money."

'The Deep State used the US Dollar to punish the regimes that did not agree with their agenda or demands. The US Dollar has been, until recently, the only global trade currency. So, when Libya's ruler, Muammar Gaddafi developed a plan to sell oil in Dinars and to move away from US Dollars… or Saddam Hussein of Iraq, who had plans to quit US Dollars and sell oil in euros… the Deep State saw to it that both these leaders were removed. But now the Saudi-backed Petro Dollar has gone, and that has certainly disturbed the Deep State… and its plans.'

"There is a lot more that can be taught about the Deep State, but it would be better for you to read everything in detail and compile your own notes, views, comments. I will be giving you a list of major references that you must read, and there is, of course, more literature on Deep State activities which you can find on your own."

"Any questions?"

Lots of hands went up, and questions started popping out like cornflakes popping...

- Does it happen in every country?

- What about banks?

- What about people like Borge Ross who give funds?

- What about Cobblestone?

- What happens if there is eventually de-dollarization?

- You said there is a nexus between Wall Street and the Pentagon... can you explain in detail?

Prof. Matthew raised his hand and said, "Hold it. Put down all your questions on one sheet of paper and hand it to me in my room. I will begin the next class with answers to your questions. We have just covered the basics; there is far more to it. We must stick to the syllabus first."

With that, he collected his papers and books and walked out of the class. Jerry immediately got up and went after Prof. Matthew. He caught up with Prof. Matthew just at the end of the corridor.

"Hi... just wondered if you have a couple of minutes... I need to discuss something with you."

"Is it related to today's topic?"

"No... actually, it is related to what is happening on the campus... the demonstrations. I wanted to get your inputs, thoughts or whatever."

Prof. Matthew stopped in his tracks, turned to Jerry, and said, "If you want to be safe, please stay away from these demos and don't spoil your career."

"Oh no... I did not participate. I just watched it... and had a brief argument, um... discussion with Cathy Dexter... heated discussion, that is."

"Interesting."

"What I failed to understand is what the point of doing the demonstrations here is when I know for sure 99% of the guys demonstrating cannot and will not be able to point out Palestine on the world map."

Prof. Matthew laughed... "Yes, that is correct."

"Then why the heck are they resorting to this drama?"

"What do you think?"

"Publicity for themselves."

"And?"

"I don't know for sure, but someone must be paying them to do this. Cathy mentioned Borge Ross as one of the main contributors, supporters. Is this part of the Deep State?"

Prof. Matthew laughed again and said, "I am advising you to keep away from these guys and their agenda. All I can say is, it will be dangerous to you and your career, your future. As they say in Star Wars, don't go to the dark side. Any altercations or arguments with them will put you at risk, as you would be considered their adversary."

"Yes, I understand. So, are they part of the Deep State then?"

"Have you seen an octopus… I am sure you have. It has. These guys have countless tentacles. So, every other person you meet on the street could be working for these guys. Please keep your thoughts to yourself. Someone may pretend to agree with your thoughts… but he or she may, in fact, be a tentacle… you will never know. Be careful and avoid talking about this subject. Do not speak to Cathy again… Even if she wants to speak to you. Just tell her that she had been right… and that post-demo lecture you agree with her thoughts."

"Understood. Thank you very much, Prof. Matthew."

Jerry stood there like a statue, looking at Prof. Matthew as he disappeared around the corner. Jerry was still in shock because he had not expected such a warning from Prof. Matthew. The question he wanted to ask Prof. Matthew was… "Why did he think these guys were so dangerous? What force is driving them? Why was the institute not ready to take any action on these guys… or punish them?" Perhaps these people had much deeper roots in society, in the establishments where people were scared to take any action. "Scare the hell out of the people." Jerry shuddered at the very thought, turned, and started walking back to the class.

New York, US

January 9, 2024; 11.30 AM

Borge Ross was trying to get his hands around Gregory Brink for a while now. Over the last few years, Gregory Brink had become too big for Ross to contain him or Cobblestone… and he loathed it. Way back in September 2021, he had tried to warn publicly about the investments Brink's Cobblestone had made in China… stating that "The investments of Cobblestone in China are akin to supporting an oppressive regime." He had also warned that "it's likely to lose money for Cobblestone's clients and, more importantly, will damage the national security interests of the US and other democracies." Ross had felt that Cobblestone was funneling billions of American dollars into China — a move he had felt imperiled clients' money and US security.

Borge Ross always believed right from his childhood that he was "anointed" by God and that he had to be the creator, and he must have complete control over all matters. He felt comfortable when he could feel that he was God… the creator.

Ross has spoken out against repressive regimes before. He survived Nazi occupation during World War II and moved to England after the war. He focused his charitable giving on organizations that "build vibrant and inclusive democracies whose governments are accountable to their citizens." Borge was a mega donor to Democrats. In 2020, he injected about $30 million into various Democratic campaigns. He also supported various liberal causes.

In the recent weeks, Ross had come out strongly against China. He felt that Xi's dictatorship threatened the Chinese state and that investors in Xi's China would face a rude awakening as Xi did not understand the market economy. Ross had given away over $35 billion through his philanthropy, the Free Society Establishment, and felt that he had to have control over all global matters by controlling the presidents and prime ministers of various countries… because he understood everything more than them.

Now in July, Ross had come to know about the letter the US Congress House of Representatives- Select Committee of the Chinese Communist Party had sent to Gregory Brink of Cobblestone…requesting information about Cobblestone's facilitation of American capital flows to Chinese companies that have been blacklisted by the US government because of their role in fueling the People's Republic of China's (PRC) military advancement or in facilitating the Chinese Communist Party's (CCP) human rights abuses.

A few of Cobblestone's funds revealed that Cobblestone facilitated American capital flows to more than twenty-five blacklisted PRC companies. Across just five funds, Cobblestone had invested more than $400 million in PRC companies that pose national security risks and act directly against the interests of the United States. As a direct result of decisions made by Cobblestone, these Americans were unwittingly funding PRC companies that developed and built weapons for the People's Liberation Army (PLA)—the PRC's military and advanced the CCP's stated mission of technological supremacy. Cobblestone was the world's largest money manager, with $9.5 trillion under management.

Ross remembered how he had manipulated and provided all the data to his "contacts" in the US Congress, which had led to this inquiry. Ross knew that Brink and Cobblestone were quite big for him to handle but, nonetheless, he would make their life difficult as Ross saw them as his nemesis.

The Israeli lobby had always been strong, and US Govts… whether Dems or Reps, always gave unconditional support and aid to Israel… even if Israel openly defied some of the US's mandates. This preferred treatment given to Israel was something Ross loathed even though he was a Jew. He felt Israel was a dictatorial state and not a democratic one. But Ross could do nothing and felt miserable.

Ross sought complete control over his scheme of things… including running proxy governments in various countries. Chaos, he thought, was the best way to govern any country. Currently, his immediate focus was the elections in India. He wanted to get rid of the current nationalistic government and replace it with one that would lead to chaos, thereby giving Ross the ultimate control he wanted.

"Indian politicians and people can be bought for pennies," he thought to himself and smiled.

New York, US

January 11, 2024; 04.00 PM

Lemur had managed to transform himself into a media reporter with an "authentic" ID hanging around his neck. It was almost 4 PM when he went to the venue of the demonstration arranged by Cathy Dexter and her Society for Civil Rights. There were, as Lemur had expected, the pseudo-liberals, mostly the young intellectuals with zero real-life experience, gathering around the area… carrying Palestinian flags and some placards with slogans.

This was too familiar to experienced guys like Lemur. "If I show these chums the world map and ask them to pinpoint Palestine, I can bet my underpants, no one will be able to show it," Lemur thought to himself.

Lemur had decided to move behind the crowd to have a bird's eye view of the demonstration. Lemur had noticed the smart young brunette going around giving orders to her group members. "She seems to be the queen bee," Lemur muttered to himself.

"She is quite a smart girl," Lemur said to the student standing near him.

"Who? Cathy Dexter… you bet!!! Wait till you hear her… she will tear apart anyone who makes a noise against the Palestine issue." The guy said with pride in his voice.

"Looks like you are in love with her," Lemur remarked.

The guy gave a sheepish smile and slowly moved ahead, mixing in the crowd.

Lemur laughed aloud and looked around himself. His attention was drawn to a man standing a few feet away from him on his right side. He was standing under a tree with a young guy at his side. The young guy appeared to be a student as he was carrying his backpack on his shoulders and his laptop in his hands. The man appeared to be in his early thirties. Lemur searched his mental database to check if he had seen the man before… and if his face looked familiar.

Lemur decided to move closer to the guy and the student so that he could listen to their conversation. Lemur's mind was busy searching his mental database. After about five minutes, Lemur had understood from their conversation that the name of the man was Leo and that of the student was Jerry. Leo was a journalist working with some media houses.

With the name Leo, Lemur searched his mental database again but produced no results. Lemur now moved just behind Leo and Jerry so that he could hear their conversation properly.

By the time Cathy had taken to the small makeshift dais and started speaking, Lemur had understood that Jerry's last name was Carson, and his family had some kind of publishing business which his parents wanted him to look after… but the boy was interested in Journalism… touring around the world. Leo was trying to get more information about Cathy Dexter and the demonstration.

Cathy Dexter was in full flow… Lemur recalled the remarks… "She will tear you apart!!!" Cathy was quite an orator. Lemur could see that Cathy's speech was arousing the emotions of the crowd and the students were getting excited. Cathy was tearing the right-wingers and the supporters of Israel to pieces. More claps and more shouting followed.

Leo was possibly video-recording Cathy's speech. He had held his iPad in such a way that no one would suspect that he was recording. Lemur laughed to himself. "Amateurs!" Lemur muttered to himself.

Unknown to Leo and Jerry, Lemur had also captured their faces on his cell phone because he thought that it was an interesting pair... an odd pair. Lemur had a distinct feeling that Jerry was being used as an informant. But then, since Leo was a journalist, he was "cultivating" his contact... Lemur thought.

There were loads of claps and shouting in support of Palestine. More placards were waved in the air. Cathy had finished her lecture, and some other guy had taken her place on the dais. Lemur was now certain that there was something interesting cooking here; otherwise, why would Nash ask an ex-FBI person like Lemur to investigate privately?

"But what am I supposed to be looking for?" Lemur thought to himself.

"I am not in support of these demonstrations," Lemur heard Jerry expressing his views. "We are students. We don't have the power and the means to enforce anything on the US government or on the Israeli government. Plus, it was an act of terrorism carried out by Hamas. Israel did not initiate this," Jerry was blunt.

"So, you are against these demos then?" Leo asked.

"Yes. For sure. It is such a waste of resources. Maybe that Dexter girl wants to become a career politician and hence, she is showing off her skills. Maybe someone like that Ross guy is supporting her Society for Civil Rights or whatever. I dunno... and I don't care."

"But there are so many here who do care," Leo said.

"Yeah… well, then there are so many who don't care. We have better things to do in life," Jerry said.

"Well, if you want to become a journalist, you can't be passive about these things… sentiments of the people. You've got to exploit them," Leo remarked.

"Well, I will see when the time comes to cross the bridge. Right now, I have no interest," Jerry said.

"But then you came here anyway," Leo remarked.

"Yeah. I thought I might find you. Guess you seem to be quite impressed with that Dexter girl," Jerry said with a smile on his face.

"Hey, I am doing what I am supposed to do. Period," Leo said, clearly indicating that the conversation had come to an end. "In any case, you have my contact number… call me if you have any new developments," Leo said as he turned to leave.

"Yes. Will do. See you!" Jerry shook hands and left… walking towards the university building. Lemur turned his back towards Leo, pretending to observe another group of students.

Lemur then quickly turned and started following Leo… who was walking towards his parked car. As Leo was entering his car, Lemur quickly took a picture of his car and the registration plate. He would certainly find out where Leo worked… who he was really representing. Lemur did not see any point in following Leo.

Lemur walked towards his parked car, making sure that he was not being followed. He took two rounds of the area where his car was parked, again making sure that no one was observing him. He quickly entered his car; it was cold inside, almost frigid. It had already become dark by now. Lemur started the car and waited until the inside of the car had warmed up.

"I am not sure if there is anything fishy going on there. Or maybe I need to dig more and find out. From the face of it, it is all kid stuff," Lemur's train of thought had begun. "But then why Nash… and why me? I need to find that out first."

Lemur left the parking lot wondering if he should call Nash and inform him that it is useless to follow up on such demos.

New York, US

January 11, 2024; 08.00 PM

Cathy was back in her dorm room. She was very excited. She had received a message from the Free Society Establishment congratulating her on behalf of Borge Ross for the stupendous work of public awareness towards the persecution of the poor Palestinians. The lady who had personally visited her after her lecture had also told her that the Free Society Establishment would support her movement to the hilt… and that after she finishes her graduation, there will always be a place for her at the Free Society Establishment. Someone with her set of skills would be an asset to FSE.

This meant a lot to Cathy as she felt that her dream had come true. Publicity, name and fame, a big position, money, world travel, everything would follow. All she had to do was to pretend that she truly believed in uplifting the poor devils of this world. "Who the f*** cares about the Palestinians? I am interested in making a name, fame, and tons of money for myself." She stood in front of the mirror and laughed. "Babe… you are going to make it one day very soon," she said to her image in the mirror.

While Cathy was enjoying her accolades, Jerry was sitting in his room wondering if he really wanted to be a journo. He wondered if he would be able to create the false narratives which the media houses desired. They were interested in creating sensation… creating mass euphoria… increasing their TRP. Jerry abhorred all that. Dejected, Jerry decided to finish his undergrad first. "Will take a call once I am done with my undergrad," Jerry said to himself. He had lost his mood and appetite after listening to Cathy Dexter and watching the euphoria of his fellow students. "I don't belong there," he said to himself.

New Delhi, India

14 January 2024; 10.00 PM

Pranab Ramaswami was busy poring over various reports. He had been at it for over two hours now. He had returned from the RAW HQ where he had received a briefing about the areas that he, Pranab, needed to concentrate on.

The Parliamentary general elections were due in less than three months, and the political atmosphere was reaching its crescendo. It was absolutely dirty.

"People can go to any extent; they can even sell their mother if there is money to be made," his boss had remarked. "Lies, lies and more lies…even the media sets up false narratives as their masters, who are sitting overseas, pay them and order them to do it their way," his boss had commented.

"Why can't we take action against them?" Pranab had asked, although he knew the answer.

His boss had given him a weird look and said, "because we are a democracy."

"But we do have proof… don't we?"

Pranab's boss had not heard his question. He continued to look at the dark ceiling and continued his monologue… "They want to instill fear in the minds of the people against the patriotic leaders… like the democracy is in danger… or the constitution is going to be changed completely… well… you know it already."

"Yeah… these two pennyworth politicians," Pranab remarked.

"No Pranab, I am not talking about these tiny weeny politicians… I am talking about those who manage these politicians… they are big and dangerous people. Extremely powerful people. They can make or break governments in any given country… including India. Just the difference is… before 2014, it was easy to topple the governments in India. Now it has become difficult… though possible."

"Deep State."

"Umm hmm. That is why I keep reminding you to watch your back."

"Yes."

"Divide and rule is the basic game or strategy. You know… SC/ST versus OBC… reservation in government and private jobs. Vote banks… rather religious vote banks. In addition, there is this Venezuela Model… give free stuff to get votes and get elected. Even if you don't fulfill your promise after you get elected, it is okay. The organizations that help such corrupt politicos have been very well researched by you. I have read all those reports."

"And?"

"There is very little that we can do. Our own people… Indians… local or overseas are traitors. If we take action, the international media will make a big noise about 'democracy under threat' in India, and that is exactly what the opposition desires. If we don't take any action, that is great for the gang… the opposition, their masters, and the media and their masters. It is a win-win situation for them. The G-7 countries consider it as their birthright to interfere in others' matters… as it is an age-old habit, and no one has challenged it. Someone has to do it… sooner than later. Unfortunately, all the previous

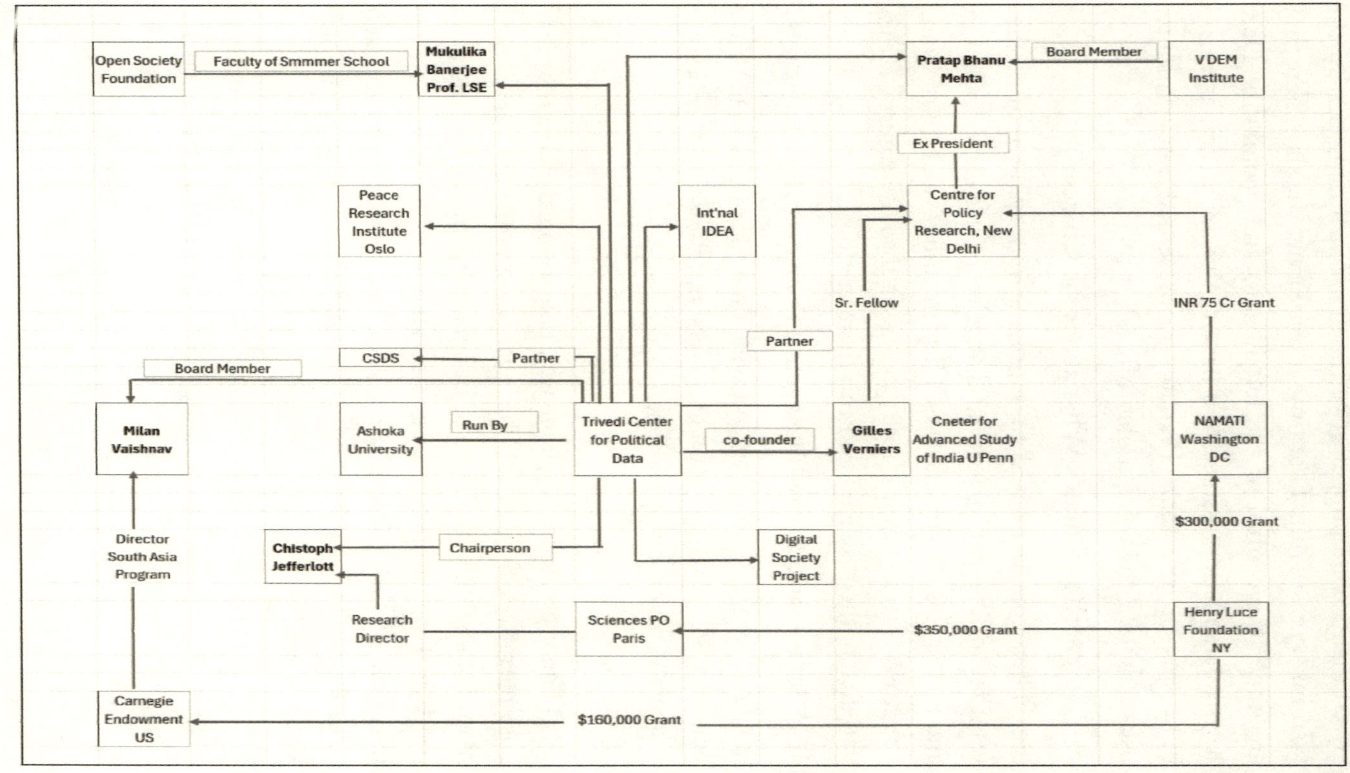

Open Society Foundation
Faculty of Smmmer School
Mukulika Banerjee Prof. LSE
Pratap Bhanu Mehta
Board Member
V DEM Institute
Ex President
Peace Research Institute Oslo
Int'nal IDEA
Centre for Policy Research, New Delhi
Sr. Fellow
INR 75 Cr Grant
Partner
CSDS
Partner
Board Member
Milan Vaishnav
Ashoka University
Run By
Trivedi Center for Political Data
co-founder
Gilles Verniers
Cneter for Advanced Study of India U Penn
NAMATI Washington DC
$300,000 Grant
Director South Asia Program
Chistoph Jefferlott
Chairperson
Digital Society Project
Research Director
Sciences PO Paris
$350,000 Grant
Henry Luce Foundation NY
Carnegie Endowment US
$160,000 Grant

governments were puppet governments… including that of the Nandhi Dynasty rule. That time it was Soviet Russia… now they are under the control of the left liberals and people like Dam Keytruda and Borge Ross. We have the proof… such as this… indicating on the chart Pranab had presented a few minutes back… but…" the voice trailed off.

"Sorry state of affairs. What about the Chinese?"

"Their role is limited to supplying money. In return, they want favors like getting your land on a long-term lease… and free and easy access to your markets. They are unlike the Keytruda and the Ross of this world. Those guys want absolute control… they will dictate their policies and run their agenda."

"But we can't do anything against them even if we know this."

"Yes, for the time being. We will come out of this web. While you are at it… it will be good to understand the 'social media well-wishers'… and their operations."

"What is that?"

"There are plenty of people who take to social media to spread false narratives. Some could be local… here in India, some could be overseas… like in Pakistan, Bangladesh, England, Canada, or the US. If we can get them geo-located, then we will know the locations of the 'infected' areas. We can cleanse them up later once we are back in the saddle… which I hope we will… we will know it by April…"

"It is difficult… from the point of view of time… because such bloggers could be in many languages spread across India… Plus, social media spread is quite wide… I mean you are talking about YouTubers, Facebookers… Tweeters… WhatsAppers…!"

"Yes, we will give you some pointers, keywords… and some specific access to break into the system… we need to understand the sort of heat map of these bedbugs. The sooner, the better."

"Can be done, but again, what is the use? Because if we cannot take any preventive action against them, then these bedbugs will still be around," Pranab tried to protest.

"Just do it. We will see how best we can control this. We might hear some interesting chatter. Anyway, keep digging. It is getting late, and it is cold outside… you better leave and watch your back."

Pranab was on his feet… he had pondered over going home… but decided otherwise and had come to his office. He was busy poring over the reports prepared by his team. He was going to have a busy night.

"You can't satisfy everybody in the party… some unsatisfied souls will always play the backstabbing game. Who you can control and satisfy… it is a futile game. Frustrating," Pranab thought to himself. He knew he had limitations… even if he could manage to wield a machine gun and shoot all the traitors… there would be a new breed springing up the very next day.

"Why can't we be like the Japanese or the Germans or even the Israelis… patriotic to the toe," Pranab said aloud. There was no one to hear him.

Beijing, China

January 23, 2024; 10.00 AM

Zhou Xuebin, the Minister heading the Ministry of Water Resources (MWR), and Tian Xuewen, the Minister heading the Ministry of Agriculture (MOA), both cabinet-level executive departments of the State Council of China, had just come out of the meeting with the Chinese Premier, who had clearly informed them that both their departments must concentrate on ensuring Chinese government control over both agricultural land and water... including seas and oceans. If they are unable to perform, they will perish.

Also, in attendance was Wu Youxia, Head of the China National Space Administration (CNSA), which was the Chinese government agency that managed the country's space activities, including the country's satellite fleets. Wu was directed to provide a specific official to coordinate all satellite activities related to agricultural land and water... rivers, lakes, seas, oceans... everything.

"We need all the seas... Yellow Sea, East China Sea, The South China Sea, Philippine Sea, and part of the North Pacific till the Marshall Islands under our control. Period. We will control that piece of earth. The Himalayas... extremely important for the freshwater, drinking water sources... the rivers, the lakes... all that must be under our control. Remember, oil will not be the most important thing on this planet... water and food will be.

Our satellites will watch over all these resources 24X7X365 and even if there is a small encroachment, they will inform my office directly."

"The same is true with agricultural land… we would like to turn part of the Gobi Desert into cultivable land, and we will need water to be made available for this venture. You will soon receive the specific directives on this."

"What is going on?" Zhou asked Tian and Wu once they were out of the meeting. Wu was in a hurry to leave as he had to attend a meeting with some German and Russian visitors. But he remarked softly, "Keep your heads down and do what has been told. Learn not to ask questions. You are senior guys… I don't need to tell you this… but our satellites have the capability to listen to your whispers also… even from space." Indicating with his eyes the cameras monitoring the area, Wu said, "They can also read your lips."

Bidding them a good day, Wu entered his waiting car and left. "Hope I will be able to reach in time," Wu said to himself. He was not exactly sure as to why he was invited to the meeting, but he did not bother to inquire. "Perhaps because I can speak German fluently," Wu thought to himself.

Wu's father was a military attaché posted in Germany. Wu had attended Aachen University…Rheinisch-Westfälische Technische Hochschule Aachen and completed his graduation in Mechanical engineering. RWTH Aachen University has been the largest university of technology in Germany and one of the most renowned in Europe. Wu wanted to stay back in Germany and not return to China. He had picked up the German language quite well. However, as always was the case, Wu was required to come back to China and serve in some government job.

Due to his Aachen University credentials, Wu was picked up by the newly formed and cultivated Chinese National Space Administration… then a poor equivalent of NASA… as Wu had thought at the time. However, over the years, Wu had proved to be quite an asset, and CNSA had progressed by leaps and bounds. Wu was now heading it. His father had told him only one thing: "Keep your mouth shut and nod your head in agreement." That helped a lot.

The meeting was in the office of the Ministry of Commerce, PRC and would be attended by Wang Gengxin, International Trade Negotiator; Tu Wentao, Minister of the Ministry of Foreign Trade and Economic Cooperation; Zhang Qian, Chinese People's Liberation Army (PLA) Rocket Force; and Jian Fung, Chairman, CMC (Central Military Commission) Equipment Development Department.

Wu was shown to the conference room and led to his place at the table. Wang Genxin was yet to arrive. Wu figured he would be bringing in the guests. There was one lady sitting at the far end of the table… it was not a familiar face to Wu. But then, it was a common practice to have some such Chinese Secret Service persons present in the meetings. The lady was concentrating on the folder she was carrying with her.

Momentarily, Wang entered with a tall, white, blonde guy. He had blue eyes. He was wearing an elegant, expensive yet casual jacket, slacks and did not wear a tie… which was rather surprising. Everybody at the table was wearing expensive suits and ties but… their guest looked far more handsome and dashing.

Where is the other one… the Russian… Wu wondered because his brief was that he would be meeting a German and a Russian. "Maybe there is a change of plan. Why would a Russian meet a German… they are at war," Wu thought of NATO versus Russia fighting over Ukraine.

"Gentlemen, I have the pleasure of introducing Herr Ludolf Hoffmann, who is an entrepreneur and has developed multi-billion-dollar global organizations in Germany. We have been in discussions with Herr Ludolf over the last few months and we would like to seek cooperation between Herr Ludolf's organization and the People's Republic of China for mutual benefits and the benefit of mankind. May I request you to please welcome Herr Ludolf Hoffmann."

Everybody had stood up and clapped. After they had all occupied their respective chairs, they were all asked to introduce themselves. The translator, sitting next to Ludolf, would translate what was said to Ludolf... who was making a note of everything on his iPad.

"Benefit of mankind!!! My foot. You guys don't care two hoots about anyone, including your own people... where is the question of mankind?" Ludolf had said to himself. "Pretentious guys!!!"

Ludolf could hear the introduction of his company... which the translator was muttering...

"LH Raumfahrt, the leading manufacturer of Satellite radar and space components, successfully entered the long-range missiles segment a few years back. LH Raumfahrt also develops solar panels for the International Space Station and other satellites."

"Immuno-Biotronik is a leading global biotechnology company that pioneered multiple breakthrough innovations. The company is a provider of biological therapeutics derived from human plasma. The company specializes primarily in the areas of clinical immunology, hematology, and intensive care medicine. It has also developed an advanced pipeline of potential novel therapies across neurology, neuropsychiatry, specialized immunology, and rare diseases."

"We would certainly like to explore the areas of interest for cooperation in the fields that Her Ludolf's organization has expertise."

"What cooperation are these guys talking about? How can there be cooperation when there was no one from the German government present at the meeting?" Ludolf wondered.

It was Wang Gengxin, the International Trade Negotiator, who had done all the talking till now. It was Wang who had received Ludolf at the airport, taken him to the hotel, and brought him to the meeting.

Wang looked at Tu Wentao, Minister of the Ministry of Foreign Trade and Economic Cooperation, anticipating Tu to take over and steer the discussions further. After all, it was Tu's turf.

Tu cleared his throat and spoke… "We welcome you to PRC, Herr Ludolf. Your country is a pioneer in many fields and has cooperated with PRC a great deal in the last few years to increase mutual business."

Ludolf laughed to himself… "Bloody liars." Ludolf knew that between Jan 2023 and Jan 2024, the exports of Germany had decreased from €8.27B to €7.97B, while imports had increased from €12.8B to €14.2B. The balance of trade was negative as far as Germany was concerned.

"As you must have seen, we all drive Mercedes and BMW… we love the German cars. Our manufacturing companies use German machinery, and we also use a variety of chemicals imported from Germany. We would like to extend this list to other products such as the ones manufactured by your esteemed organization."

Ludolf kept a stern expression with no emotions showing. "Why are they beating around the bush?" he thought to himself. Ludolf did not say anything. His silence was disturbing the people around the table.

"It would immensely benefit both Germany and China to cooperate in the fields of space and biotechnology… the benefits of which can be reaped by mankind."

"Benefits… such as?" Ludolf suddenly asked. The translator translated to Tu.

Tu was not prepared for this question. He was dumbfounded. He fumbled for words. He felt extremely uncomfortable answering the pointed question. "Well, you have products and therapies in neurology, specialized immunology, and rare diseases… which can be of great help to a populous country like China… if they are manufactured here, they can be made available to even the poor people at an affordable price…. This is what I meant by benefits."

"What percentage of the population is suffering from neurological-related issues or rare diseases for that matter? I would like to understand the ground reality," Ludolf said, emphasizing the importance of "the need to get them manufactured in China."

Again, Tu felt quite uncomfortable. "We can share that data with you while you are here. This is just an exploratory meeting. We do not have to decide anything in a hurry. This is your first visit to China; we would like you to get acclimatized to the environment here… understand our asks and then we can decide."

Tu's reply said everything… that the meeting was not going the way the Chinese had imagined. Wang was feeling uncomfortable as the main question regarding the critical missile components and also the radar components had not come to the table. Wang looked at Wu.

Wu was not sure what and how he could approach the topic. His brief was simple… under the pretext of helping Iran build the long-range cruise and ballistic missiles… hypersonic, if possible, China should get hold of the technology developed by LH Raumfahrt… and not waste time on developing it themselves.

The Chinese could not care less about Iran and could provide them with some obsolete technology free of charge, which the Iranians would love, and the Chinese could then negotiate better rates for their energy needs.

Wu was not sure how he could open the topic. "Could you please tell us a little more about LH Raumfahrt and its operations? We would like to understand more about the Satellites radar systems and the long-range new generation hypersonic missiles," Wu said in his accented German.

Ludolf laughed to himself. "The cat is out of the bag. Finally," he thought to himself. "At least there is someone who speaks German."

"What exactly do you want to know? Because I am not a technical person to explain to you the details pertaining to the technology. I can tell you the product specifications and the prices just like any of my sales guys. The products are for sale… not the new gen technology. I am sure even China will not share the details of the new gen fighters that your country is working on," Ludolf replied in German and paused.

"But tell me why you need the details when you, China that is, are manufacturing everything yourself. Although, how much research and development you have really done I have no idea about it, but considering that you did, you will know that technology cannot be replaced with a snap of a finger. You are possibly having technology quite different from what we are using. So, I am not sure as to how you can benefit by knowing the details of Satellite radar systems and new gen missiles." Ludolf stopped.

"Well, we don't need your technology, Herr Ludolf. We would like to provide it to one of our allies who could benefit from it. We would buy it from you, but we will route it to our ally through somebody. We can assure you; it will be used against the enemy you and many others dislike... hate perhaps." Wu had decided to try a direct approach.

"Interesting... but why don't you give your stuff... manufactured by you to your ally? That would be straightforward. You are talking about Iran... as I understand. Well, either China or your close allies like Russia or North Korea can help Iran. Why come to me? I don't see the rationale," Ludolf said.

"Well, Herr Ludolf, you must understand... neither of us can provide our stuff, as you call it, to Iran because when they use it, it will be deemed that we ... that is, China or Russia or North Korea have directly invaded the country... Israel in this case, as you know. So, we would like to buy your stuff; someone else would 'manage' to lay their hands on it and the stuff will end up in Iran. Neither you nor any of us will be blamed."

"Sea Pirates?"

"Yes. Your understanding is quite quick, like German products," Wu commented.

"I am not sure at this stage. 'Cause naturally I alone cannot decide about such a sale. The German government has to be brought in to make the final decision."

"Come, come, Herr Ludolf. You have the German government in your back pocket. You live in Germany and not in the PRC. Anything and everything is possible for you. If we had known that you are not the ultimate decision-maker, you would not be here with us now. We understand you quite well," Wu said.

"You mean you have made a dossier on me... via your spies who live in Germany," Ludolf laughed and spoke.

"We have our ways... Argentina to Zambia, we cover everything in between," Wu smiled.

"Still, I will have to follow the protocols. I will not be able to decide during my stay here. It will not be considered appropriate. It is only after I have gone back to Germany that I will be able to decide," Ludolf said bluntly.

"We understand. However, during your visit here, we would like to introduce you to someone who will be 'managing' the sea piracy. It is better that you know each other... because you both have a similar mindset... although not identical," Wu said.

"All right," Ludolf agreed.

The lady who was sitting at the end of the table was not taking any notes. But Wu suspected that she might be recording the conversation... and would make her own report to the Chairman... the Chinese Premier. "He will understand that I managed the German quite well," Wu thought to himself and felt happy. "Wang and Tu had issues managing the German. They are softies. A bunch of suckers," Wu thought.

Ludolf was thinking ahead... "I would not give the latest stuff to this bunch of suckers. I know what they would do... They would take some stuff and do reverse engineering and then develop it themselves. I will provide them with the old stuff; after all, who the heck is going to check... and who will understand? Everything is shrouded in mystery. Let me meet this Russian character and gauge him before I do a handshake with him."

After the customary thanks, the meeting ended. Ludolf wondered why so many people were attending the meeting when only one was needed. "Perhaps that is how these guys work."

Beijing, China

January 23, 2024; 02.00 PM

Wang had invited everyone who was at the meeting, except the woman, for a working lunch with Ludolf. Wang made sure that everybody interacted with Ludolf on a one-on-one basis. Ludolf found it quite boring, but he had decided to go through the motions.

Wu had kept his distance because he did not want to appear overbearing to either Wang or Tu. It was their meeting. Ludolf had also kept away from Wu on purpose… because he did not want more questions. However, Ludolf also noticed that Wu had a certain air of superiority around him.

"He has graduated from one of your top universities in Germany… Aachen. He is a German engineer," Wang had told him and had laughed. Ludolf could not figure out why Wang laughed. He thought it was sarcastic… but let go.

After lunch, they all said goodbye and left. Only Wang and Tu remained with Ludolf. Ludolf was then taken to a different government building which was about a 15-minute drive. Ludolf felt he was in some place in Frankfurt… a similar environment, albeit filled with Chinese people. They were met by a well-dressed official who escorted them to the 7th floor of the building. After passing through several corridors, they arrived at a corner office.

Ludolf felt he had been taken to his own office. The setup was almost identical. "Are they trying to tell me that we have you covered from your toe to your head?" Ludolf was surprised but did not show it on his face.

Wang and Tu were looking at Ludolf's face to see his reaction… but there was none. "This way, please…" Wang said to Ludolf, pointing at a door on his right.

"Looks like a private meeting chamber," Ludolf thought to himself as he proceeded to the door held open by Wang.

There was an oval-shaped table inside the meeting room. The room was very elegantly decorated with antique Chinese items. A tall, well-built, hefty, white Caucasian man was sitting at one end of the table with a Chinese official.

"Herr Ludolf, we would like to introduce you to Mr. Alexei Mikhailovich Zakharov, from Moscow… Mr. Alexei… we take pleasure in introducing Herr Ludolf Hoffmann from Frankfurt, Germany." Tu made the introduction… the translator translating it almost immediately.

Alexei had stood up and walked a few steps to meet Ludolf. He extended his hand and said in his accented English, "It is such a pleasure to meet you, Mister Ludolf Hoffmann."

Ludolf accepted Alexei's hand and found that Alexei's grip was warm and firm. That meant "a man of commitment" to Ludolf. Ludolf had gained the experience of judging people by their handshakes. So, the first impression of Alexei was quite positive for Ludolf.

"Pleasure to meet you too, Mr. Zakharov."

"You can call me Alexei. I prefer that. Isn't it funny that our governments are fighting, and we are shaking hands to do business together… Ha ha ha ha… and what is funnier is your government has stopped buying my gas and frozen my assets... Ha ha ha ha... Never mind. There are no permanent friends and no permanent enemies in politics... ya? Ha ha ha ha," Alexei said.

Ludolf could not hold back his laughter. He had liked Alexei's style of being frank and jovial even about serious issues. "Yes, unfortunately we all are affected by our respective governments' problems... or rather lack of willingness to solve the problems. I agree with you," Ludolf said with a hearty laugh.

"I am told that I have to rob your ships and divert the... what you call it... yes... defense material to another country. Is that correct?" Alexei directly came to the point without beating around. Ludolf liked it. "This guy means business. No politics." Ludolf thought to himself.

"Well, in principle, yes. But it is not going to be easy, and first I need to check if the deal can be done with the Chinese government or not. Once that is okayed, then what you said is expected to be done," Ludolf chose his words carefully.

"Yes, I know, and I understand that... it is the basic... yeah? I will arrange everything once you confirm a go ahead... yeah? But who pays me... you or these people? You know this can't be done for free... this is not United Nations' charity work... yeah? Ha ha ha... Serious stuff... Dangerous stuff. We will have to switch off all the global satellite functioning for a few hours to make this happen... otherwise big brothers are watching from the sky.... Yeah? Ha ha ha ha..." Alexei said.

Ludolf was shocked... because he had never thought of what Alexei was saying. "It is indeed an extremely risky maneuver. How come I never thought of it? I should have been the first one to think about it," Ludolf thought to himself, and suddenly his respect for Alexei went up. "This man is very practical... down to earth."

Ludolf remembered having heard about Zakharov… a story of rags to riches. But the man appeared to be rooted to the ground.

"Yes, you are right again. But I will not be the payer of your fees… shall we say… it will be these people…" Ludolf moved his palm in the direction of the Chinese.

"Fees… ha ha ha ha… I like the word. Fees. Yes… Okay. I will demand my fees from these guys. But the robbery on the high seas, which I have to discuss with you. Because I will be the one providing you with the sea transportation… ships, that is. My ships will be easy for me to steal… yes? Ha ha ha ha."

"Ahhh!!! Well, I am okay with that. But you have to make sure that those vessels will be legal to enter German ports," Ludolf said.

"Ha ha ha ha… Mister Hoffmann… Alexei is very legal in every deal he makes. Nothing illegal… ask anyone… they will tell you… yes? Ha ha ha ha…" Alexei said.

"Which means you convert every illegal thing into a legal tender through your network," Ludolf thought but did not express it. "This means personally I will be safe even if I do this deal," Ludolf thought.

"That is fine. If this deal happens, who will contact you?" Ludolf asked.

"There will be no direct contact between the two of us. Never. Only through these Chinese, and we will have different names. Ya? For our safety," Alexei said.

Ludolf was impressed. "This guy thinks ten steps ahead… seems like a KGB-trained person," Ludolf thought, but openly he said, "Good idea."

"We plan to call you Lu Hoy Tun, Herr Ludolf, and we will be calling Alexei… Xiānshēng Xīlà Shīzi," Tu interrupted.

"What? Can you not have simple names… something like Iron Man or James Bond…" Alexei sounded upset.

"These are literal translations of your names in Mandarin… and in any case, you will get used to the names. These names are for your understanding… not ours," Tu emphasized.

"Okay… anything else?" Ludolf demanded, looking at Tu and Wang.

"No, I think we have made progress. We will start working now," Tu said.

"Are you not forgetting something important?" Alexei said.

"What?" Tu asked.

"What is the timeline? When do you think this will happen? In 2024, 2025, 2026? I need to know well in advance… at least 6 months in advance… along with the payment. I will let you know my… what… fees… yes and once I get paid in advance… full amount… yes… then I will start making plans," Alexei said firmly.

Ludolf was surprised. He could see that Alexei could think rationally even during such weird meetings. "The man has guts," Ludolf liked Alexei. "This guy could be a good friend," he thought to himself.

"Of course, Mister Zakharov. We will discuss that and agree once Herr Ludolf leaves," said Tu.

"No discussion. I tell you my fees… you accept. Simple. No negotiations," Alexei said firmly.

"Yes, Mr. Zakharov," Tu had no choice but to say. He would need to go back to the supreme commander… the Chinese President…. "He may talk to the Russian President and agree on something…. Or maybe not. They might just put our heads on the block."Tu could feel the fear running through his spine.

Ludolf got a piece of paper and a pen from the translator, scribbled something on the paper, and gave it to Alexei. "Whenever you visit Europe, call this number. If possible, I will come to meet you. It was a pleasure meeting you in person," Ludolf said.

"Likewise… Mister Ludolf. You are a nice guy," Alexei said. "I will meet you someday somewhere for sure." Alexei took the piece of paper, opened his cell phone, typed the number, and tore the piece of paper into pieces. He put them into his mouth, chewed them, and swallowed them. All this happened in less than a minute. Everybody, including Ludolf, was completely taken aback by what Alexei had done.

Ludolf realized that it was only Alexei who would know the name under which the number was saved. So, it was safe, and there was no proof left either. "This guy is a pro… I am sure… or he has learned all the tricks of staying alive, even in the most adverse conditions… A real survivor," Ludolf thought to himself.

They said goodbye, and Ludolf and Wang departed. Now Alexei took a piece of paper and a pen from the translator… wrote an amount on the paper and gave it to Tu.

"My fees. Once you are ready, I will let you know who and where to send them," Alexei said firmly.

Tu's eyes tried to read the amount again and again. He was sure he would be hanged by his President either way. But presently he just nodded and kept the paper in his pocket.

Alexei got up from his chair, headed to the door and said to Tu, "Can we go now?"

Beijing, China

January 23, 2024; 06.00 PM

Alexei had boarded the flight and settled down in his massive, soft leather chair with a glass of vodka in his hand. The aircraft was waiting at the entrance of the runway for instructions to take off.

Alexei was already lost in his thoughts. When he met the President, he received his briefings. The instructions were simple.

"Play the game without really coming into the picture. Earn money and get out. The Germans are not idiots. They will never give their 'next-gen' technology to the Iranians… knowing well that the Chinese are involved. We don't need German technology because we are already experts in that field. And even if we come to know it, we are not going to dismantle ours and accept theirs… no way. Let the Chinese and the Iranians enjoy. Ultimately, we will sell our products to Iran because in a make or buy situation, it will be easier for the Iranians to buy from us than to make it themselves… or with the help of the Chinese or the Germans. Let others get exposed. You stay out of it. Ask for more money… so that you can earn and give some to others to die. Proxy is the name of the game."

"That is good advice. I will follow it. But I still do not understand… Iran has developed its own missiles… why do they need the "technology" now when they have the basic technology," Alexei had asked.

"Missile in General is a complex subject… and it is dynamic… in the sense that the development is always ongoing for better effectiveness, better range, better accuracy… better everything. Iran has developed perhaps the 1st or 2nd generation missiles… maybe third. I have no idea. But what the West, including us, has is a much more advanced version. Then, there are varieties of missiles… Ballistic missiles, Cruise missiles… and then passive systems, semi-active systems, active systems and so on. What the Germans have is the active system… what is perfected is G&C… Guidance and Control. With G&C in place, speed can be increased… to a hypersonic level. The German company is already in radar systems… so for them G&C was never an issue. They will keep on improving on it." The President had paused.

"The Germans will never sell their current-gen or next-gen products either to China or to anyone… except perhaps NATO and the US. So, forget about getting new stuff. The Germans will provide earlier generation products at current costs… They will get paid. You arrange shipment via someone… you get paid, the shipping company gets paid. End of story. What happens to the cargo is none of our business. Let them do whatever they want. Yes, we will keep an eye on it because we don't want that stuff to be used against our assets… via Ukraine. That is something you've got to make sure of."

Alexei had finished his drink; the flight had already taken off. Alexei had asked for a whopping six hundred million dollars. After all, what was six hundred million for Iran… or even for China? Alexei would give one hundred million dollars to the ship company and the rest he would pocket. Alexei had other plans… which he had not told even the President. Alexei had intentions of using real sea pirates for this job. This would be the surprise element. A real heist after the fake heist.

Alexei had to work out his plan quite carefully. He would keep his plans ready and put the plan into action only after he had received the money in advance.

While Alexei was sitting in his aircraft and thinking about the plan of action, Ludolf had just boarded his aircraft. He wanted to get away from the maddening crowd as fast as he could. Although, somewhere in his mind, he had made a note of the wealth and the mega cities created by China over the last twenty-odd years and their quest for global control, dismantling the West, the US in particular, from the position of the ultimate superpower.

However, somewhere underneath the glamour and the show of power, Ludolf felt that there existed another world… which the Chinese had hidden or had kept secret from the global view. Ludolf had sensed "fear" in the minds of the people he had dealt with… that had made Ludolf wary of dealing with the Chinese. "Untrustworthy" … the word that had come to Ludolf's mind after all the meetings and interactions he had with the Chinese.

The Guidance and Control systems used a combination of tracking, computation, and steering to achieve pinpoint accuracy and speed. Ludolf had wondered why the Chinese could not give the technology or the weaponry systems they already had to Iran… what was the need to do all this drama… what was the hidden agenda? Was it to turn the worldview against Germany or maybe Russia? His opinion about Alexei had become quite positive after the first meeting itself.

Ludolf could not put his finger on the main issue that was bothering him… What was China's ultimate game plan? Space, Satellites, Cyberspace, missiles, Bioweapons… What was China trying to accomplish in the near term and long term? He was not sure and that made him uncomfortable. He, Ludolf, had no controlling stake in that relationship and that bothered him a lot.

"I do not wish to enter into a relationship where I do not have direct control," Ludolf reminded himself.

Ludolf remembered the case of the Chinese spy Xu Yanjun who was caught in October 2021 in the US stealing the secrets of the new advanced jet engine GE9X General Electric was developing for the Boeing 777X. The advanced engine's fan blades were made of composite material which was developed by GE, and that technology was not available at that time outside GE. China was trying to make its own commercial aircraft like Boeing and needed this technology. They had lured one of the engineers working on that specific project at GE to provide the details.

Ludolf was quite aware of the operations of the Chinese spy network and had ensured that all his companies had all the required protections. "The Chinese Deep State is deeper than the Mariana Trench and it is wider than the Pacific Ocean," Ludolf said to himself.

Given the fact that China infiltrated various countries via student networking, tourists, asylum seekers, defectors, migrants, and workers/laborers, not just the Chinese diplomats in the Chinese embassy, but all the Chinese diaspora, Ludolf made sure that the engineers his companies employed had no "Chinese" friends… more so during their university days. So, when he came to know that Wu was an Aachen University graduate, he instantly decided to stay away from him. As such, Ludolf also stayed away from employing anyone from Berlin and typically an "East German" of origin because he knew that Berlin and Austria were known to be Spy Capitals. Ludolf also avoided employing people of color or those with left-liberal mindsets.

Given the state of the economy in Germany, the high cost of energy due to the Ukraine war, and the looming recession, German industries were looking to cut costs and stay afloat. Outsourcing to China had registered an increase. So, Ludolf was sure that the German government would agree to this "supply" proposal of the Chinese… when they would approach the German government. Ludolf wanted to stay away from this deal. He would not mind dealing directly with Alexei… if it were possible.

By the time the aircraft took off, Ludolf had dozed off.

Virginia, US

January 27, 2024; 06.30 PM

It was a cold, frozen evening, but Martin Kingston was engrossed in his own thoughts. He was meeting Nash that evening. Martin was still debating on how to open the topic with Nash. It was a very sensitive subject, and Martin was therefore hesitant.

They had decided to meet at Waterman's Surfside Grille near Cape Henry Lighthouses as Martin wanted to be away from places like Arlington or Fairfax even for that matter. "I don't want to be anywhere near the CIA HQ," Martin had told Nash when he had called for a personal meeting.

Nash had understood that Martin would have nothing personal to discuss. He was not the kind of man who would discuss family matters outside the doors of his own bedroom. Knowing too well that this time of year, there would hardly be any crowd at the Waterman's Grille… and no one would pay any undue attention to two oldish-looking folks enjoying their drink and food, Nash had suggested the place. Martin had arrived and was waiting for Nash to arrive.

In the rear-view mirror of his parked car, Martin saw a set of bright lights approaching his way. "That must be Nash," Martin said to himself and heaved a sigh of relief. Momentarily, the car arrived and parked near Martin's. Nash got out of the car. He was wearing a long coat, a monkey cap pulled over his ears, and a woolen scarf around his neck, shielding his chin. Martin also got out of the car.

"Hey there, good to see you after a while. You look the same," Martin said, extending his gloved hand.

Nash shook his head and said, "Guess I am like the fir tree, never changing my colors." Martin laughed.

"Hey, thanks for coming. Really appreciate it," Martin said. "Hope the place is safe from onlookers."

"Ah, don't worry. The place is safe at this time of the year... no crowd. I am sure you will find the place almost empty," Nash showed the parking area... there were just six cars, including theirs, in the parking lot. "Come, let's get inside."

Looking at their attire, they were seated near the fireplace. They ordered their drinks and appetizers and asked for the mains to be brought after 40 minutes. Perhaps they would have a second round of drinks. The waiter nodded and left them.

The drinks and the appetizers were on the table... by then, Martin had already started to feel like a baked potato in his Eskimo-ish clothing.

"Okay Martin, shoot. What's on your mind that is bothering you? I am sure if it were not something critical, you wouldn't be driving down here in this weather," Nash said, sipping his drink.

"Yes... I think it is critical... but I am still groping in the dark," Martin said and then quickly narrated his meeting with Abe Williams and the mention of DARPA.

Nash was listening to Martin's narration attentively, looking into Martin's eyes all the time. Once Martin finished his narrative, Nash said, "Interesting. But where do I come into this? What is it that you want from me?"

Nash knew that there was something sinister about the whole thing. He knew Abe extremely well. Abe was one of those no-nonsense guys… and meant business. He was not a part of any politics nor belonged to any political party or aligned with any specific politician or senator. That was one of the reasons that after all these years, Abe was still kept away from the top position… Director of CIA… because he would not be politically manipulated.

Nash knew that after the Iraq war, Abe had become quite bitter about the agency and its operatives. Privately, he had once remarked to Nash that "Iraq was a bogey… there was nothing like WMD… all made up 'cause Vice wanted to get there and get his hands on oil." Later, Nash had come to know that Abe's only son was killed in Iraq.

Abe's family was always associated with the armed forces. His own father was a West Point man. Abe was an oddball to have joined the agency. So, when Abe is involved in any inquiry, it meant a real problem. Nash would not dare to touch… but would like to understand the undercurrents because that was his job.

"Well, for starters, I would like to understand the CIA's role in investigating the State Department's discussions with various lobbies. I don't see any connection. And even if someone has to look into it, I guess it would be the FBI and not the agency folks." Martin paused.

"And?"

"Where does DARPA come into these lobby discussions?"

"Martin, all I can say is, the lobbies you deal with are all full of powerful people representing some extremely powerful organizations. And they are all global… you know it… The defense, The Pharma, The Biotech, The Silicon Valley, The

Oil... and then you have the foreign lobbies... The Chinese, The Arabs... So, it is not just 'local' per se. It is global for sure, and I don't see any reason as to why the CIA would not be ... let us just say 'Curious' about what these guys are up to?"

"Nash, you know these... these lobby discussions are all above board," Martin said.

"Really?!" Nash looked hard into Martin's eyes. Martin felt uncomfortable.

"Well, at my level at least."

"Martin, if you need my help, you need to come clean. Only then can I help you. Otherwise, you know how the wind blows once it starts blowing. You are inching towards your retirement. So, you need to decide what is best for you," Nash was blunt.

"Yes... I see your point. That is why I came to you. This is causing me a lot of sleepless nights. What do you want to know?" Martin's tone had changed. He sounded like a worried man.

"Everything... who, what, when, how much, why... Where... etc., etc."

"Nash, you know that all these lobbies... The Defense Giants, The Biotech Giants, The Pharma Giants, The Tech Giants... they all have one common thing... The major stakeholder in these companies is...."

"Cobblestone," Nash said softly.

"Yes. And then there are some lobbies... "Charitable, Human considerations, Equality, democracy kind of organizations... who are bothered about everybody living in the Third World countries... even though they themselves live in homes worth millions of pounds and would not know who lives next door... but are worried about democracy in some godforsaken tiny country."

"Borge Ross," Nash said softly.

"Yeah… that guy and his stupid org. They get on my nerves more than the others. The others are not pretentious at least." Martin seems angry.

"Okay… I knew the Who part… but I am more interested in What, where, when, how and maybe how much."

"The defense ones are the ones going bonkers… they would like to set the world on fire if they could… Because every bullet fired, or every missile fired, brings money to their pockets…!"

"Martin… What, When, Where and How…"

Martin suddenly went quiet. His face looked worried. Nash could see fear in his eyes. The wood burning in the fireplace crackled, sending a few sparks flying. Martin kept staring at the fireplace.

"Nash, this Cobblestone guy… Brink… is hell-bent on acquiring real assets… land, water bodies, mines… mountains… all over the world. Take over the country by making the country lease out every bit of the real asset to Cobblestone. If it means one has to create a war, so be it. When Soviet Russia dissolved, there was an agreement that NATO would not expand beyond the then current geography. But as soon as the ink dried, the US started adding more European countries to NATO. So, obviously, it led to war in Crimea. Then came the Minsk accord… but the US never wanted that accord to be successful… so Ukraine started… I guess you know the story that now Cobblestone "owns" 70% of the Ukrainian real assets… and wants more… Entire Russia, Central Asia, the Middle East, Africa… even Latin America. So, there is no "When" it is already on… Where… I just told you… How… I told you. What more can I say?"

"You told me nothing, Martin. This is all known stuff. You mentioned DARPA. That is the key. Abe was there with you because of that word DARPA. So, stop beating around the bush and tell me the real stuff," Nash sounded harsh. He was tired of Martin's "hide and seek" approach.

"I don't know what Cobblestone is doing with DARPA. None of the other lobbyists have anything to do with DARPA... of which I am sure. Ross Orgs wants easy access to various countries to open their offices and make a mess there. I am sure he is at loggerheads with the Brink guy. Both guys want to own and control the world... both think they are Gods."

"DARPA Martin. Cobblestone... What connection... What projects?"

"Frankly, I have no clue. Defense lobbies are like octopuses... they are and want to be on land, in water, in space, in mountains... everywhere... and I don't know what. They are already there everywhere... but I have no clue... why would they want exclusivity in places like Hudson Bay or the Labrador Sea or the Beaufort Sea or the Gulf of Alaska or Lake Superior. Why do they want exclusivity in the Northwest Territories near Great Bear Lake? That is in Canada... but they said the Canadian government is in their hip pocket. Go figure. Same thing in the space program, Satellite Program... Exclusivity. I don't know what it means. I am not the decision-maker. I just know the peripherals. Trust me," Martin said.

Nash was quietly listening to Martin and making mental notes.

"Was DARPA mentioned during any discussions?"

"Not to my knowledge."

"Is it just the defense lobbyist or anyone else?"

"Just the defense… but my sense is the Biotech guys, and the Silicon Valley guys were part of that during some of the meetings… Though nothing specific was discussed related to Biotech or Hi-Tech."

"I see," Nash said softly under his breath.

The main course was served, and they ate silently… each one immersed in their own thoughts.

"Who were all the beneficiaries of this exclusivity?" Nash suddenly asked.

Martin was jolted. "I am not one of them. Period," he said, even without looking at Nash. "I would not know."

"Has it been approved… the request I meant?" Nash asked.

"Possibly. I don't have any directive on that, but denial was never on the table."

"All I can suggest, Martin, is… this 'whatever related to DARPA' thing will take another 5 years, perhaps, to come to fruition… the way DARPA works… by then you would have retired, and it will not be your headache anymore. So, stop worrying and go with the flow. In any case, you don't know who will come to power in the next US election and what their agenda will be. So, chill," Nash told Martin.

Nash's face was slightly brightened up. "I hope you are right. I don't want to have any hassles right now. But the issue is, what do I tell Abe?"

"Nothing. Just say you are a small fry, and you are not involved in such matters," Nash advised.

"I had told Abe, but he did not accept it."

"He is doing his job. You do yours. Period," Nash said. "Should we?" Nash indicated that the meeting was over, and he wanted to leave.

"Yes. Hey, thank you for hearing me out. I wanted some advice for sure. At least I am feeling okay now."

"Tell Abe seriously... that you have absolutely no clue whatsoever. The matter is handled at the WH level. He will understand it."

"Will Abe accept it?"

"Yes... if you tell him sincerely and not with authority. Do you understand?"

"Yes. Thank you, Nash. It was really great meeting you. I will be in touch."

After wishing goodnight, both went off in their own directions. Nash was now going over what was discussed during the last couple of hours.

There is something definitely going on... 'What' Nash did not know. 'Where' ... Nash had a fairly good idea of the geo-locations. 'When' ... this was critical... it depended on how long ago DARPA had envisioned whatever they had... so, if it was in the initial phase or the final phase, Nash had no idea.

'How' depended on 'What' and that was something bothering Nash. He decided to find out. He would not be able to do it alone. He needed help from 'inside.' 'Will see,' Nash thought to himself as he steered his car on the freeway towards his home.

Richmond, Virginia, US

January 29, 2024; 06.25 PM

William Byrd Park was deserted. There was still some snow on the ground. It had been a sunny day, and the weather was improving… albeit it was still cold. Lemur, as always, arrived early and assessed the area carefully. Now he was waiting for Nash to arrive. "Another 5 minutes to go," he said to himself.

Lemur had been busy doing his research after his visit to Columbia campus. He had found out who Leo was… his real name was Don McIntire. He was a freelance journalist. "Investigative Journalism" was his "specialty." He wrote articles in various news journals and weekly magazines under the pseudonym Leo Tracker. The guy had a flair for writing… no doubt. But Lemur felt that he still lacked maturity and seemed to be heavily influenced by Churchill and his writings.

He already knew about Jerry Carson and his parents' publishing company. He had known more about Cathy Dexter and her association with Borge Ross's organization… and how she was being "groomed." She had all the characteristics of becoming a tyrant… Bold, Beautiful, Sexy, Go-getter, demanding… ambitious and hostile too.

Lemur did not expect the meeting to last more than 10 minutes. Lemur checked the time on his cell phone… It was exactly 6.30 pm. "Nash should be here any minute," Lemur thought to himself as he looked around and saw the silhouette of Nash walking towards him.

"Hey there," Lemur said.

"Thanks for coming. What's the news?"

Lemur quickly narrated the information to Nash, who listened quietly. Then he said, "Yes, I know that publishing company. I have used them in the past. They are good people. So, his son is at Columbia. Interesting."

"Yes, quite a sharp guy. Has his brain in place. Does not belong to the protesters' gang. I wonder how he knows this journalist. Need to know that."

"Hmmm… go meet him, talk to him. Find out what his ambition is. Maybe we can use him," Nash had suddenly thought of something.

"Like what?" Lemur asked.

"I don't know… I will know when the time comes. Just cultivate him. Make it natural. The same goes for that Leo guy… find out everything about him, including what kind of underwear he uses. Okay? And yes, I have another, additional assignment for you… this time a paid one," Nash said.

"I am all ears," Lemur chirped happily.

"Not now. Perhaps in a week's time. I will let you know where to meet. But it will be critical stuff. Till then, do something with this kid and get deeper with this journo… Investigative Journo is interesting. Find out more about this guy. His hobbies, girlfriends, eating habits, his friend circle, if any… his family… parents, siblings… his earnings. Does he get motivated by money at all? His political views… inclination. I need to know everything. Okay? I will let you know when and where to meet next."

"Got it, boss," Lemur said with a salute.

Both departed their own ways… Lemur making sure no one was observing them, following him.

"What's with this Jerry boy? Why does he need to know him more?" Lemur thought as he drove his car away. "Your job is not to think… but to do what has been told… so just do it," Lemur told himself.

Washington D.C., US

Tracy's pod was just a one-bedroom unit in the Georgetown area. It was the closest thing Tracy could afford with her salary as an admin assistant to Brian Smith, the chief attorney of a renowned lobbying firm who represented some of the Biotech companies from the West Coast.

Sergei had met Tracy during the undergraduate years, and both had fallen for each other. But Sergei chose a different path and had decided to remain "unattached" for a while. The time had passed, and both Sergei and Tracy had stayed "separately together," … as Tracy had once told Sergei.

Sergei would always visit and stay with Tracy whenever he was back in the US and seldom went to visit his parents and siblings. Both would spend time together at home or venture out to Adams Morgan exploring the numerous bars, live music venues, and various international dining options along 18th Street.

However, today Sergei had made a special request to Tracy to step out alone and let him be at home because he wanted to meet a special guest to discuss "business." Sergei had never done this sort of "thing," but looking at Sergei's face, Tracy could feel that there was something serious on his mind. So, a little after 6.30 pm, Tracy had stepped out. It was a cold but almost clear night.

Precisely at 7.00 pm, the buzzer sounded… Sergei had let the guest inside the apartment complex. Soon, there was a knock on the door. Sergei opened the door and welcomed his guest.

"Mr. Nash, how very nice of you to accept my invitation and come to my poor fellow's pod," Sergei said warmly, shaking Nash's hand.

"Poor fellow? Is that how you get paid at the agency? I bet you must be traveling at least business class and staying in some star hotels. I can find that out tomorrow," Nash said with a hearty laugh.

Sergei laughed loudly and asked Nash to make himself comfortable on the couch. "What would you like, Nash?"

"Actually, a cup of coffee would do. Just black… if you can," said Nash.

"Not an issue. Give me a minute… would instant be okay?"

"Anything."

After a couple of minutes, Sergei came out of the small kitchen with two cups of coffee… handed one over to Nash and sat down.

"Meeting after a long time… aren't we?" Sergei said.

"Yes… It has been a while. A lot of changes have happened… and will possibly happen… depending on who will be in power after the next election later this year."

"Yes, everything is so uncertain. I wonder who is running the US?"

"It is a simple question with a complicated answer. States, organizations, corporations, individuals, who control global events and narratives are not exactly acting in your best interest. After WW2, the US emerged as the dominant global power exercising its might across the world. But now that influence has slowly declined over the last few years. The US had the IMF, WTO, and the World Bank at its disposal to exercise control over the world. Satisfying the interests of the elite is at the heart or core of any government that comes to power. So, in short, it is they… the elite… individuals, organizations, corporations who run the US. Period. They always did it and they will continue to do it."

"Always did it?" Sergei seemed baffled.

"Oh, come now, as if you don't know. Our agency is quite famous for what… Staging coups across the globe and installing puppet governments who would be favorable to us and let us do anything that we want and still support us. That is dictatorship but we call it democracy. We preach democracy. When our political leaders say… 'we are doing it for the betterment of the world'… the term 'world' referred to by our government refers to the political and media elites in Washington D.C. and London and their supporters. It is the way Anglo-American Politicos operate. It serves their purpose. When militants kill, it is called an act of terrorism. But when our forces go to Iraq, Afghanistan, Vietnam and kill more people than the terrorists, the narrative is quite different… It does not fall under the act of terrorism… right? So, the world is ruled by organizations, Corporations who have their interests at heart and also by individuals who own these organizations or corporations… and have their own vicious ambitions at heart. They control our politicians and our policymakers."

"Yeah… I know. It is frustrating sometimes. We are naked, but we forget that and tell others that they are naked. Well, not the right way of putting it, but you get what I mean," Sergei said.

"Yes. True."

"What is it that you want my help with? I will do anything possible for you within my limits or power," Sergei said.

"Thank you. I really appreciate it," Nash said. "I need you to dig in and get me some intel from within the agency."

"What? Within the agency? Oh boy! From where… which departments or divisions or individuals?"

"DARPA."

"What? DARPA? That is out of my league, you know."

"Sergei… I need to know what DARPA is currently working on… they are usually 20 years ahead of the world. Their projects will be in various stages… but which of the projects are now coming to fruition or going to get implemented? You need to find a source within DARPA and get me the intel. ASAP." Nash paused…

"Also, I need to know who from DARPA is a 'contact person' to organizations like Cobblestone or the companies owned by Cobblestone… in the defense sector, Biotech sector, Pharma Sector… Also, where does the Director of the CIA fit into this equation… that is also critical." Nash stopped. He was looking at Sergei's eyes.

Sergei was sitting with his mouth open, holding his coffee cup tightly in both his palms. He was looking at nothing… just a blank stare.

"Sergei?" Nash asked…

"Well, what you have asked is like trying to move the entire Baikal Lake from Russia to the US… which is almost impossible. If I start asking questions, sooner or later someone is going to raise an alarm. Remember, I am 'Russian' to these folks."

"I need the intel ASAP, Sergei. Maybe it will be a shock to you as well. What, who, when, and how. Those are the four things I need to know."

"How fast?"

"Yesterday."

"I am serious… how fast?"

"In the next couple of weeks… 15 days or so. Before you get shunted out to Europe," Nash said.

"You have more powers than I; you can get it easily," Sergei said.

"Precisely, since I have more powers, it makes me a 'person of interest' to them."

"Them?"

"Yes, those specific elite individuals, organizations, corporations… whoever they are. Those with enormous financial power."

Sergei thought of Alexei, Ludolf and some other heavyweights… who wielded such power.

"Ok, I will need time to prepare… but I would appreciate some pointers, hints of what I am looking for…. Buzz words," said Sergei.

"I don't know the buzzwords or project names like operation this or that. But the point is… the projects may have to do with water… lakes, seas, oceans… and land in the wilderness. Maybe some space program related to some military project… like Iron Dome or whatever…. Or Bioweapons. The list could be endless," Nash said, finishing his coffee.

Sergei's eyes narrowed as he heard space and Bioweapons. "Jeez," he said under his breath. "This is sounding dangerous…"

Sergei thought. He recalled the Chinese wanted to collaborate with Ludolf's companies… Space and Biotech. "Something sinister is going on. Perhaps it is time to wind up instead of getting butchered in the fight of the two monsters," Sergei thought to himself.

"Okay Nash. I will work on it and get back to you. Perhaps we will meet in person here, in this apartment. Hope this is not too inconvenient for you. It is absolutely a safe place," Sergei said.

"No problem. I trust you. I don't expect any hidden microphones or video cams," Nash said, smiling.

"You are so funny sometimes," Sergei said.

"Please keep it simple and confidential," Nash said, getting up from the couch.

"Yes, obviously. I never heard, and you never said," said Sergei.

Nash laughed, shook hands with Sergei, and left the apartment, quickly vanishing in the dark.

Sergei sat in the chair holding his head in his palms… "What the heck is going on?" he wondered.

Biotech suddenly reminded him of Tracy. Sergei picked up his cell phone and called Tracy. He hung up after 2 rings. That was the signal for Tracy to return to the apartment.

"Heck, Tracy perhaps will be able to give some intel… because they represent some Biotech companies. Perhaps… they may have something to do with this DARPA. But I've got to be careful," Sergei thought to himself.

New York, US

February 6, 2024; 01.00 PM

Lemur had been following Leo since morning. He had gone and parked himself outside Leo's apartment, just close to Leo's car. It was an area that housed predominantly lower-middle-class residents, mostly in the nearby boroughs and in parts of eastern Inwood. Given Leo's status, Lemur figured that he must be living in a shared apartment… otherwise, Leo would have to make at least £60-80K annually to afford an apartment here.

It was almost 9.30 am when Lemur saw Leo walking towards his car. "Here we go," said Lemur to himself. Lemur followed Leo. Leo seemed to be heading towards the city center…. Soon, Lemur realized that Leo was heading towards Fifth Avenue, Manhattan. "Where the heck is he going…," Leo wondered to himself, then suddenly it occurred to him that Leo must be going to the New York Public Library located in the Stephen A. Schwarzman Building.

"This is on 42nd Street while the cheapest parking would be on 46th Street… nothing less than \$25 for two hours… Why the heck did he not take the underground? Perhaps he might be going someplace later on." Lemur thought to himself as he followed Leo. Lemur saw Leo going to 46th Street and entering the Public Parking there. Lemur drove on. He did not want to waste \$25 on parking. He went ahead and drove to 5th Avenue, 46th Street, 6th Avenue and was back on 46th Street. Lemur managed to find a place just before the entrance/exit of the Public Parking. Sitting in his car, he would be able to see Leo come out of the parking. "Two hours max… he can't stay there the whole day long," Lemur thought to himself.

It was around 12.15 when Lemur saw Leo coming out of the Public Parking. While Leo was waiting to turn right, Lemur brought his car to life and was ready to chase Leo. After following Leo, Lemur realized that Leo was heading towards Brooklyn. Lemur wondered why. "Maybe he has some work there, who knows," he said to himself.

Leo crossed over to Brooklyn and headed towards the Brooklyn Botanic Garden. Then he turned south and proceeded down Prospect Avenue. At the corner of Prospect Park West, Leo suddenly pulled into an empty parking space. Lemur, accustomed to such things, slowed down, and moved ahead to keep Leo in view. Leo had crossed over and entered Bedaw Café, a Mediterranean eatery. Lemur found a parking space, got out of the car, and followed Leo into the restaurant.

It was still lunchtime, and as such, the place was crowded. From the appearance, the place seemed to be catering to lower-category people… low-wage earners. The prices on the menu seemed quite reasonable. Leo had ordered and was waiting for his food at the delivery counter. Lemur went ahead, ordered his lunch, and stood near Leo… pretending to wait for his lunch.

"Bit crowded today," Lemur said to Leo.

Leo turned his face, smiled, and said, "It usually is. Lunchtime, you know."

"Yes, I love the Mediterranean stuff. The Kebabs are great with Hummus," said Lemur.

"Yes. Ditto," Leo smiled back.

"I am Peter... Peter Parker," Lemur introduced himself, picking up one of the names from his tradecraft basket. It was the name of Spider-Man... Peter Benjamin Parker. Easy to remember.

"Leo... Leo Tracker."

"Tracker... that's an unusual name... what do you track?" Lemur said with a smile, making it sound like a joke.

"Oh... Real stuff... Real news. These days everything is a fake narrative doled out by politically aligned media. I try to track the reality and report that."

"Interesting. I would like to hear more about it... maybe we can eat at the same table and chat if that's okay with you."

"For sure... why not," Leo said.

Both carried their trays to a corner table and sat facing each other. Lemur had achieved his first objective... to get introduced.

"And what do you do... Peter?"

"I am associated with a start-up organization in the field of education. We are developing products that would help the students to find global opportunities... both employment and entrepreneurial. The world is a village now and every nook and corner of the village is 'under development,' including the so-called developed world. The needs have changed along with the time."

"Yes, that is so true. Great concept," Leo remarked. Lemur had said it with such conviction that he himself could not believe it. "Looks like I am getting better at bullshitting," Lemur thought to himself.

"So, you were telling me about fake news and real news," Lemur brought the topic back on track.

"Yes. Most of the narratives run by the mainstream media are aligned with some political party, heavyweight individual, or organization that actually owns that media house," Leo said.

"Like… for instance?" Lemur poked further.

"Oh… like Fox News is Republican… CNN is a left-winger… etc. Some media houses are owned by someone like Borge Ross or Gregory Brink. So, they run their narratives, their point of view. Let us say that one of these folks, either an individual or an organization, wants to tarnish a specific country… let us just say, for example, Mexico… all I've got to do is find a couple of unemployed Spanish-speaking guys, pay them some 100 bucks, tell them what answers they should give when interviewed… and then put them in front of the camera. They will say how bad the conditions in Mexico are… and how they have suffered. That is how you run a fake narrative. But that is not the real stuff. That is not the reality." Leo paused.

"Like the Iraq war. There was no WMD. These politicians and the oil companies wanted to go after the Iraqi Oil… that was the main target… not the WMD. But back then, when you opened any channel or news media, you would see or hear about WMD. The Iraq war is long since over… where are the WMDs? This is what I mean. These big corporations or organizations like the Open Society Foundation, which funds the protests against Israel in big Ivy League universities, have an agenda… a political one in this case… Their ultimate objective is to control global events and global governments. They can go to any extent to destroy the socio-economic fabric of any country." Leo stopped.

Lemur was impressed. This guy knew his stuff. "Yes. What you say is true. But how do you get the real stuff?" Lemur asked.

"Well, I read various newspapers from other countries… watch news from other foreign news media. Speak to people… like you when I get a chance to meet them."

"Do you publish these findings?"

"Yes, I write for a couple of magazines and periodicals."

"Do you get paid well… if you don't mind me asking this… I am just curious."

"Well, I am able to keep myself afloat… head above water. But I can do better after some time. I am not for sale to this fake media. I am in investigative journalism, you see. Someday, I will get a break… either here or abroad. I don't know."

"Where do you live… are you from New York?"

"I live in the eastern Inwood area as a PG. Only bed, no breakfast. Since they know my condition, they charge me a nominal amount. Rest is all for gas and eating… which I do once a day. I am from Minneapolis…. Father retired from the local municipal corporation, mother no more. One elder brother… died in the Iraq war. Life is simple…. Practically no strings," Leo said.

Lemur thought that the guy was genuine and straightforward… could be cultivated if trained properly. Perhaps Nash was right. Good that I spoke to him. But openly he said…

"Oh, I am sorry to hear that. But let us stay in touch. I will try to help you wherever and whenever I can. Can you possibly share your cell number… if I need to contact you…I will give you mine," Lemur said.

Leo reached into his pocket and brought out his business card… "Here is my cell number. By the way, my real name is Don McIntire. Leo Tracker is my pseudonym."

"Oh, okay. I understand," Lemur brought out a piece of paper from his pocket, scribbled his name and number on it, and gave it to Leo. He did not bother to write his real name. It was not required. "Here it is… if you are in any difficult situation, just pick up your cell phone and call me. I will help you. Consider me your Man Friday," Lemur said.

"Oh, that is very gracious. Thank you. It was indeed nice meeting you, and I look forward to seeing you again," Leo said.

"Definitely. You will be hearing from me as well," Lemur said, getting up and picking up his tray as he proceeded to the trash can.

They had a handshake, and both departed their own ways.

"One main task accomplished," Lemur muttered to himself as he walked towards his car. "Now I need to catch hold of Jerry… perhaps I can finish it today… it is just about quarter past two now. It will take an hour or so to get there," Lemur thought to himself.

Lemur started his car and began driving towards Prospect Expressway north. While driving, Lemur was wondering how to get hold of Jerry. Columbia was a big campus, and finding one student was like finding a needle in a haystack. Lemur had his way of getting things done, which he had learned in his tradecraft.

Lemur had hit the traffic as he got onto the FDR Drive. It took him an hour and a half to reach the Columbia campus. "90 minutes to travel fifteen miles!!! Jeez. I hate this traffic," Lemur muttered to himself as he found a parking space.

Lemur decided to try his luck at the admin office. He thought it would be the best place to start. He had already thought of the "story" he would tell to make sure the guys in the admin felt that Lemur was legit.

The admin office was huge and busy, as always. Lemur went to the inquiry counter and stood in the queue. There were 3-4 guys ahead of him, mostly wannabe students. After about 15 minutes, Lemur was at the window.

"Sorry to bother you, but I am looking for Jerry Carson... the one who has a publishing company... I mean, his father has one. Where can I find him? I came to know about Jerry from a journalist friend of mine. I would like to see him if he is available."

"In what connection?"

"I am associated with a start-up organization in the field of education. We have products that would help the students to find global opportunities... both employment as well as entrepreneurial. We would like to publish some of our materials, and we were scouting for a publishing house which would not charge an arm and a leg. My journalist friend informed me that Jerry Carson could possibly help. I just want to check with him and if he could make intros to his father. That's it. It won't take more than 10 minutes, I would say," Lemur finished his monologue. He was not sure how much of it was understood by the lady sitting on the other side of the window.

"Let me check his whereabouts... Jerry Carson, you said, right?"

"Yes mam."

"Political Science?"

"Perhaps... possibly."

"He has a class until 4.30 PM... I will text him a message to come here. I can't guarantee... because if he does not see the message until after he goes to his dorm... then he may not come."

"Okay... Thank you."

"I have sent him the text. You may want to wait," the lady pointed towards the chairs.

"Thanks again. You will let me know once he is here, won't you?"

"Yes."

Lemur had no alternative but to wait.

It was close to 5 PM when Jerry showed up. The admin office was about to close. The lady at the inquiry counter was no longer in her seat.

Taking the chance, Lemur called out… "Jerry Carson?" Since Lemur had seen Jerry, he had no difficulty in recognizing him.

"Yes."

"Peter Parker. I wanted to speak with you. Can we find a place? I need no more than 15 minutes… if you are okay."

"What is this regarding?" Jerry asked.

"I will speak to you… if we can find a place."

"For sure," Jerry said and led Lemur outside. It was still cold and getting dark.

Jerry found an empty bench on the lawns of the campus and indicated Lemur to sit.

"I am associated with a start-up organization in the field of education. We have products that would help the students to find global opportunities… both employment as well as entrepreneurial. We wanted to print some promotional material and were looking for a publishing company which would charge an arm and a leg… so a journalist friend of mine told me about your parent's company. Perhaps you could introduce me to your father, I can take this forward."

"That can be done… who is your journalist friend who knows me?" Jerry asked.

"Well, in business, we prefer not to share the names because it is considered unethical. I hope you do understand the professional ethics," Lemur made a sorry face.

"Well, yes. I wonder who that might be," Jerry said.

"You live on campus? In the dorm?"

"Yes… but I will shortly be moving as it is quite expensive, and I don't want to be a burden to my parents."

"A kid is never a burden to his/her parents. Never. They would do everything possible to make sure you get the best. Trust me."

"Yes, but I would like to study for my postgrad and will need funds. So, I am trying to save as much as I can."

"What do you want to study?"

"Journalism. I want to travel the world… Investigative journalism… Cover the real stories," Jerry said.

'That is a good field. I am sure you can get good stories here in the US too.'

"Maybe, but here there is a lot of competition… and already some bigwigs like Christian Amanpour are there in the field. So, I would prefer to go global."

"Great idea. You said you will be shifting… where to?"

"Oh… nearby. Jersey City. We have an old house there. It is lying unused because it requires lots of repairs. I will be using it… Sometimes my mother can come and be with me for a couple of days. It will save a lot of money. The dorm is expensive."

"Oh great. In fact, my family also has a place in Jersey City. Where is your house?"

"The street name is Clerk Street… 213 Clerk Street. It will take me an hour to reach the university if I take I-95. Yes, there is travel, but it is much more economical."

"You know, I really appreciate your candid nature. Not many are so mature at your age. Your parents are lucky," Lemur said.

"Well, I have to be practical."

"So, will you make the introduction?"

"Yes. I will speak to him and ask him to call you if you can give me your cell number," Jerry said.

"Oh yes," Lemur took out his pen and asked Jerry for a pen.

"That is so old-fashioned… like my father. Please tell me your cell number." Jerry took out his cell and entered the number as narrated by Lemur… "Peter Parker, right?"

"Yes. It is."

"When are you moving?"

"Another week… by the 15th, I will be gone."

"Can you give me your cell number in case I have to contact you?" Lemur asked. "I won't be bothering you in your studies. Trust me."

"It's okay," said Jerry and gave his number to Lemur, who typed it into his cell phone and saved it. When he looked at Jerry, Jerry was smiling.

"What do you think of the demonstrations that are going on here?" Lemur asked.

"Stupid guys. There is a girl… Cathy Dexter… she has gone bonkers. She thinks she is kind of a politician. Maybe she will become one someday. But she has no maturity. She is just a bumblebee… a puppet in someone's hand. I detest it and am not paying any attention to it. All fake. I can bet you, if I open a map, 95% of the guys would not know where Palestine is. And what is the big deal of protesting here at Columbia University? They should go to Israel and protest and then see what happens." Jerry seemed agitated.

"You are absolutely right. Demos here are such a waste of time and money. I wonder how the university allows it."

"Democracy contains the word demo! Now you see the connection," Jerry started laughing.

Lemur also laughed. He got up from the bench, thanked Jerry profusely, and left. It was already dark and cold. Lemur wanted to have a hot cup of coffee… "Need to find either a Dunkin or a McD nearby," he said to himself and went towards his parked car. Both of his objectives were achieved today.

Richmond, Virginia, US

February 9, 2024; 06.30 PM

William Byrd Park was the venue decided by Nash. Lemur, as always, arrived early… went around checking for any signs of being observed. By the time Nash arrived, Lemur was ready.

After initial small talk, Lemur narrated the two meetings in detail. Nash had listened to everything Lemur had narrated but had not spoken a word. He was still sitting quietly.

Lemur wondered if Nash had been paying attention to what he had been told or if he was just preoccupied with his own thoughts. Momentarily, Nash just made a "Hmmmm" sound but said nothing.

Lemur knew that Nash's brain must be working out the plan… which he may or may not share. There was nothing else but to sit quietly and wait for Nash to say something. After about ten minutes, Nash said, "Great job. Keep working on both. Keep meeting them under some pretext… More concentration on Leo. Give him some money if he needs… My understanding is he may not take the money just like that. So, take him out for lunch or dinner. Give him some useful gift… keep him under surveillance. Do not lose him. As regards Jerry, same thing. Under surveillance. Do not lose him either." Nash paused, looked at Lemur and said…

"I will have other work for you soon. I will let you know," with that Nash got up and started walking towards the exit. Lemur slowly followed him.

"I will be damned if I do not think that there is something serious going on."

Washington, D.C., US

Secretary of State Bob Mayers was having a private dinner with Russ Pankrats, Director of the CIA. Bob wanted it to be a clandestine meeting because technically, the Director of the CIA reported to the Director of National Intelligence (DNI), who in turn reported to the President. Although the Bureau of Intelligence and Research reported to Bob, the objectives Bob had in mind could not have been achieved by the Bureau. Hence, he had requested Russ for a private dinner meeting away from prying eyes and ears.

Bob knew from experience that this "reporting" hierarchy was just a façade. In reality, the CIA ran its own little government… as per their whims and fancies, likes, and dislikes and formed their own narratives for their bosses. But who actually "managed" the CIA was always a million-dollar question. There were powerful people outside the government who had more power and authority to direct and manage the CIA. Bob always felt that the CIA stylishly "ignored" the State Department.

This particular meeting was taking place in DC's affluent suburb, Kalorama. Kalorama's tree-lined streets and elegant architecture, its spacious homes with meticulously landscaped lawns and carefully tended gardens had made it a natural fit for affluent families. The neighborhood's history of housing ambassadors and dignitaries had solidified its reputation as a diplomatic hub, attracting a select cadre of residents. Unsurprisingly, Kalorama's discreet atmosphere and security measures catered to those who valued privacy and exclusivity.

Bob had a clandestine place tucked in one corner in Kalorama which he used on special occasions such as this. After dinner, the two men had carried their Cognac glasses to the library section of the living room… which was an L-shaped room, and the small end of the room was converted into a library.

"Alright, shoot. What is it that you want to talk about?" Russ asked once they were seated. Russ had no interest in the State Department's objectives or plans. They, the CIA, had already worked out their plans and some of them were already initiated in conjunction with the Pentagon and, of course, some other key special stakeholders… which Russ had no intention of informing Bob about. He just wanted to know what the State Department was thinking that had prompted this meeting.

"India," Bob said.

"About what?" Russ suddenly became alert. He did not want any overruns with whatever the CIA was already involved in. He was already weary of RAW.

"Well, you know their general elections are beginning in April, and it is likely that the current ruling party will come back to power."

At the back of his mind, Russ could recall Ross's directives on how to destabilize the current Indian government of Prime Minister Dodi… whom Ross immensely hated. "Implode them from within," he had demanded. But presently Russ said, "So, what is the problem? They are okay to work with… yes, they are not timid like the ones before, and I for one, would like to deal with someone who is a toughie and not a jelly man."

"True. However, the US administration is not used to having someone telling us to 'shove it up'… and the continued imports of Russian oil by India under our very noses are hurting the egos of our policymakers. I am being open about it. Let us face it… only the current government in India has the capacity to deal with China with an iron fist. Any other government would have wiggled long back. Definitely, we need an ally like India in that part of the world. We learned our lesson with Pakistan. They will take our money and use it to screw India… rather than defend US's interests."

"So, what's the problem? I still don't get it."

"We don't want another China in the form of India. We already have one monster to deal with… then there will be two. If they fight with each other and finish each other off, then we can heave a sigh of relief… but that may not happen… anytime soon. So, we would like to keep some pressure on India. That way, they will not be able to see us eye to eye and say shove it up."

"What about imposing some sanctions? You guys are pretty good at that."

"Nah… that does not work anymore. We need… or at least I need something that would keep India under pressure. I think there are quite a few other ways or methods."

"For example?" Russ appeared curious. Because the CIA had its network widely spread in India. Several state ministers, opposition leaders, and cabinet ministers were either directly or indirectly employed by the CIA web. But sometimes Russ wondered if the intel provided was genuine or fabricated, "made for spies." India had changed a lot, and RAW had become quite agile and powerful.

"Use Canada as a proxy... we can ignite the Khalistani movement. The Canadian PM is an immature person... in my personal view. Because if you are keeping snakes in your backyard as pets, they are sure to bite you one day in the future," Bob suggested.

Russ kept quiet. He did not want to admit that the CIA was already fostering the Khalistanis in the US and even in Canada. Managing the Khalistanis in Canada was a "piece of cake" for the CIA because Russ, like Bob, also thought that the Canadian PM was just a clown, a dimwit.

'Or we can reignite the Pakistan-Occupied Kashmir issue and force India to open its doors to the spillover from POK. We can ask our Ambassador in Pakistan to take a tour of POK. Then, create unrest in POK and send those guys from POK to India. Once there, they can mess up inside India. That should divert attention from the elections.'

"They may just cancel or postpone the elections... no big deal," Russ pointed out. "And if that happens, the current ruling party will become stronger... because they will say... see, we have been telling you about this all the time... now it happened."

"Yes, that is possible," Bob paused.

"The issue of St Martin's Island!" Bob said.

Russ wanted to tell Bob that whatever he was suggesting had already been initiated by the CIA and they did not need any input from the State Department. But openly he said...

"That is the Bangladesh issue with Myanmar. The International Tribunal for the Law of the Sea (ITLOS) has already recognized St Martin's Island as part of Bangladesh, but Myanmar still sees it as its own territory. There is nothing we can do."

"We can occupy St. Martin's Island. The US wants to build an air base on that small island. It is situated just five miles away from Myanmar, even though it falls under Bangladeshi territory. Bangladesh can lease out that island to the US. The biggest advantage for anyone with a military base at St. Martin's, despite its small size, would be the strategic presence it would have over the Strait of Malacca, which the Chinese use mainly for their transportation. The island would also prove to be a pressure point to the Cox Bazaar port in Bangladesh that the Chinese are building. The island can be turned into a good listening post for surveillance activities, focused not just on China's and Myanmar's activities, but also on India's."

"Sounds good. So, why not ask the Bangladeshi PM? She will not refuse to lease out," Russ said.

"Well, she did refuse. Even when it was conveyed to her that leasing St Martin to us would ensure your smooth return to power."

"And?"

"And she said, 'over my dead body.'"

"Atta boy!!!"

"Yes, so we would like the CIA to create some sort of implosion there. There is already some unrest and uncomfortable feeling among some ultra-conservative Muslims. We can also use the Pakistani ISI folks who already have the web at the ground level. Pakistan will be too happy to help us because their economy has tanked and that of Bangladesh is thriving. So, they would want to tank even Bangladesh's economy. We can drive out this lady PM and bring someone who would listen to us. We don't want China to grab them like they have grabbed Pakistan," Bob paused.

"Okay, I will see what can be done. But your concern was India, I thought," Russ said.

"Or there is this Kuki land issue in the Northeast part of India. They want a separate Christian state. We can support that and make it happen," Bob said.

"Well, easier said than done. We haven't got any ground intel there," Russ avoided a yawn.

"Yes… I have given you my options; you can try yours. Money works magic in India. Everybody is for sale there. In my opinion, an implosion is the only way. I am sure others like Borge Ross must be working their bit as well because he hates the current Indian PM. He wants someone "liberal" … not a nationalist," Bob said.

The Mention of Borge Ross made Russ uneasy. "This means even the State Department was supposedly 'reporting' to Ross," Russ thought to himself. But openly he said…

"Well, from my perspective… the current India will prove to be good for the US when we take on China. It is not if, but when we take them on. That clash will happen someday in the near future. At that time, the current Indian government will back us up all the way. Keep that in mind," Russ said.

"I understand, but let us try to tone them down and not allow them to become formidable," Bob said.

"BTW… I believe Abe had met Martin but came back empty-handed," Russ said. "Apparently, Abe 'heard' something about DARPA… not sure if there is any leak somewhere." Russ wanted to keep Bob completely out of this matter, but he was not the decision-maker here.

"Certainly not here. And in any case, Martin would not know and would never tell even if he knew. That is why I had asked Abe to meet him. No damage done," Bob said.

They spoke for some more time. By the time Russ left, it was well past 10.00 p.m.

Langley, Virginia, US

February 23, 2024; 07.00 PM

Abe was still sitting at his desk, trying to finish some pending work. He hated meetings. He felt meetings were unproductive and took away a lot of "workable time." Being Friday, there should have been hardly any meetings, but Abe had spent almost the entire day running from one meeting to the other. He was now at his desk trying to finish the pending work before he could head out for a quiet weekend.

In reality, there was never a "quiet" weekend. There were always some "urgent" jobs which would spring up at lunchtime or even at dinnertime. Many a time he had left the barbecue half-done, much to the annoyance of his wife.

After his last meeting… which was with the Director of CIA, Russ Pankrats, Abe had returned to his room a little frustrated. When Abe had brought some of the key issues to the notice of the Director, all he said was, "Just put it aside for the time being," "Don't lose your sleep over it," or "Ohhh, that is not a critical one to worry about." Abe wondered if Russ was on the CIA's payroll or working for somebody else.

"Or maybe he knows that next year, by this time, he will not be in that chair… Hence, he does not want to indulge in any major issues. Let the next man bother about them." Abe tried to rationalize his thoughts.

Abe's first project at the CIA was way back in 1962… Project Coldfeet. Their team had picked up the Soviet Drift Station NP8 Soviet's Arctic research activities on an acoustic system to detect under-ice systems. Project Coldfeet was a CIA operation to extract intelligence from an abandoned Soviet Arctic drifting ice station. Due to the nature of its abandonment as a result of unstable ice, the retrieval of the operatives had used the Fulton surface-to-air recovery system.

What became known as Operation Coldfeet had begun in May 1961, when a naval aircraft flying an aeromagnetic survey over the Arctic Ocean reported sighting an abandoned Soviet drift station. A few days later, the Soviets announced that they had been forced to leave Station NP 9 (a different station, NP eight ended up being the target) when the ice runway used to supply it had been destroyed by a pressure ridge, and it was assumed that it would be crushed in the Arctic Ocean.

Those days were fun… Abe was lost in his thoughts. CIA then worked on Mass Psychosis. Abe's stay in Berlin during the Cold War had taught him some very practical lessons of his life. Some of his own colleagues turned out to be Soviet agents. Money changed hands and no one was "clean."

During the first Gulf War, Abe was posted in the Middle East. That was another experience. That war had changed the CIA forever. The CIA had become the de facto operating arm of the US armed forces.

The Counterintelligence Center (CIC) was a part of the Central Intelligence Agency (CIA) that protected CIA operations from foreign adversaries. The CIC was established in 1988 and later transformed into the Counterintelligence Mission Center (CIMC) in 2015.

"CIA had now become like an octopus," Abe thought to himself. "So many bloody departments." Departments suddenly made Abe remember DARPA. He immediately straightened up in his chair. He had completely forgotten about it.

If Martin really did not know about the possible discussions some interesting parties had with DARPA, then who would know? "Wish I could know the names of those lobbyists… or even the lobbies… I would find out what's going on," Abe muttered under his breath.

"DARPA will not get involved unless someone from the top… either at the Pentagon or from the Director of National Intelligence office had directed the guys at DARPA to get involved. Now, what does that mean?" Abe was lost in his thoughts.

"There are several areas that DARPA worked on… what would the lobbyists want? Biotech, Bioweapons? Let me do that process of elimination… Oil lobby… no, Automobile… no, Pharma… no, Wall Street, Banks… no, defense… Yes, Biotech… Yes, Hi-Tech… maybe."

"So, there would be only three lobbies who could 'communicate' with guys at DARPA. But why? What do they want to develop? Or… maybe it is already under development since the last few years and that I am coming to know just now… just by accident… Is that the truth? This means something is going on at the very top level. But since when… because the governments to have changed multiple times in the last 12 years… and may change again. So, does this mean that it is happening behind the back of the POTUS and SecDef?" Abe suddenly felt the blood rushing to his head.

"If I am the only one with this knowledge outside their ring, and since I have asked the Director of CIA… who in turn asked me to go and see the Secretary of State…. And then his deputy… which means now three top guys know that I know something fishy is going on. Jeez… this means I am now the 'dangerous' man or 'person of interest' from those guys' point of view. The question is who 'those' guys are?" Abe was now sweating, and his heart was pounding hard.

"I made a mistake. I should have thought before opening my trap. Assuming I am at risk… let me do my risk assessment… The risk will be greater if I pursue this topic or speak about it again. But if I don't speak about it and just pretend nothing has happened, then maybe I will be on safer ground. Hopefully. Let me think this over… because I need to find out if anything sinister is being worked out." Abe looked at the watch… it was past 9.00 pm.

He shut his laptop off, took his stuff, put it in his backpack, turned off the light and left the room, pulling the door shut behind him. It was cold outside… but Abe was feeling numb, frustrated, and betrayed. Betrayed by his own people.

Arlington, Virginia, US

March 5, 2024; 04.30 PM

DARPA director Albert Powell was busy poring over the details of the three mega initiatives that were presently of paramount importance. These initiatives neither appeared on the regular reports to SecDef nor were discussed during the regular meetings. There were only a handful of officials working on these initiatives.

DARPA governed six technical offices that managed the agency's research portfolio, and two additional offices that managed special projects. All offices reported to Albert Powell, the DARPA director, including:

The Defense Sciences Office (DSO): DSO identified and pursued high-risk, high-payoff research initiatives across a broad spectrum of science and engineering disciplines and transformed them into important new game-changing technologies for US national security. Current DSO themes included novel materials and structures, sensing and measurement, computation, and processing, enabling operations, collective intelligence, and global change.

The Information Innovation Office (I2O) aimed to ensure US technological superiority in all areas where information could provide a decisive military advantage.

The Microsystems Technology Office (MTO).... core mission was the development of high-performance, intelligent microsystems and next-generation components to ensure US dominance in command, Control, Communications, Computer, Intelligence, Surveillance, and Reconnaissance (C4ISR), Electronic Warfare (EW), and Directed Energy (DE). The effectiveness, survivability, and lethality of systems related to these applications depended critically on microsystems and components.

The Strategic Technology Office (STO) mission's focus was on technologies that would have a global theater-wide impact and that involved multiple services.

The Tactical Technology Office (TTO) engaged in high-risk, high-payoff advanced military research, emphasizing the "system" and "subsystem" approach to the development of aeronautic, space, and land systems as well as embedded processors and control systems.

The Biological Technologies Office (BTO) fostered, demonstrated, and transitioned breakthrough fundamental research, discoveries, and applications that integrated biology, engineering, and computer science for national security. This was created in April 2014.

Albert was aware that the Pentagon had a whole nine yards of issues currently on their table... the wars in Ukraine and in the Middle East... NATO's "I scratch my back, you scratch my back" attitude and its less than active role in the Ukraine war, the ever-increasing threat coming from China... the Taiwan issue... the South China Sea challenge... The possible recession in Europe and the threat of Islamic radicals... the list was endless.

"They will not have time to divert their attention to these prime projects of ours." Albert looked at the two project update reports... Operation Castillon (Otho Gunga) and Operation Taranis.

Albert was quite sure that the way he had selected the project names, it would be quite difficult for anyone to understand the nature of these projects. Money was not an issue because these projects were not "funded" by the Feds. Although privately funded, once the projects went on stream, even the Feds would reap the benefits. "After all, the Feds are just the puppets," Albert thought to himself.

The proposal to manage these projects came out of the blue. Albert was scared to get involved in any such "Public-Private Partnership," as he termed it. But when he was made to realize that the answer cannot be a no… because if it came to it, perhaps Albert may cease to exist. So, Albert had to say yes and now Albert was in it deep up to his nose.

Albert remembered the way it was informed to him… a big world map had been spread over the large table. "This, this, here and here…. we need it. Get it," it was ordered. The man who had ordered it was quite a powerful man… more powerful than even the US President, in a manner of speaking.

"This is what we want, this is how we want, this is where we want… and this is when we want… So, get it accomplished." The message was plain and simple.

Albert had pulled in senior officials from DSO, MTO, and BTO… He had explained to them about the secrecy, urgency, and the serious nature of the projects. "Strictly… no copies, no discussions, no brainstorming with anyone outside this group."

These projects were not something out of the world; conceptually, Albert thought they were picked up from some sci-fi movies. Yet, given the nature of the global circumstances, the projects seemed to be quite relevant. However, to put these concepts into real use was the real challenge. Once completed, they would be deemed "personal property." And Albert did not like that.

However, Albert had no choice but to get it done… Even if he hated the lobbyists and the man whom they represented. Only once had he made a snide remark about the lobbyists to one of his peers but without giving any reference. Albert later regretted his remark and hoped that it did not create any ripples. So far, it had been all quiet.

Albert went back to reading the reports he had just received. The projects were progressing well… at least in the lab.

Beijing, China

March 11, 2024; 10.30 AM

It had been over an hour since the Chinese President had been rattling off instructions to his ministers from various ministries.

"Water, Land, and space. We want complete control. Unchallenged control. These are the three essential areas of human existence, and the Chinese government should have complete control over them… globally. Not the US nor any country in the West or East, nor any rich individual from any country." He had avoided mentioning Elon Musk.

"We want complete control over the land to grow and transport food and extract the mineral wealth. We want complete control over water… Rivers, Lakes, Seas, Oceans… for the same reason… Food, Drinking water, minerals, and maritime transportation. We want complete control over the space… so that we can keep an eye on others and not let others keep an eye on us. We should be able to identify any threat from space and should be able to destroy it from space."

"So, global acquisition of land, water resources and space is of paramount importance to us. We have initiated various projects to achieve these objectives. At the same time, our adversaries would also be working on similar projects, and if they are, we should know and see how to subvert them. Whatever we say or do on the global stage is just a show. But this… what I have just narrated…

is the real goal… and we shall achieve it. This is of paramount importance, and I need not stress the urgency… because you all understand it."

Ministers sitting around the table just nodded their heads in agreement. Some of these objectives were near impossible… but saying no or questioning the directive was akin to a death sentence.

However, the question that nagged everybody was… "Why this urgency?"

"Acquiring world assets… land or water… is something we have been trying via BRI. If the government in any country is unfriendly towards us, create an environment in the country through the locals to throw out the unfriendly government and establish one that is friendly towards us. The US and the West have followed this strategy for a long time. It is our time now to implement it. We should concentrate on port cities, fertile land, sites with water resources, and those with rich mineral wealth."

"I need this accomplished in a year from now," the President looked at Wu Youxia, Head of the China National Space Administration (CNSA), questioningly.

Wu nodded his head in full agreement. There was nothing to say… except "Yes, Sir." Wu was fully aware of what the President wanted. While Wu was skeptical, he had no choice. The Chinese Deep State was so deep and wide that Wu would not even trust his mother completely… forget about trusting his wife.

Having lived in the West, Wu was of a "live and let live" nature. Extreme dominance was not something Wu appreciated. But he had no choice.

Wu had known that the President's immediate mission was acquiring Taiwan. His other important mission was destabilizing

India. Although the President did not admit publicly, he was weary of the current Indian politicians and their eyeball-to-eyeball kind of attitude. He wanted to destabilize India so that he could break India apart… an implosion. However, the President's main worry was if India retaliated with full force, China would lose some of its teeth and would come across as a toothless dragon to the US forces… which was quite dangerous.

Wu also knew that the President was biding his time to invade Taiwan because he was worried about facing the US head-on. It would disturb the trade. Wu also was aware that the President preferred the current US President rather than the previous one… as the current President or the VP were very docile and would not confront China should it invade Taiwan.

So, as an "Insurance," the President had asked Wu to work on something that would give China an edge over either India or the US. This was a clandestine project… a dark secret… which is what the President was asking Wu to agree on.

Wu was aware that if he did not do it, someone else would and by then, Wu would be gone forever.

"The Hamas and the Hezbollah have built an underground infrastructure of immense complexity. It is really worth appreciating and learning. It is essential for us to plan to build underground cities… not just bunkers or tunnels. Having underground cities in secret places will serve us well in case of any emergency. Obviously, such underground cities will not be open to every citizen. We will have to differentiate and give preferences. However, it is necessary that we start working on this immediately." The President stopped and looked around the table.

Everybody seemed completely surprised… as having an underground city for a select few people meant something serious was expected to happen in the near future. "Who would be these select few?" was the question on everybody's mind.

Wu knew exactly what it meant. That was a clear hint of the space attack. Space warfare.

Space warfare made use of space weapons. There existed and still exist three kinds: space-to-space weapons, earth-to-space weapons, and space-to-earth weapons.

Space weapons included weapons that could attack space systems in orbit, such as anti-satellite weapons, attack targets on the earth from space, or disable missiles traveling through space. In the course of the militarization of space, such weapons were developed mainly by the contesting superpowers during the Cold War, and some remain under development today.

But Wu knew what the President had in mind... Orbital Weaponry. Orbital weaponry was any weapon that is in orbit around a large body such as a planet or moon. Several orbital weaponry systems were designed by the United States and the Soviet Union during the Cold War. During World War II, Nazi Germany was also developing plans for an orbital weapon called the Sun Gun, an orbital mirror that would have been used to focus and weaponize beams of sunlight. Silbervogel was the name of the Nazi German space weapon project.

Several nations deployed orbital surveillance networks to observe other nations or armed forces but not orbital weaponry. Development of orbital weaponry was something the President had been forcing Wu to concentrate on... with both laser and nuclear options.

It was common knowledge that China's development of an orbiting nuclear strike weapon was also designed to target all 50 US states. The China Aerospace Studies Institute had once revealed, "The use of an orbital bombardment system could increase PLA power projection capabilities against bases and territories globally, including targets in the 50 states."

Wu also knew that Chinese military researchers could easily disable systems such as the over 6,000 orbiting Starlink satellites deployed by Elon Musk's company, SpaceX. But orbital nuclear weaponry was a different ballgame.

"And what if the US, Russia, and even India are also thinking about the same?" Wu shuddered.

Frankfurt, Germany

April 30, 2024; 10.30 AM

Ludolf had spent the last few weeks upon his return from China to thoroughly understand the arms needs of Iran. He noticed that Iran had been running two major programs simultaneously… the Missile Program and the Nuclear Program. Their Missile Program had been quite elaborate and included both Ballistic and Cruise missiles. In addition, Iran had also developed their Drone Program quite successfully. This meant Iran either had the technology and the skill sets to develop everything internally or some country had been helping Iran in their development despite the sanctions on them.

During his research, Ludolf had learned that Iran had forty-three missile sites spread out within the country and possibly had a couple of thousand missiles ready to be deployed. If that was the case, Ludolf wondered why Iran would need missiles and related hi-tech stuff from Ludolf's firm. Unless…. "Either Iran would be using it for their nuke warheads, or they might be selling their existing missiles to Hamas, Hezbollah or the Houthis," Ludolf muttered to himself.

"But what if the shipment does not go to Iran and goes to China instead, then the Chinese will obviously resort to reverse engineering and develop on their own. Well, the Iranians would do the same," Ludolf was lost in his thoughts.

"And if the stolen shipment does not end up in Iran or in China, then where would it go?" Ludolf shuddered. "If Alexei could manage the heist at mid-sea, he can divert it to any other country… but where?" Ludolf wondered.

Ludolf had thought about making a clandestine sale, an unauthorized one, and giving that money to the III Way (3 Path) party… which Ludolf admired and secretly supported. Monetary support would give them the necessary boost to propagate their mission throughout Europe as they had already begun spreading in the Nordic countries.

"Do I really care where the shipment goes… after all, the number one buyer of German arms was Algeria, which was not a very credible state. Perhaps Alexei may play a game and divert it to Cuba… which would be a spoiler as it would create political issues between Germany and the US." Ludolf was weighing his options.

"Having missiles does not mean anything, one needs a delivery mechanism… and this would mean the sale will be made to a country which has already acquired the delivery mechanism. It would also mean Alexei could sell the stolen cargo to anybody in the Middle East… like Syria or Iraq. I would rather not take the risk and wait for the right opportunity… and I am sure I will get one because the current German government is damaging the economy… and they haven't got a clue how to revive it," Ludolf thought to himself.

"Perhaps it would be a good idea to meet this Alexei guy and get to know him a wee bit more before I make any decision," Ludolf muttered.

Langley, Virginia, US

April 30, 2024; 06.30 PM

Nash was heading towards the Georgetown area. Sergei had sent a buzz asking him to meet at Tracy's pod, the one-bedroom unit in Georgetown where they had met before.

"Unless Sergei had any intel, he wouldn't call," Nash had thought before accepting the invitation. In another 5 minutes, he would be at the one-bedroom unit.

Nash had applied his mind to the brief information that he had received from Martin… but it was rather too vague. Nash knew that Albert headed DARPA, but he was not close to Albert to approach him even socially. The only thing Nash could think of was the project or projects, if any, would be managed by DSO… and he had no contacts at DSO. This was quite frustrating… and the time was of the essence. He had to find a source who could provide the intel.

"Hey there," Nash said as Sergei opened the door of the apartment.

"Hey… good to see you… come on in. Tracy has ventured out… It is a nice spring evening," Sergei said.

Nash smiled and sat on the chair.

"Coffee?"

"No, thanks. I am good," Nash wanted to get on with the topic.

"Fine… but if you need it, just say it," Sergei laughed.

"You seem to have unearthed something. You seem to be quite pleased with yourself."

"Nash, Nash, Nash… You will never change. You are so effing perceptive. Yes, I do have something for you," Sergei said. "Operation Castillon (Otho Gunga) and Operation Taranis are the two projects managed by Albert… well, how should I put it… under the radar… clandestinely… With the help of DSO, MTO, and BTO."

"Interesting. How did it originate… I am sure you must have figured it out," Nash asked.

"Well, it is like this Nash… Tracy works for a legal firm that represents a couple of Biotech firms from the West Coast. So, I asked Tracy to do a little bit of snooping. Mind you, she is pretty good at that…"

"Maybe she picked it up from you."

"Absolutely… I love that Nash!!! Anyway, the grapevine is the funding of the project is coming from one specific resource… which controls one too many industry segments… such as Biotech and Defense in particular."

"And… the name of this controlling unit is…" Nash asked.

"It is an extremely powerful organization, Nash. I would be careful," Sergei said.

"The name starts with a C?" Nash asked.

Sergei just smiled.

"Okay, next…" Nash asked.

"Next what?"

"When, Where, How, What?"

"Hey, that is something you've got to figure out. I got what you had asked for. Yes, there are projects... not on record anywhere.... All are extremely classified. Only three teams consisting of seven people and Albert have any knowledge of these projects... Operation Castillon (Otho Gunga) and Operation Taranis."

"Oh, for God's sake, Sergei... those names don't mean anything," Nash said.

"Oh, but they do, Nash... They absolutely mean something. I simply Googled both names and this is what I got..." Sergei said and went on to read from a printout. "I am sure you have seen Star Wars."

"Castillon... Castillon actually, is an Ocean Planet located in the galaxy's Mid-Rim and is located close to the borders of Wild space."

"Naboo is another planet located beneath the surface of Lake Panoga. On Naboo is the spectacular Gungan city. The bubbles are hydrostatic force fields that contain a breathable atmosphere... Gungan submarines... moth moth-shaped. Vegetation growth underwater... Underwater town...."

"And... Taranis... is a Celtic God of lightning and thunder."

"WTF... this is insane.... Underwater town, underwater vegetation.... Are they thinking of Captain Nemo or something? And the Celtic God of thunder and lightning.... Now wait a minute... are they thinking about creating artificial thunder and lightning?" Nash asked, exasperated.

'No, Nash... this is what I think: perhaps the project is to create large-scale fires, shock waves, environmental change as severe thunder and lightning would do. This is possible via a space-based nuclear explosion... which could generate a powerful electromagnetic pulse that could severely disrupt electric grids across large areas of earth, causing power outages and damaging electronic systems.'

"Oh boy… I know what they are thinking of… Space-to-earth nuclear weaponry… missiles. That would do the damage you just described. Bloody clever in naming the projects. Star Wars… that's where it originated. So, space to earth nukes and Underwater city and blue sky research technique… the Bio Hybrids, that is."

"Yup."

"But why underwater cities and vegetation? That would explain wanting exclusive rights over large water bodies across the globe… freshwater bodies, I can understand, but seas and oceans? What kind of towns and cities are they planning?" Nash wondered. He looked quite disturbed.

"Not sure… but if they can have seed banks in Norway where nothing can ever grow… it is okay to have a city underwater where one can grow some seaweeds and catch some fish," Sergei laughed.

"Sergei, this is damn bloody serious. What kind of underwater cities… creating bubbles with breathable air… and growing vegetation. The depth at which the underwater vegetation is currently done is around 650 feet under the surface. This is too shallow for a city to sustain any natural or manmade calamity. How are they going to protect it… and why underwater in the first place? What are they anticipating… An all-out nuclear war? If so, when? Nash looked very perturbed.

"I don't know Nash. I did not think about all this. I just got you the titbits. You are the one imagining all this," Sergei said. "But it makes sense, though… Coz Yes, it is dangerous. And who will all be permitted to live in the underwater city or town? Will you or I get a place there? I don't think so. I am sure that city will be well protected… from either natural or any manmade disasters."

"Bloody clever…. This is not official… not on record. So, the Senate or the Congress will not know. I bet even the POTUS or the VeeP would not know. I guess it would be under wraps… only SecDef, Albert, the team of 7-8 guys and perhaps the Secretary of State might just know…. And yes, Russ Pankrats, Director of the CIA, for sure. He would be the one who would be doing the 'cleaning operation' and providing safe ground or water bodies outside the US." Nash thought to himself.

"So, what do you think, Nash?" Sergei asked.

"I don't know. The only thing that can be done is to expose this to the public."

"What will happen then? Nothing… they will officially say 'Yes, we are doing it'."

"Sergei… there will be worldwide competition… Russia would want to put nukes in space too… China as well… there will be no end. Salt II treaty gone to dogs. And also, Russia will say okay… we will build a city under Lake Baikal… the Chinese will say No Entry to the South China Sea. When I say expose it, I mean get their plan out in the open… not just the idea… the real plans… drawings, blueprints, worksheets… out in the open… it will shock them…. And we need to do this before the election in November."

"Oh okay… I understand… that would be fun," Sergei said. He had a different idea already brewing in his mind.

"Thanks, Sergei, for all the help. I will be in touch and will let you know the Path forward. I am sure we can turn this around."

"For sure Nash. Just one thing… be extremely careful. This is dangerous stuff," Sergei said.

"I will," said Nash as he got up to leave. "See you soon," he said and left quickly.

"Boy!!! I did not know this darn thing was so serious. I need to quietly work out my plans," Sergei said as he picked up the phone and gave a missed call to Tracy… a signal to head back to the apartment.

Sergei was worried.

Beijing, China

May 2, 2024, 10:30 AM

It had been over an hour that the Chinese President was reprimanding his army commandants. Chen Wenhua, General of the Southern Theater Command, General Huang Jiangshan of the Central Theater Command, General Zheng Weidong of the Eastern Theater Command, Zhou Xuebin, the Minister heading the Ministry of Water Resources (MWR), and Tian Xuewen, the Minister heading the Ministry of Agriculture (MOA) were in attendance.

Southern Theater Command's area of responsibility (AOR) included the South China Sea, Myanmar, Laos, and Vietnam (Mainland Southeast Asia). The command's primary missions were maintaining security in the South China Sea and likely supporting the Eastern Theater Command in any major amphibious operation against Taiwan.

Eastern Theater Command's area of responsibility (AOR) included the East China Sea, the Taiwan Strait, and East China. The command's primary missions were maintaining security in the East China Sea and the conduct of major operations against Taiwan, including the Penghu, Kinmen, and Matsu Islands. They were also responsible for matters relating to Japan, including the Ryukyu Archipelago, the Tsushima Strait, and the disputed Senkaku Islands. Its jurisdiction included Jiangsu, Zhejiang, Anhui, Fujian, Jiangxi, and Shanghai provinces and the East China Sea to include the Strait of Taiwan.

The Central Theater Command's area of responsibility (AOR) consisted of the previous Beijing Military Region, including the capital Beijing and the neighboring provinces, and directly governed municipalities of Tianjin, Hebei, Shaanxi, Shanxi, Henan, and Hubei. The command's primary responsibility was the defense of the nation's capital, Beijing, and it served as the national strategic military reserve.

There was a digital map displayed on the huge screen, and all three Generals were standing and explaining their point of view… which, of course, was not accepted by the Chinese President.

General Chen Wenhua of the Southern Command had explained that…

"The South China Sea's major feature was a deep rhombus-shaped basin in the eastern part, with reef-studded shoals rising steeply within the basin to the south near the Reed and Tizard Banks and the Nanshan Island area, and in the northwest, the Paracel Islands and Macclesfield Banks."

"Along the northwest side of the basin towards the mainland is a broad, shallow shelf as wide as 150 miles. This shelf includes the Gulf of Tonkin, the Taiwan Strait, and the large islands of Hainan and Taiwan."

"To the south, off Vietnam, the shelf narrows and connects with the Sunda Shelf, one of the largest in the world, which covers the area between Borneo, Sumatra, and the Malay Peninsula and includes the southern part of the South China Sea, the Gulf of Thailand, and the Java Sea. This broad trough is about 130 feet deep at its periphery and up to 330 feet in its central part. On the bottom of the shelf is a network of submerged river valleys that converge into the Sunda Depression and then into the China Sea Basin."

General Zheng Weidong of the Eastern Theater Command had explained that…

"Most of the East China Sea is shallow, with almost three-fourths of it being less than 660 feet deep, while the maximum depth, reached in the Okinawa Trough, is nine thousand feet. The Korean peninsula, China, Japan, and Taiwan lie within or border the East China Sea."

"Your explanations did not answer my question," the Chinese President barked. "Show me the area which can be up to six thousand feet deep where we can certainly have a permanent base for the Shenhai Yongshi's newer version. The Shenhai Yangshi just returned to Sanya recently, as you know, after the completion of its deep-sea in-situ scientific research. It is just 13000 feet manned submersible. What I asked for was a permanent manned submersible station, like a space station but in water, which can be operational at a much deeper level, operating on a continuous basis and not on an experimental basis, and will be twice as big as the current Shenhai Yangshi. We would like to have that installed by the end of this year and no later."

General Zheng Weidong wanted to say something but kept quiet. The President looked at him, probing.

"Xiānshēng (Sir), I applaud your vision. It is indeed a great feat that we have achieved with Shenhai Yangshi. For the newer version, I do not have any concrete plan on the security aspect as you very well know the danger of having the underwater base near the Okinawa Trough… which is where the depth is nine thousand feet. For the South China Sea, I would refer that to

General Chen Wenhua. Considering the fact that Xiānshēng is thinking of having two such bases."

"We shall worry about security once we have decided on the exact area. Don't worry about the Americans. We can make sure that they have their hands full with other things. I do not want these new stations as experimental bases. It is important that we expand our footprint underwater to get the edible vegetation farms established as well as seafood farming... plus, of course, there will be other research programs. If necessary, one can live there for an extended period of time... say 6-9 months."

General Chen Wenhua was skeptical about the whole thing but remained quiet. Security apart, he was uncertain how these permanent stations would respond to earthquakes... which happened quite frequently, though on a minor scale in that region. He also wondered about the vegetation angle because it did not make sense. Rice... which was the main staple diet, could not be grown underwater... yes, things like lettuce, seaweeds and a couple of similar vegetables could be cultivated but it was of low value. "There must be some hidden agenda," he thought to himself.

"You have seven days to prepare a complete plan and present it to me. Is it clear?" the President asked and without waiting for an answer, he turned to General Huang Jiangshan of Central Theater Command and barked, "You show me what you have about the underground city projects that I had spoken to you about."

General Huang Jiangshan bowed and went to the digital map and expanded it. "Xiānshēng, we have located two areas for building two underground cities. One is here... between Beijing and Langfang in Hebei.... Closer to Langfang... about an hour's drive from Beijing. And the other area is here... Nanchang...near Wuhan. It is also near Shanghai and Shenzhen. Actually, it is at the center of the triangle of Wuhan, Shanghai, and Shenzhen. The cities will be at a depth of 1000-1200 feet, fully protected with reinforced steel and concrete structures… and earthquake shockproof. The underground cities will have all the amenities as above ground and can accommodate 300-350 people… about 100 families."

"The Hamas guys have built it so well under the very noses of the Israelis. Why don't you get some of their labor force and get started? We need to complete this ASAP. Also, is there a provision for farming there?" the President asked.

General Huang had not investigated this area at all and hence did not know what to answer. All he could do was to cast a glance at Tian Xuewen, the Minister heading the Ministry of Agriculture (MOA), and say, "We might have to do some experiments to be sure."

Tian Xuewen nodded in affirmation.

"Get the damn experimentation going… for what are you waiting? You should have thought about all these aspects right at the conception. We are not building any underground bunkers… these are underground towns. We can have more in the course of time," the President roared.

Somewhere in the corner of his mind, the President was worried about the possible outcome of the US elections. If the Dems came to power, China would do well because most of the Dems were on the Chinese payroll. The Chinese Deep State had spread its roots extensively in the US over the last twenty-odd years. But if the Reps came to power, there would be some issues with respect to tariffs. As such, the economy was sluggish, and with India starting to grow in the manufacturing segment, it had impacted the Chinese manufacturing sector somewhat… but the President thought this was a danger sign.

The President was also worried about the slowdown and the Islamic fundamentalist issues in the EU countries. That would also affect the business in the coming year. He was also suspecting that some of his men were working clandestinely for the CIA. "Can't trust the white guys," he repeated to himself. "Not sure who really is managing the US now. Wonder which dark force runs it," he muttered.

There was also the issue of having nukes in space… Space-to-earth nukes. The President suspected that the US was secretly working on it… and one day in the near future may surprise everyone… He made a mental note to take this topic up with Wu as a topmost priority. The US was losing heavily on the international front. The US Dollar had lost its shine, and the World Bank and IMF had lost some of their teeth. "The Ukraine war was an eye-opener," he said to himself.

The President wanted to get ready with the underground project first… the underwater was a little vulnerable from a security point of view. Because Shenhai Yongshi could not possibly defend a missile fired from the air. After all, it would be on a fixed platform… like a sitting duck in the water. It would need a different kind of defense system… which Wu's team was working on, but it would take some time. "There would be ways to protect the station… but it was way too early," the President thought. "But this would be important from a future perspective."

Presently, he barked his orders… "Okay, one week from now, I want the final plans." And with a wave of his hand, he dismissed them all.

Jersey City, NJ

May 4, 2024; 12.00 Noon

The weather had warmed up. Jerry had moved out of the dorm at Columbia and had shifted his stuff to his family's old place on Clerk Street in Jersey City on April 30th. He had just dumped his stuff then because he was too tired to arrange it. He had decided to do the cleaning and arranging over the weekend.

It was almost noon when Jerry had finished putting the stuff in place as best as he could. He was hungry and was contemplating either going out or calling Uber Eats. He was standing at the French window in the living room enjoying the afternoon sun when he noticed that someone had just moved into the house across the street… Jerry remembered that the house at 208 had been unoccupied for quite some time.

"Interesting. Perhaps somebody like me must have had an intelligent idea to move into that house," Jerry now noticed that the house did not have a wired compound like other houses. The front stairs looked broken at the edges. The paint on the front door had long lost its shine.

"Maybe someone took it on rent," Jerry thought to himself. "I am sure I will know who the heck that person is… it is just a matter of time." Jerry smirked and went back to his cell phone, browsing Uber Eats.

After ordering, Jerry started figuring out which mode of transport would be the cheapest for him to travel to Columbia and back. He looked at the 3-4 options: NJ Transit, MTA, or Path, which would cost the same $3 one way. However, the MTA's frequency was every 10 minutes, while NJ Transit's was every 20 minutes. There was also the option of Bus line 119 and then the Subway from Midtown Manhattan, which would take half an hour longer than the MTA or NJ Transit but cost the same.

"Oh, well... I can try them all and then settle on the cheapest and the fastest. In any case, the travel cost would be like $120-$150 a month... which is a lot cheaper than the dorm." Jerry smiled to himself and looked out of the window for the Uber guy.

Jerry suddenly remembered the visit of Peter Parker who had come to visit him at Columbia. "I wonder if he ever contacted dad. I had completely forgotten to mention him to dad," Jerry said to himself. "I will ask dad when I speak to him next. I wonder who recommended my name to Peter." Jerry shrugged his shoulders and forgot about it as he saw the Uber guy pulling up in front of his house.

"Ah, food. Finally," Jerry said and went to the door to receive it.

Moscow, Russia

May 5, 2024, 0830 PM

"You wanted to see me immediately," asked the President of Russia.

"Yes, something important and urgent from our man," replied Alexei… still standing.

"Go ahead."

"Our friends are contemplating building underwater habitats and also revoking… or rather ignoring the 1967 Outer Space Treaty."

"I see. What is the status?"

"DARPA is still working on it. It is clandestine… under the radar."

"Details?"

"Our man says he is at it. It may take some time to get his hands on both."

"Interesting. Underground, yes… I can understand. Underwater… what is the benefit?" the President asked.

"Not sure. We don't know the objective," Alexei replied.

"Our Chinese friends already tried the underwater thing. So did we… but for research and not as a habitat. The Chinese think they can have something like an International Space Station underwater. We shall see. The outer space thing is interesting. We can do it… it is not that difficult. How to keep it under wraps is the question. Anyway, convey thanks to our man," the President said. He did not seem perturbed at all. Not a single line had moved from his face after hearing the news. Alexei was surprised.

"By the way, what happened to that German-Chinese deal?" the President asked.

"No idea. I have not heard from either party. Maybe the deal is off," Alexei said.

The President smiled and said, "Iran already has its missile and nuclear program, and they have developed it quite well. They do exports. Yes, the quality may not be like the German ones… but it delivers results. You have seen the Hamas and Hezbollah attacks… pretty accurate. Why would Iranians buy expensive stuff? They can get it cheaper from North Koreans or even us. I think there must be something else involved in the deal. Be careful before you do anything."

"Yes, I am and will be careful," Alexei said.

"You can contact the German guy and feel the wind," the President said.

"Yes, I will," Alexei said, wished good night, and left the meeting room. "Message delivered," he muttered to himself.

Langley, Virginia, US

May 6, 2024; 01.30 AM

Nash was still in his study, poring over various reports from the recent past. He also had the North American map displayed on the big digital screen on the wall. He had circled Hudson Bay, Labrador Sea, Beaufort Sea, Gulf of Alaska, Lake Superior, and the Northwest Territories near Great Bear Lake.

He had printouts of the reports on Shenhai Yongshi and a report on a Russian project for a submersible underwater power module featuring two nuclear power units with a total capacity of 20 MWe, that could dive to a depth of 1200 feet and provide energy in the Arctic regions. It was being worked on by the Malakhit Marine Engineering Bureau in St. Petersburg, Russia.

Nash had been studying various reports on underwater habitats but had come to the conclusion that a permanent or long-term underwater habitat was nearly impossible because it had lots of limitations. Depth was the first and foremost. Then there were other issues… safety, security, waste management, health… both physical and mental, corrosion of the habitat and the moving parts of any equipment… etc.

Nash felt… as a research vessel the underwater habitat for a couple of months would be normal, but making an underwater colony for a long-term stay was not a feasible option. Nash had gone near to the display monitor on the wall, zoomed in and had closely looked at all the water bodies named by Martin... not once but multiple times, and he had come to the conclusion that the bubble-shaped or dome-shaped habitat... like in Star Wars was not practically feasible.

"Either Martin had it all wrong, or Sergei did, or both. This Castellion project seems to be either an eyewash, or it is something else that Sergei completely failed to understand." Nash once again went to the map displayed on the screen....

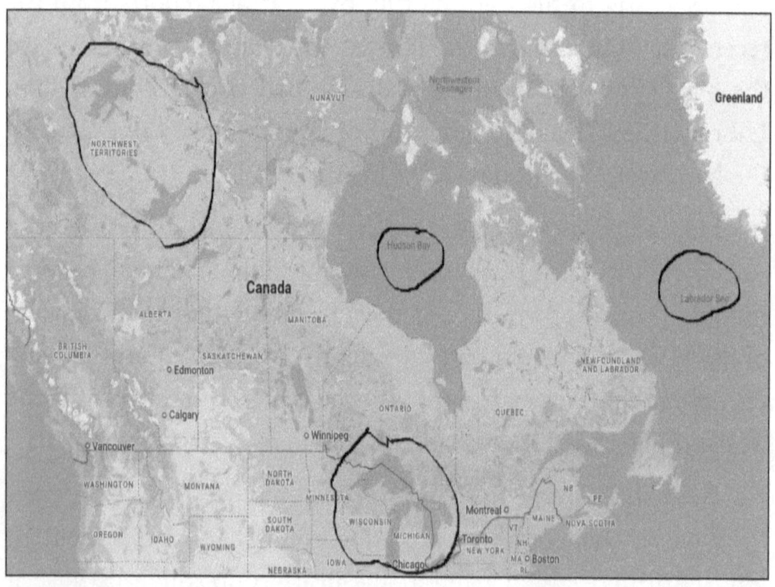

He circled the three main names mentioned by Martin... and stood there thinking. Then he took a pen and jotted down some points on a piece of paper...

1. What is common in these water bodies?

2. What is special about these water bodies?

3. What purpose would they serve in case of an emergency?

Nash noticed that apart from Lake Superior and Great Bear Lake, the other two major water bodies were of saltwater. Lake Superior and Great Bear Lake were of freshwater.

"I can understand Lake Superior and Lake Great Bear... 'cause they both provide potable water. But why Hudson Bay and Labrador Sea? Also, if someone has to deploy a permanent underwater base, it cannot be deeper than one thousand feet at the most. This means that the underwater base would be closer to the shores... shores of Canada... obviously!" Nash thought to himself.

So, what is common in these water bodies is Canada. They are all in and near Canada.

What is special about these locations... they are all manageable by the US.

Nash wrote down the answers next to his questions. "What purpose?" he wondered.

"Emergency hideout? What emergency? The worst-case scenario would be a nuclear strike. Water readily transmits shock waves, so while being underwater and in a ditch may shield someone from infrared and gamma radiation, shockwaves may crush... unless... unless you are under a protected shield underwater....!!!" Nash stood near the map, deep in thought.... Then suddenly, it came to him. "Jeez. This has nothing to do with an underwater habitat for long-term dwellings. That is just an eyewash. The project is initiated by someone powerful, so he is making sure that his life remains safe in case of an emergency. The space missiles are easy to understand. Now the picture is clear."

"WTF...!!!" Nash exclaimed... and then he zoomed in on the locations... he observed the landscape carefully... quickly jotted down his thoughts on paper... and then turned off the screen.

Nash then gathered all the papers he was poring over, stacked them, put them in the paper shredder, collected the shredded papers in a garbage bag… went to the living room, lit the fire in the fireplace, and then slowly added all the shredded papers to the fire. He waited until all the papers were burned and turned to ashes. Then he put out the fire, turned off the light, and went to the bedroom. It was almost 4 AM. Nash knew what his action plan was. Nash decided not to share his thoughts with anyone… not even with Martin. It was way too dangerous. That was why he had destroyed all the evidence of his "research."

Sergei had duly passed on the intel that Ludolf was meeting Chinese leadership in China, and the discussion topics were missile and radar technology as well as Biotech.

That was just enough for Langley to send a lorry load of field agents to keep Ludolf under surveillance. From experience, Sergei knew that the Chinese would have also employed their net of spooks. Sergei had also sent a signal to Alexei to be on guard if he intended to meet Ludolf.

However, today, Sergei was a bit disturbed because he had come to understand that Nash had called in sick. He was apparently down with flu. After Covid, everybody was weary of anyone with a cold. Sergei thought, "Better to let the weekend pass by and it is even better to wait for a week."

But at that precise moment, Nash was on his way to Bear Island in Newfoundland and Labrador… on the Canadian shores of the Labrador Sea. He intended to visit Nunalla Egg River in Caribou River Park Reserve near Hudson Bay and Délı̨nę in the Northwest Territories near Great Bear Lake during his visit. Nash was quite sure that his trip would be quite productive.

New Delhi, India

Pranab Ramaswami, acting as the Chief News Editor of Laser Media House's News section, worked for RAW in reality. He had seen the rule of Indian Congress regimes and had corroborated evidence of them having worked hand in glove with Pakistani politicians and the ISI. Pranab had seen innocent people getting killed due to the two regimes' selfish agendas. "Creating anarchic conditions in India and the subcontinent and not allowing India to progress had always been the agenda of the Western powers." Pranab had shared his opinion with his colleagues many times.

If the ongoing elections were anything to go by, Pranab had his own thoughts. Based on the evidence he had; the substantial interference of the US-based Borge Ross and his agents had spread throughout India. Pranab had decided to write down his thoughts in the form of a report… which could perhaps start off another debate in the media… and Pranab certainly wanted that to happen. He was editing what he had written…

"A man known to harbor hidden agendas, Ross had always been quite vocal about his 'mission' or 'dream' for India, that of dislodging the current Prime Minister, Mr. Dodi, and 'making democracy flourish again' in India. This, to some analysts, might appear to be nothing but an open threat to meddle with the electoral process in the world's largest democracy… while some analysts, employed on Ross's payroll, may take a very passive view."

"Ross's dubious China link, which became public in the 1980s, also raised questions about the reason behind his interest in India and its neighbors. The timing of the smear campaigns launched by the 93-year-old philanthropist's dirty tricks gang—just before parliament sessions and now just before the grand G20 Summit—raised doubts about a larger conspiracy aimed at discrediting Indian institutions, the economy, the corporates and above all the Indian Prime Minister, who had personally scripted the revival of the economy from the gloomy situation in 2013 when India had slipped into the category of 'fragile five' economies—a group of nations that had become increasingly reliant on risky foreign investment to fund their growth."

"Free Societies Establishment remained one of the major global donors that had consistently funded causes and individuals working on so-called accountability and inclusion, in the stated (vested?) interest of greater democratization… a 'free for all' utopian concept. This motivation often had been equated with support for dissidents and political opposition to power, had traditionally landed him in the crosshairs of political leadership wherever his funding went. India had been the only major power that had pricked the 93-year-old billionaire…. Other countries were all minnows. Russia and China were far too big and shielded for Ross to even try."

"One is compelled to see Ross's work on 'free societies' as either a penance or a smokescreen for larger global domination. The two themes that had been consistent in Ross's detraction were… the first being his idea of free societies, which, in its pursuit of inclusion, was generally seen as a gateway for diluting the dominant groups in the political systems. Thus, a range of causes, such as minority rights, immigration, gender diversity, which tended to be driven by progressives, were on the wrong side of conservative politics. These helped cement the notion of Ross as a manipulator from the outside, attempting to change the fundamental nature of social and political systems. The second theme was Anti-Semitism, which while rarely spoken out loud, fed on the idea of Ross as a Jewish financier with evil unstated intent and perhaps it had something to do with his disturbed childhood as a Jew in the Nazi-occupied country."

"While several countries in the West, most prominently Hungary, Poland, and the US, had seen strong campaigns presenting Ross as an alternate villain during elections, he had for the first time become a widely talked-about figure on social media in India. In fact, he was made bigger than life by the Indian media. This was driven by his comments on the current Indian Prime Minister and democracy at a conference in Munich, where he specifically had called into question the quality of Indian democracy, especially for Muslims, under Indian Prime Minister Dodi and the role of crony capitalism in its continuity in India. In any case, Ross had no business to comment on a country to which he neither belonged nor was associated either by birth or by religion if he practiced one."

"The EU had banned Ross, but politicians in India wanted to believe him and convince the Indian voters that the messiah of humanity and transparency had found a 'corruption angle' in the superb performance of a top company and that the government and their watchdogs in the country were at fault for not clipping the wings of the company."

"With an annual outlay of $1.5 billion, the Ross family's FSE claimed to be on a self-proclaimed crusade against human rights violations and upholding of democratic institutions and practices. It had been a known fact that Ross had signed a pact with a Chinese spy operative in the 1980s and had pumped substantial amounts of money into the country for economic system reform. Going by Ross's network's ambitions to spread its tentacles in India, the easiest way for it would be to install a puppet regime… and who better than Mehul Nandhi would be an ideal puppet. Dealing with the current Prime Minister, whom even China wants ousted, appeared to be giving Ross's network a nightmare."

"A weak India would not be able to highlight the cause of the Global South, and Ross's network wanted to use its hit jobs to spread confusion about the country and its capabilities, notwithstanding the success of India's moon mission and the growth in the fields of UPI, financial inclusion, the space industry, and poverty alleviation. Forces outside India—and those within the country that had allegedly coordinated with Ross's network—must also have had a shock that the OCCRP allegations against an Indian corporation had not caused upheaval similar to the one caused by a similar report earlier this year."

"The notion of behind-the-scenes management of affairs was commonly attributed to Ross wherever he was seen to have had funding. The presence of the VP of the Free Society Establishment- India Branch in the Bharat Jodo Yatra, where he walked directly next to Mehul Nandhi, access to whom was quite controlled, had presented strong evidence of a definite link."

"Overall, the focus of this messaging on Ross is that he is a backer of Mehul Nandhi's party. Since Mehul is being presented on multiple social media with the metaphor of a puppeteer, it amounts to Mehul as being controlled by Borge Ross. Several reports suggest a connection between the Nandhi family and

Ross. Given the broad range of investments made by Ross in the past, also his own access to political and business elites over the years of Mehul's party's rule, there are connections between the Nandhi family and Ross."

Pranab reread the report, smiled, and muttered to himself... "Let the fireworks begin now. It would be fun to watch. Who knows, Ross may someday send his henchmen to get rid of me!"

Moscow, Russia

May 20, 2024; 06.30 PM

Alexei had just returned from his weekend stay at his dacha, which was situated in Peredelkino, to the southwest of Moscow. It was quite relaxing, and he needed that break. Before he left, he had received the intel from Sergei that Ludolf was under constant surveillance. This meant that it would be way too risky for Ludolf to meet Alexei… even if he tried.

Alexei had read Ludolf quite well during his China visit and had seen Ludolf somewhat differently. Alexei opined that Ludolf was a daredevil and did not care two hoots for anybody or anything. He would do what he wanted to do irrespective of the circumstances. Ludolf's background and his support, inclination, and sympathy towards the extreme right-wingers… the Neo-Nazis, made Alexei think that Ludolf was a no-nonsense go-getter. The way he had built his empire and the way he ran it with tight control proved his mental strength.

"No harm in trying… but what are we going to discuss? In any case, Ludolf must have guessed that the Chinese guys were creating a smoke screen," Alexei thought. "It is actually the Biotech that the Chinese were keen on collaborating with Ludolf. Possibly, the Chinese are developing some bio-weaponry and need some help. But the missile thing seems to me just hogwash."

"Even though the relations with Germany are strained due to the ongoing Ukraine war, the business, except for the gas, is going on as usual… so, calling Ludolf and meeting him should not be an issue," Alexei was trying to convince himself.

"Alright, let me take a chance and call Ludolf. Let me see what he has to say." Alexei brought out his cell phone and started pulling out Ludolf's number, which he had stored under a different name.

After two rings, the phone was answered.

"Hello there!"

"Hello, hope I am not disturbing you during your dinner meeting," Alexei said lightly.

"No. You are welcome to speak," Ludolf replied.

"Is there a possibility of meeting in the coming weeks… perhaps in Austria… or have you now been put under the microscope?" Alexei said.

Ludolf laughed loudly. "You are very perceptive and also direct."

"Well, yes. Because when you deal with the Chinese, you are already under two microscopes… the Chinese and the Americans," Alexei replied.

"Yes. I know, but I don't care because I have my things to do… whether they like it or not. And frankly, who cares? I am not going to ask their permission and wait for them to say yes or no. No way. I don't give a damn," Ludolf said. His voice had hardened.

"Great. I like that attitude and approach. So, is a meeting a possibility?" Alexei reminded Ludolf about the meeting.

"Ah, yes. The meeting… Austria, you said… It should be possible. If you can call me tomorrow morning, I should be able

to tell you the day and the time. You be ready with a place to meet. Since you suggested Austria, I am guessing it is Vienna and that you must be a frequent visitor and know the place well," Ludolf said.

"Yes, to all. I will call you tomorrow morning at 9.30," Alexei answered.

"Okay. I will wait for your call. Thank you, and good night."

"Good night," Alexei cut off the call.

"The guy is quite sharp. It would be fun to deal with him," Alexei said to himself as he cut off the call.

Langley, Virginia, US

May 31, 2024; 07.30 PM

Nash was at his desk in his study. It had been a couple of weeks since his return from Canada. He had been to all three places… Bear Island in Newfoundland and Labrador … on the Canadian shores of the Labrador Sea, Nunalla Egg River in Caribou River Park Reserve near Hudson Bay, and Délı̨nę in the Northwest Territories near Great Bear Lake.

He had seen first-hand what was happening on the ground there. Pretending to be a tourist and dressed like one, he had captured the ground reality in some photographs, in some videos. He had spoken to the workers working on the ground there… which is what he had expected to find before he had traveled there. He had seen the construction drawings, clicked pictures. He was just a curious tourist awed by nature and the amazing work that was being done in the natural environment.

"Seriously, you mean people would come and live here? Is this some kind of a hotel or a tourist resort," Nash had quipped.

"Maybe. We haven't got a clue, Sir. But one thing's for sure… people like us can only build this kind of stuff… but can't afford to stay in them… never," the man on the site replied.

So, now Nash knew exactly what Operation Castellon was. Nash knew quite well what Operation Taranis would be. It was quite obvious now as to who was financing these projects and why. The way things were now, Nash was quite sure about the "when" part of it. Where and how he had already figured it out.

Nash had decided not to reveal anything to anyone and not keep any evidence of his "knowledge" of these "operations" anywhere… either at his office or at his residence. He had decided not to tell even Sergei because it was dangerous. If anything, he would tell Sergei that he had decided to let it pass.

His excuse of being "down with flu" had worked well, and no one had any reason not to believe him. Overall, Nash was happy with the outcome. Nash expected Sergei to call sooner rather than later because Nash knew how Sergei worked and also where his loyalties lay.

Operation Taranis was just putting the nukes in space… in short. Nash suspected that both the other parties… the Russians and the Chinese would also be at it. The nuke in space need not have to be of a Tsar Bomba size 'cause even a small-sized missile hitting the Earth with force would make a solid impact.

Any missile fired from space impacting Earth would cause a devastating localized explosion due to its high velocity, potentially creating a large crater, significant shockwaves, and extreme heat at the impact site. The severity would depend on the missile's size, composition, material, explosive or radioactive, and impact location. Also, depending on the missile's design, it could cause widespread damage through secondary effects like firestorms and atmospheric disturbances. If the material of the missile had radioactive components, it could amplify the damage significantly.

If a nuclear bomb were detonated in space, aimed at Earth, the primary impact would create a massive electromagnetic pulse (EMP) that could induce high voltage surges, crippling electrical grids across large areas of the planet, causing widespread power outages and potentially disrupting critical infrastructure. The higher the detonation altitude, the larger the area affected by the EMP.

Even if the blast itself didn't directly hit a populated area, depending on the altitude of the explosion, the affected region could be continent-wide, with further damage from intense heat radiation and potential radioactive fallout depending on the detonation point and atmospheric conditions.

If the nuclear explosion happened in the low earth orbit, it could severely damage or destroy nearby satellites, impacting communication and navigation systems. A large-scale nuclear detonation in space could potentially disrupt the Earth's climate by altering atmospheric conditions. The type of nuclear warhead and its yield would significantly impact the severity of the effects.

Nash understood the consequences… but what he did not understand was who would have control of the nuclear button… who would have the authority to push the button when the time came. Because the project was privately funded, it was likely that the Feds did not approve the idea. If it wasn't theirs, then it was obvious that whoever in private had control over the button would be the King because he could destroy the earth-based nukes and nuke sites from space effortlessly.

"But then, there is SpaceX… a private company operating in an area which hitherto had been dominated by NASA. So, why not Raytheon or Lockheed Martin or their major stockholder or owner… decide to put and control the nukes in space? Possibly, the Feds can't afford it or don't want to be seen as an offender of any treaty… and hence collaborated with someone like Cobblestone to do the honors… but by staying behind the curtains. Quite possible. Perhaps that is where DARPA comes into the picture." Nash thought to himself.

"Operation Castellon is the logical outcome of Operation Taranis," Nash said to himself. The race for "global control" had now passed from key political players to private organizations… who had the money and the resources to twist anybody's neck if they did not fall in line with their agenda.

Nash laughed to himself and muttered, "Now the Rosses of this world look like insects who could be crushed easily." Nash had read about the sarcastic remarks made by Borge Ross on Gregory Brink when Brink had entered the Chinese Housing Market. "That 93-year-old guy has gone nuts. I guess all these old billionaires, who think they are demigods, should get their nuts checked twice a day."

More than scared, Nash was amused because he could imagine the scenario when the cat would be out of the bag and the Feds would know that someone had put nukes up there in space and also had control!

"It would be fun," Nash smiled to himself. He had his plan in place now and would start working on it.

"Just one last piece… I will have to involve Lemur to get it done," Nash muttered to himself as he started clearing his desk.

Salzburg, Austria

June 2, 2024; 07.00 PM

Alexei had changed the venue to Salzburg rather than going to the crowded Vienna. Even in Salzburg, Alexei reckoned that the tourist season would have started, and hence, he had selected an upscale restaurant situated on the top of a building… IMLAUER Sky… located on Rainerstraße. Ludolf had liked the idea as well.

Ludolf was the first to reach and was duly directed towards the reserved table. Alexei, who was standing on the pavement opposite the building, was observing the crowd and making sure that no one was following them or keeping an eye on them. After Ludolf entered the building, Alexei waited for five minutes to make sure Ludolf was not followed. Then, he entered the building and joined Ludolf.

"My apologies for being late… but I was making sure that no one was following you," Alexei said, shaking hands with Ludolf.

"No worries. Have you served in the armed forces or in the KGB?" Ludolf was direct.

Alexei laughed… "No… that is not my area of expertise. But during the Soviet occupation of Afghanistan, I was there doing my trading business. So, I learned the art of survival. This is a part of that learning."

"Makes sense. I like it. Survival of the fittest," Ludolf said.

Looking at the menu, they zeroed in on "Castello di Ama, Gaiole, Tuscany 1995 Chianti Classico Gran Selezione 'Vigneto Bellavista'."

"Should be fine," Ludolf said.

The waiter bowed… and left. He came back with the bottle and two wine glasses. Obviously seasoned, he poured a little into the glasses for tasting. Both Ludolf and Alexei tasted and nodded in admiration. The waiter filled the glasses, leaving the bottle in a holder beside the table.

Ludolf and Alexei discussed the menu and agreed on one starter and selected their own main courses.…

They ordered… Zweierlei Von Der Steirischen Kumer Lachsforelle… a duo of Salmon and Trout with sour cream terrine, orange-fennel salad & red radish.

And for the main course, Ludolf ordered… Geschmortes Rinderbackerl.… A Braised Beef Cheek with truffled polenta, roasted celery & herbs.

Alexei selected… Im Ganzen Gebratene Lammkrone.… A Roasted Rack of Lamb with Ratatouille, potato soufflé, and tomato gravy.

The waiter nodded in appreciation of the selection and left.

"I was not sure if you would accept to meet since you are under constant surveillance," Alexei opened the conversation, making sure that they would not be overheard.

"I don't know because even if I am… I don't seem to know it or sense it… the surveillance I meant," Ludolf replied.

"There are various means of surveillance these days… I am sure you must know them all. But it is and must be obvious to you as well," Alexei replied.

"I don't give a damn. They can't do shit. They need me, I don't need them. Period." Ludolf was blunt.

"I like that attitude," Alexei raised his glass and said, "to your fearless attitude." Ludolf toasted as well.

"Whatever the Chinese discussed never made any sense to me… the missile deal I meant. It seemed to be an eyewash. The real purpose of the Chinese inviting you there must have been different. I was an afterthought, I felt," Alexei said in an extremely low voice.

"Yes. I also feel so. I guess the main purpose was to discuss with me about a possible tie-up for their Biotech research needs… that is what I felt. But since I declined to accept their reasoning, they shifted gears to this phony Iranian deal. Although…" Ludolf halted as the waiter approached and laid down the starters and served them on their plates.

"Although… what?" Alexei asked as soon as the waiter left.

"This is my own thinking. I have no proof or any evidence… but I felt that the missiles they had in mind did not make sense if they had to be used by Iran on Israel. You see, the ones the Chinese are interested in are those ultra-modern 6th Gen lightweight, super precision missiles… which would hit the target with 200% accuracy… not a millimeter here or there. But they are not the long-range hypersonic heavyweight missiles that would cause heavy damage to the area." Ludolf stopped.

"Go on… I am listening," Alexei said.

"I mean where Iranians would use these missiles. For what purpose? On what targets? It simply did not make sense to me. Then something struck me. What if the Chinese are trying to put the missiles in space, directed towards the Earth… then these missiles would be perfect… lightweight, super accurate… no need for fuel or oxygen for release and take-off. If you fix a nuke warhead, you are done. The Chinese can send these to space with their rockets… satellites… and can install them on their space station… or on any military satellites. Who is going to check? A shipload of missiles would serve them for a long time. They can reverse engineer and invent their own types… who knows? But, of course, this is my assumption. I could be wrong too." Ludolf stopped.

Alexei had stopped eating and was intently listening to every word Ludolf was saying. "Interesting… makes sense. Quite probable, quite possible," Alexei commented.

"I am sorry, but you would not be able to make the money you would have made," Ludolf said to Alexei.

"Oh, no worries. Money is the least of the botheration. I am happy that I have not signed my own death warrant… and you, too. I would have never thought about it… that angle, I mean, because I don't understand the technology part. So, what next?" Alexei asked.

"Well, let them come back and ask… I will tell them that I am not interested. If they increase the stakes and demand… then we are sure. But in any case, I will not be ready to provide them with the 6th Gen stuff. It is like you said… signing our death warrant. But let me ask you this… Russia had these plans in the past… yes?" Ludolf asked.

"Yes, Russia was then Soviet Russia. Not today's Russia. We had the plans… then plans are always there in one form or the other. The question is implementation. If China implements it… then all the bets are off both for Russia and the US. Oh yes, they would also jump at it… maybe they already are at it… who knows… because they probably knew why you were in China," Alexei said, looking into the eyes of Ludolf.

"Possibly. That means now we will all be at the mercy of you three," Ludolf laughed.

"Look, my opinion is simple… no empire has lasted ad infinitum. They eventually collapsed. No one can own the world. If you look at the history… the Sumerians, the Egyptians, the Mesopotamians, the Greeks, the Romans, the Mayans, the Incas, the Aztecs… and even… the Japanese, the Chinese and the Europeans… the Dutch, the Brits, the Portuguese, the Spaniards… to even Hitler for that matter… everybody tried to be the owner of the world… they all lost eventually. So… why try to be greedy? Then there is this modern breed of organizations, corporations who want to own the world… dictate their terms… like the Americans… They want to own the world by controlling dollars, the World Bank, the IMF, sanctions… I am not sure where and when this will end. It is frustrating to even think about it." Alexei said… and waited for Ludolf's reaction.

"I have no clue. Yes, it is true that I personally don't like certain sections or types of people. I believe in keeping everything in their own respective backyards… Religion, Faith, Customs, Traditions, Beliefs… Theological Ideas… Philosophies… everything. Everybody remains in their own circles and does not force their ideals on others. Remain Segregated and not integrated," Ludolf said.

"Interesting thought. I don't know how many will support that… Particularly in the so-called 'democratic' West. They are so focused on integration."

"You mean people like Borge Ross? He is a weirdo," Ludolf said. "But then, by and large, what you say is right… how many will accept it?"

The main dishes were served. The rest of the conversation was concentrated on food and wine. They talked on various subjects… including China's possible attempt at developing some new generation bio-weaponry. After having coffee, they left at midnight… promising each other to meet again soon.

Alexei was now certain of what Sergei had messaged. He would have to provide this bit of detail to the President tomorrow.

Frankfurt, Germany

June 3, 2024; 09.00 AM

Ludolf had come to his office directly from Salzburg at 6.00 am. He had been reviewing the progress of the ultra-special project which had been initiated by him after he had studied some of the technical reports on the developments undertaken during Hitler's regime.

"Those guys were f**king ahead of their times. No wonder my grandfather adored them," Ludolf had thought when he read those reports. Having selected one such unfinished project from that time, Ludolf had initiated serious research and was now in the process of perfecting the end product. He was sure that other countries like the US, Russia, or China may develop this product someday in the future… but Ludolf wanted to be the first one to have it.

Now, the efforts and the money he had invested had produced the desired results. Ludolf was ecstatic but did not show it on his face. "I want to install the product in multiple places without anyone knowing it. Only I would have the controls and would exercise my rights when the time came."

"Surprise is the key… Shock and Awe, Blitzkrieg - rapid attack," Ludolf said to himself. He had a broad smile on his face… "Grandfather would have been so proud of me," he thought.

Ludolf hated the liberal stance of the German government in letting the Muslim immigrants come into and settle in Germany. They would bring their beliefs and culture and would never assimilate with the German culture. Ludolf was certain that sooner rather than later these Islamic immigrants would ask for their pound of flesh. "Germany has not learned the lesson from the past. They are repeating the same mistake they made with the Jews. I guess I will have to use the Third Way guys to remove this infestation," Ludolf thought to himself.

He could visualize how he could use his new development/invention to get rid of these pests… And he was pleased… Because no one would ever know how the pests were removed and who removed them. It would happen in a fraction of a minute.

New York City, NY, US

June 8, 2024; 12.30 PM

The location was Prospect Park West, Brooklyn… the same eating joint, Badawi Café, that Leo frequented. This time around, Leo had another company. While he was standing to place an order, there was another man… perhaps Hispanic, in his late forties, who almost lost his balance while removing his heavy backpack from his shoulder.

Sheepishly… he muttered apologies and said in a tired voice… "Signs of getting old."

"No worries," Leo replied. He felt sympathy for the man.

"What is good in this place? It is my first time here. Have you been here before?" the man asked.

"Yes, I come here frequently. The food is sumptuous and reasonably priced. What is good… well, almost everything. I usually stick to Kebabs. There is, of course, the Falafel and Shawarma. I would suggest you try Kebabs. They are really juicy and tasty."

"Okay… as you say, son," the man said.

The place was crowded. While they were standing, the old man spotted a table with two empty seats. He said to Leo, "I guess I will go and occupy the seats when you get your order, come and join me, then I will go and collect my tray."

Leo liked the idea and said, "That is great. Thank you."

After waiting for a while, both had their trays in front of them. The man ate slowly. He seemed hungry but was eating slowly, as if the food would last him until the end of the day.

"So, what do you do for a living?" the man asked.

"Well, I am a journalist," Leo replied… unsure whether the man would understand.

"Oh… that is a very noble profession… if you are reporting the truth… which is quite rare these days," the man answered.

"Yes, that is what I try to do. I am glad you are of the same opinion. And what do you do?"

"Well, I used to own a bookshop in Boston. Over time, people started losing interest in buying physical books. They started getting everything digitally… Kindle and that kind of stuff. So, eventually, I had to close down my shop. Now, I try to do some janitorial work to keep going. It pays for my living expenses… but not beyond."

"Yes, what you said is right. People do not want to read long stuff. They need short and sweet… like the Tweets," Leo replied.

"Why don't you write books… and publish them online? People like to read real stuff… Investigative Journalism, it is called."

"Yes, that is what I am… an investigative journalist. But I don't have a real story to write," Leo said.

"What if you get one… will you not attempt?"

"Why not? I will certainly attempt. But where will I get one?" Leo asked.

"You never know. You should keep your eyes, ears, and options open… and mouth shut. You must open it only to ask relevant questions… get the real intelligence… filter out the noise, the garbage. Then you will see the real gems under the flowing muddy water," the man said.

"You speak so well… obviously you had a bookstore… You must be well-read," Leo said.

The man smiled with sadness in his eyes. "I had… past tense. It is no more. Anyway. I am sure you will get a story to write. Nobody will hand you over a story. You will find bits and pieces… You will have to connect the dots and do research and then understand and then write the real story. No point in writing bits and pieces. No one reads them," the man said. He had almost wiped his dish clean.

"Well, yes. Thank you for your kind advice. I really appreciate it," Leo said.

"I gave you suggestions, son. I am in no position to advise anybody," the man said with sadness in his voice.

"I would like to meet you again and talk to you. You are quite knowledgeable and interesting. Where do you live…?"

"Well, here in NYC but it's not a great place to meet."

"No, what I meant was you can visit my place. It is not a great place either. It is a shared one. But we can meet and chat… if it is okay with you. Perhaps on a weekend."

"Well, if it is not of any inconvenience to you… Where do you live?"

Leo quickly jotted down his address on the back of the restaurant bill as well as his phone number. Please call me during any weekend and then we can fix up the time. It was great meeting you. I learned a lot today," Leo said.

"I am happy if you feel so. Thank you. I will call you sometime," the man said, picked up his heavy backpack and left.

Leo sat there for a couple of minutes mulling over what the man had told him. Then he remembered that he had not even asked the man his name… "How very stupid of me," Leo said to himself as he stood up with his tray. He placed the tray over the bin and left.

The old man sat in his car, watching Leo leave the restaurant. The old man had removed the wig he was wearing… so Leo would not have recognized him even if he had seen him.

New York, NY, USA

June 16, 2024

Being Sunday, Leo had no specific plans. He had finished a small article he was writing for one of the agencies he worked for. Once the article had been sent, he made a cup of coffee for himself and took it to his laptop. He browsed various news items… nothing specific was of any interest… there was this interesting case of a criminal lawyer who was charged with first-degree murder. Most newspapers said that the criminal lawyer was being framed because he had raised his voice against human trafficking. The people involved in human trafficking were sending a message to him… "back off else…" There was a political angle as well… because the lawyer was a firm supporter of the Reps… a right-winger.

Leo wondered what would happen to the lawyer. Leo remembered the words of the man… write a book… "This is a good subject… but I don't think I have the power to reach anywhere near these guys."

Presently, there was a knock on the door. When Leo opened the door, there was an Uber Eats guy holding a pizza box for him…

"Leo?" he asked.

"Yes…" It is for you. The pizza guy handed over the pizza box… which was quite warm.

"But I never ordered a pizza," Leo said.

"I don't know about that. It has your name and address. I am supposed to deliver it. I did. Thank you," said the Uber Eats guy and left Leo standing at his doorstep with a warm box of pizza in his hands.

Leo shrugged his shoulders and came inside the apartment, closing the door behind him. "What the heck… somebody ordered me a pizza. Let me check my cell phone in case there is a message," Leo said to himself.

"Jeez… this is weird. There is no message. Who the hell has sent this pizza to me? Oh, well… if it is sent to me… let me eat it at least while it is fresh," Leo said to himself as he opened the box. He saw an envelope attached to the inner portion of the lid of the box. The envelope was also quite warm.

"Now, what the heck is this?" Leo wondered as he snapped the envelope off the lid and opened it. There was a note inside which read, "Pentagon's Private Operations files - Find them."

Leo was stunned… "What the hell are Pentagon Private files? Is this some kind of a joke?" He looked at the pizza… it was warm and real. He took a bite, and it tasted quite good… it was for real.

Masanielli Pizzeria… the box cover had the name printed in maroon, which looked as if it were embossed on the box.

Leo decided to call the pizzeria and ask who had placed the order for him. He opened Google on his laptop and searched for Masanielli Pizzeria. There were quite a few sundry notes on the quality of the pizza from Masanielli, but Leo could not find the website of the pizzeria.

"Maybe they are old-fashioned and maybe they don't have a website," Leo thought to himself. He then tried to find the address of the pizzeria. There was no mention of it on the pizza box.

Since the aroma of pizza was quite tempting, Leo decided to eat the pizza while searching on the web. By the time he had finished more than three-quarters of the pizza, he found a mention of Masanielli in one of the comments: "Pity that such an age-old wonderful pizzeria had the misfortune of going out of business."

Leo had suddenly stopped eating and reread the comment… it was dated December 1997. "WTF… I will be damned," Leo said to himself. After searching for over an hour, he did find the address of Masanielli Pizzeria. Leo jotted it down on his cell phone, closed his laptop, got dressed, and left the apartment. He wanted to go and check the address and ask questions.

What puzzled him is… how come the Box of Masanielli Pizzeria surfaced in 2024 when the pizzeria was closed in 1997? Who would have the old stock of the pizza boxes… and more importantly… who would put a fresh pizza in the box and deliver it to his address… pretending to be from Uber Eats? And more importantly… why would someone play such a game with him… that too about the Pentagon?

The address belonged to that part of NYC known as Little Italy. It was on the Lower East Side in the southeastern part of Manhattan. Leo decided to park his car at a Public Parking lot and walk to Mulberry Street.

When Leo reached the specific address, there was a leather shop specializing in leather goods. Being a Sunday, it was closed. There were a few people walking on the street. Leo looked around, trying to find an elderly person because Leo felt that an elderly person would know about Masanielli.

Finally, Leo found an elderly man sitting on the doorstep of what appeared to be a grocery store. Leo approached him… wished him, and said… "By the way, would you happen to know where Masanielli Pizzeria is located? I have been trying to find it for the last half an hour."

The old man looked at Leo with surprise on his face.

"Oh… it is just that someone gave me an address saying opposite Masanielli Pizzeria," Leo tried to clarify.

"That place doesn't exist anymore. It closed down a long time ago… maybe 30 years ago," the old man said.

"Oh… was it very famous?" Leo tried to probe.

"Well, he made good pizza for sure. But when Georgio's young son died in a car accident, he got shattered… He just sat there staring at the ceiling. Made no pizza no more. He died too in a month. Did not eat, drink… no sleep. Had no wife."

'Oh…sad to hear that. So, who took over his shop?'

"The bank guys. They took over. Some people came, cleaned up the place and then some other shop opened in its place." The old man got up and slowly started walking away without saying another word.

Leo wanted to ask… which bank, etc., but thought otherwise. He slowly started walking back to the public car park. This whole thing was quite intriguing.

"Maybe you will get a book to write someday… it will come in bits and pieces." Suddenly, the words of that old Hispanic man sounded in Leo's ears.

"Perhaps… who knows. I need to find out what that note means…" Leo had already forgotten the name Pentagon Private files!

New York, NY, US

June 18, 2024, 03:30 PM

Jerry had planned to leave early for his home as he had no classes in the afternoon. However, the demonstration staged by Cathy Dexter had rocked the campus.

"She has gone bonkers over the Palestinians," Jerry said to himself as he saw the crowded campus with placards, Palestinian flags, and students wearing headgear with anti-Israel slogans.

"This has gone way too far. Not sure why the university authorities can't stop this madness." Jerry was furious as he tried to find his way out.

As Jerry came towards the rear of the crowd, he heard his name being called out. Jerry looked around. He saw someone waving at him from the extreme rear end of the crowd. Jerry recognized the face. "Oh, it is that journalist guy… Leo whatever," Jerry said to himself as he started moving towards him.

"Hey there, how are you? What brings you here… this demo? Our campus should be renamed "demo-land." Jerry's voice was quite sarcastic.

"That it is. There is no doubt. I am sure Mr. Borge Ross must be paying enough dough to the university folks to allow this circus to go on unchecked," Leo said.

Both Jerry and Leo were unaware that a set of eyes was watching them from a distance… albeit due to the noise, it would be difficult to hear Jerry and Leo's conversation... a good lip reader would have easily understood the conversation.

"So, what's up? You came here to cover this... this shit?" Jerry asked.

"Yeah... trying to keep myself current. Up to date, which is. Oh, by the way, a weird thing happened the day before yesterday... on Sunday.... Want to hear?" Leo asked.

"Shoot."

Leo narrated the pizza incident, including his visit to Mulberry Street to find Masanielli Pizzeria.

"What bothers me is the note... I am not sure what the "Pentagon's Private" part is. What is private about the Pentagon? It is a federal agency," Leo asked.

"Well, I have no clue. But the very fact that it has come to you is because you are an investigative journalist... so that somebody is asking you to investigate... privately. Maybe there is an issue with the Pentagon or at the Pentagon. Maybe they deal directly with the arms suppliers who belong to private firms. Isn't there an arms lobby or something... Heck... I don't really know. I hardly get time to read even the WhatsApp messages... forget the news items," Jerry replied.

"Hey, your father has a publishing company, right?"

"Yes... so what?"

"Will he publish my book whenever it is ready?" Leo asked.

"Your book? Have you written one, or are you writing one... I guess you will have to ask him. But I don't see why not," Jerry replied cautiously.

"Just inquiring... I may write eventually. But seriously, what do you think about this pizza thingy?"

"Look, my guess is if somebody wants you to investigate, then he will provide you with more clues in the future," Jerry said. "But think of it this way, Leo… why you? Who knows you as a hardcore investigative journalist? And last but not least… what would he or she or they… whoever it is, what the heck do they want you to do after you have investigated whatever this Pentagon thing is?"

"Hmmm… I really don't know, Jerry."

"Well, maybe they want you to write the book you are talking about… like 'All the President's Men' …. Isn't it a possibility?"

"Yes, that is quite possible. I will have to wait and see," Leo said passively. He did not know where to start.

"Hey, I meant to ask you… did you happen to tell any of your contacts that my father has a publishing company?" Jerry asked.

"No. As a matter of fact, I had forgotten about it… Just this book idea brought back the memory. Why?"

"Someone had come to find me here at Columbia… asking me to introduce him to my father. When I asked him how he knew about my father's business, he said his business associate told him. No names were mentioned. Later on, I felt it was quite suspicious… in fact, fake."

"Oh, you've got to be careful. No, rest assured I haven't told anyone."

"By the way, I have now shifted from the dorm to Jersey City. My family has a place there."

"Is that so? Hmm… how long does it take for you to commute?"

'About an hour and a half… it is okay,' Jerry replied.

"There seem to be a few Islamic radicals present here right now. They don't belong to the university," Leo pointed to a few guys shouting against Israel.

"Well, this is supposed to be a democratic way," Jerry said, outright sarcastic.

"Yeah. Yeah. Human rights and all that crap. Did you hear about the criminal lawyer getting charged with first-degree murder... Man, I tell you... these folks can fix anybody. Money speaks."

"Yes... but be careful when you are researching those Pentagon files," Jerry suggested.

"Yeah... I will be... I will let you know and if you see... rather read anything freaky, please let me know," Leo said.

"Like what?"

"Anything suspicious... not normal... unusual."

"Okay," Jerry just shrugged his shoulders. "Okay, I've got to be going. See you around," Jerry said goodbye.

"Cool. Take care, Jerry," Leo replied, waving back at Jerry.

After Jerry left, Leo stood there for a while, watching the drama unfolding in front of his eyes. But his thoughts were on what Jerry had said... "Why you... what do they want you to do?"

"Funny why this never came to my mind. I should have asked this question myself. Perhaps, like Jerry said... they may send more info my way. But... why me?" Leo kept on thinking about his possible contacts who would be connected to the Pentagon.

The set of eyes that were watching both Leo and Jerry finally decided to move... because there was nothing more to watch.

Jersey City, NJ, US

July 5, 2024; 03.30 AM

It was hot and humid that night. Jerry had been to NYC to see the 4th of July fireworks. He had come back sometime after midnight. Due to the humidity, Jerry was feeling uncomfortable and unable to sleep properly. He had opened the window of his bedroom which faced the street and the opposite house, #208… Sometime later, Jerry had dozed off.

Some strange noise had disturbed his sleep. Cursing, Jerry wanted to go back to sleep, but the light coming from the window of house 208 was bothering him. Jerry, now fully awake, went to the open window. The car was now parked in front of the house. Jerry remembered that when he had returned home, there was no car parked there. He figured that it was the noise of the car that had disturbed him. He looked at his watch; it was 3.30 in the morning.

He saw a man in the room where the light was turned on. The man was trying to pull something on the floor… like a heavy bag or something similar. Jerry noticed that the man was wearing a long coat, as one wears in winter and a hat… it definitely looked spooky to Jerry. It was so hot and humid that night… why would someone wear a winter long coat… Jerry thought.

The man then bent down and tried to pull out something. Jerry realized that the man was pulling out a thick rope… like a hangman's noose. Jerry was terrified… he tried to hide in the shadows.

Perhaps there was a heavy bag on the floor which the man had tried to pull… because the man started taking out various tools from what was lying on the floor. The one object that Jerry could figure out was a pickaxe. It was then that Jerry noticed that the man was wearing work gloves.

Momentarily, Jerry's eyes caught a movement in one of the parked cars on the street. There was someone in the car. Jerry could see the faint silhouette of the man sitting in the driver's seat. Now, who would that be and why the heck is he sitting in the car at this hour… Jerry started feeling terrified.

Suddenly, Leo's words came to his mind… "If you see anything freaky… tell me." This damn thing was outright freaky. Jerry noticed that the man sitting in the car was continuously staring at #208.

"What the heck is going on here?" Jerry wondered.

After another ten minutes of activity, the light in #208 was turned off. There was complete silence thereafter. The man in the car parked on the street was still watching house #208. After some time, Jerry went back to his bed, trying to figure out what was happening… eventually he dozed off.

When he woke up in the morning, it was quarter past eight. Jerry felt tired and decided to sleep a bit more, but last night's images came to his mind, and he jumped to his feet. He looked out of the window… both the cars… the car belonging to #208 and the one keeping a watch on #208 were gone. Just then, Jerry's eyes caught sight of some strange objects lying on his front lawn… which was nothing but a small patch of grass.

Jerry quickly went down, opened the front door, and went out onto the lawn. There were a few strange items lying strewn around… Scattered randomly: a scuba mask, a Buoyancy Control Device (BCD), a snorkel, a piece of concrete, and two pieces of earth tubes.

At first glance, it appeared to be some garbage thrown onto the grass… but Jerry remembered the scene from last night and felt terrified. Not sure what to do… whether to call the police or just let the stuff remain on the lawn… Jerry just stood there looking at the stuff. Finally, he made up his mind. He went inside the house… brought out a fresh garbage bin bag and, one by one, picked up all the objects and put them into the bag. He carried the bag inside. He had decided to show this to Leo.

"Now, why would Leo tell me to watch out for freaky things? How would he know that I would see them? Is he the one making all this up? But Leo does not know where I live…!!!" Jerry was lost in his thoughts. "How the hell should I get in touch with Leo?" Then, he remembered that Leo had given him his cell number. Finally, he got up, shaved, showered, had his breakfast and then called Leo on his cell phone.

Jersey City, NJ, US

July 5, 2025; 02.20 PM

"I have no clue why and who would have thrown these on your front lawn, Jerry. If somebody is trying to send a message or messages to both of us, it means that person or set of people know us well. He or she or they would know that we have met, communicated, and linked in some way… what way… I have no clue," Leo was sharing his thoughts with Jerry. "Unless someone has seen us together at the demo in Columbia."

They were sitting in the kitchen in Jerry's house with the items spread out on the dining table. Leo had arrived precisely at 2.00 pm and had been in conversation with Jerry ever since.

"There are three different objects that I can see… one is a concrete block… this is a broken concrete piece… looks like it was broken by an axe… a sharp one… it is what… just about two inches by two inches…!!! Now, it does not tell us much. I mean, you can practically get these anywhere there is construction work… well, a Foundation being laid more precisely. Yes?" Leo was trying to examine the concrete piece.

"Then there are these scuba diving things… which means what… something underwater… what… Being researched, searched, constructed, hidden? I don't know… The main question is, where on earth? There is water all around us." Leo paused and picked up the earth Tube pieces.

"Now, what the heck are these? I have never seen them before. To me, they look like some kind of tubes for carrying water or maybe some liquid or even air… because they are made up of what… Polyethylene? I mean, these are quite common," Leo paused again.

"So?" Jerry asked.

"So what? Nothing. These tell us nothing except that it is related to construction near or under water. But where? And what is the significance… of letting you or us know? I don't see any relation to the Pentagon either," Leo said. He looked frustrated.

"Did you get any more info on that Pentagon thing?" Jerry inquired.

"Well, I searched on the net… The Pentagon deals with arms, ammunition, and wars all over the globe. They have many departments… and are quite a big entity. Yes, obviously they deal with private companies manufacturing arms and ammunition like Raytheon, Lockheed, Boeing, General Dynamics… some European companies… including firms that deal with satellite communications… food, biotechnology, energy… anything and everything in life. So… someone is expecting me to find a needle in a haystack. I think someone is just taking us for a ride. I am sure that guy… whoever it is… must be having a laugh of his lifetime looking at us running around like headless chickens." Leo sounded angry.

"Well, I don't know. But I am shaken for sure," Jerry said.

"Shaken or stirred… whatever. I don't think there is any meaning to any of these things. I don't want to waste my time chasing a wild goose… if there is indeed one." Leo banged his fist on the table. "I am out," Leo got up and picked up his backpack and started to leave.

"What do you suggest I do with these?" Jerry asked.

"Get a showcase, buddy, and keep them in it. Souvenir," Leo replied. "Okay, see you."

"Well, you had told me if I see or read or hear anything freaky, I should inform you. I did. Now you are being sarcastic," Jerry retorted.

"Look, Jerry, I am kind of frustrated… because I don't like these bits and pieces. If someone wants me to write something and expose someone or something, then they should provide me with the complete details."

"Oh yeah? Then what happens to your 'Investigative Journalism' if you get everything on a silver platter?" Jerry retorted again.

"Touché," Leo said. I am sorry for my outburst. I should not show my frustration. But you are right. I need to investigate on my own. Maybe the Pentagon and these pieces are related. I don't know. Maybe the guy in #208 must have thrown these on your lawn because he must have sensed that you were watching him last night. Well, you told me that he had a pickaxe. So, he could have broken this piece of concrete."

"Maybe. But why us? My thinking is… someone wants you to write the stuff and use my dad's company to publish it… to expose somebody or something. That is why you and I."

"Agreed for a minute. Pray, tell me… write what?" Leo said softly.

"Maybe there is more coming… patience. Let us see. Now that we know we both are in this together… by some weird luck… let us face it," Jerry said.

"Done," Leo said, extending his hand for a handshake, and then said, "Now I must leave. You take care. Call me when you have something, or I will call you if I have something. Okay?"

"Okay," Jerry said… still sitting at the dining table. Leo took his backpack, opened the front door, and left.

Jerry sat there looking at the front door. He was scared of staying alone, but he did not want to admit that to Leo.

Washington D.C., US

July 12, 2024; 08.30 PM

"Laser weapon systems will eventually replace all the kinetic weapons. It will happen sooner than expected," Krish was making a point to Nash over dinner.

They were at Nash's residence in Langley, Virginia. Krish was a college mate of Nash at Princeton. Dr. V. Gopalkerishnan… Krish, to his friends and co-workers, was the head of NASA's Pasadena Lab. After completing graduation in avionics from Princeton, Krish had gone to MIT to complete his PhD in Avionics, specializing in alternate fuel systems for long-range projectiles.

He had then joined the University of Dayton, Ohio, as an Associate Professor. During a symposium where Krish was presenting a paper, he was noticed by the then Director of NASA's Propulsion Lab and was invited Krish to join the organization.

After a couple of months, Krish had accepted the offer and had joined the Propulsion lab, shifting to California. Time passed, and Krish grew in his stature in the organization… reaching the top position. He was in DC to attend a meeting organized by DoD (Dept of Defense) as some top military official from Israel was visiting them and wanted to discuss the specific issues related to the usage of laser beams in their Iran Dome project.

During lunch at one of the restaurants in DC, Nash by chance had bumped into his old college mate and had invited him to his residence for dinner. Krish would be flying back to California the next day in the morning from Dulles.

After initial discussions about family and other topics, Nash casually broached the subject of Krish's visit to DC. Since Nash had already seen the DoD officials with Krish at the restaurant, Krish mentioned in passing the purpose of his visit.

"See, the idea of Laser Weaponry is pretty ancient... we have seen it in some Bond films, in Star Trek and Star Wars... the Death Star and all that. Why... even in Indian mythology... it may not be a mythology now... but yes, even in that era... there were Laser Weaponry. So, the concept is an old one... but it is a rather complicated subject." Krish paused.

"I mean in your backyard Nash; here in Virginia, you will see all the so-called Directed Energy Weapons (DEWs) companies... From Lockheed to Raytheon to Boeing and what have you. They are all registered in Virginia... Even the Brits have opened their shop here... BAE Systems. You know that. Globally too, there are a few firms... Israeli, French, German and Italian. Then there is one which has recently joined the race... a German company... LH Raumfahrt... Understand they have something far more advanced... the 6th or the 7th Gen. But we don't have any details."

Nash nodded and said, "Yes, I know, but I am not sure where this is all going... I mean the weaponry systems."

"The Military Laser Systems Market is segmented by technology... like, for example, Solid-State Lasers, Gas Lasers, and Other Technologies; by application... Directed Energy Weapons, Guidance Systems, Laser Sights, Designators, and

Rangefinders, and Other Applications, etc. DEWs bring benefits such as precision and rapid response. Period," Krish explained.

"Are you also harnessing solar energy for lasers?" Nash asked directly.

"Well, between us… Yes. In theory. A solar-pumped laser refers to a gaseous laser that utilizes solar radiation to energize the laser medium, resulting in high power output. Solar-pumped lasers have been studied since the 1970s and have demonstrated successful utilization of solar radiation for various applications, including carbon dioxide gas lasers and oxygen-iodine lasers." Krish paused and continued… "But as I said, this is all in theory. Nothing is in the reality."

"It will be cheaper… Laser Weaponry, I mean," Nash said.

"Maybe. I have no clue. As far as we are concerned… we are still far away from the Star Wars scenario… wherein the Death Star uses a laser beam to destroy a planet. Boom… and the planet is gone in seconds. No, we are not there yet. And may not get there at least in our lifetime. Yes, if someday they implement it, then the world will be quite different," Krish said.

"You mean a laser from space can destroy anything on earth… like in Star Wars… the Death Star concept… utilizing solar energy?"

"Huh Huh… Yup. That is right."

"But who would control it… men sitting in the International Space Station?"

"Control what, Nash?"

"Who will press the red button?"

Krish started laughing. "In real life, there is no red button. There are a series of commands that need to be executed, and those are all done from a single room or multiple locations… here on Earth. Do you remember… in Star Wars, they have control of the protective shield of the Death Star on some planet? Pretty much the same concept. Even if the laser source is in space, the controls will be on Earth. But don't worry… that is not happening in our lifetime… even if Senator Cohen is hell-bent on having the system."

"How does Senator Cohen come into the picture?"

"Hell, he is the one pushing these Israeli guys to get the laser in the Iron Dome. I just heard through the grapevine that Senator Cohen owns a major stake in C. Light Inc., which is also a DEW org… came up very fast during the last couple of years. I believe the C in C. Light is for Cohen. But I also heard that Cobblestone has picked up a major stake in C. Light and that C is for Cobblestone. I don't know what is true. These fellows are all goofballs. Thankfully, I stay away from them," Krish said. "By the way… I never said any of this, and you never heard any of this."

Nash laughed and said, "What were you talking about now? I thought you were very quiet for the last several minutes."

Both laughed. "It has been great seeing you after such a long time. But thankfully, my job is not as stressful as yours, Nash. I am glad I stuck to engineering and did not dabble in law or anything," Krish said.

"Yes, true. But you were more research-oriented type. You have the patience… I don't. Plus, I am a more nuts-and-bolts kind of person… practical. Maybe that is why I changed my line. But no regrets. It was really great to see you after such a long time. Next time you are in this part of the world, let me know. We can arrange something more interesting," Nash said.

"Yes… true. Great to see you as well. I must leave now… it is already late. Got a morning flight to catch."

"No worries, Krish… even if you miss the flight, you have a place to stay. Come over. You can take a red-eye," Nash laughed.

Krish laughed, wished Nash and his family goodbye, and got into the Uber and left.

Nash kept looking at the departed Uber until it turned and vanished from his sight. "God damn it… So, it is not the nukes that these guys are thinking about. That changes the entire perspective," he said to himself as he entered his house.

New York City, NY, US

July 28, 2024; 10.30 AM

Leo had been trying to gather as much information as he could on the Pentagon and trying to relate what Jerry had found on his front lawn. He had hardly succeeded. Even today, being a Sunday… instead of resting, he was at it again.

Momentarily, there was a hard knock on the door of his apartment. Leo was rather surprised… coz he was not expecting anyone. He got up from his desk and opened the door, but there was no one outside. Surprised, he was about to close the door when he noticed a plain white plastic carry bag lying on the doorstep. The carry bag had a pizza box, and Leo could see the Masanielli Pizzeria written on the box. Suddenly, Leo's body froze with fear. Leo quickly stepped outside and looked around but could not see anyone around who would have put the box on his doorstep.

Leo took the carry bag inside his apartment and took the pizza box out of the bag. The box appeared to be light and cold… and there was no aroma of pizza. Still frightened, Leo opened the lid of the box.

There was no pizza inside, but it had a few thick papers neatly folded and kept inside the box. Leo wondered and took out one of the folded papers… He opened it only to find that it was some sort of an engineering drawing.

There were two more inside the box. Leo opened both and found that they were also engineering drawings of some sort. Leo had absolutely no idea what the drawings referred to. He was not an engineer either to understand the details. Leo just stood there looking at the drawings.

"Who the heck is sending me these... and why? Are these in anyway related to what Jerry found?" Leo tried to think. "You may get the things in bits and pieces; you may have to join the dots and make a story." Leo suddenly remembered the words of the Hispanic old man.

"Who the heck was he? I should have taken his details... He has my details though... Is he the one sending me these? Hell, he looked quite old to do any of these shenanigans." Leo's thoughts were racing.

Leo took his cell phone and punched Jerry's cell number. A couple of rings later, Jerry came on the line.

"Yes... Leo. What's up?"

"Dude, do you know any engineer from your school? I know you don't study engineering... am just asking."

"Why?"

"Yes or No?"

"Maybe."

"That does not help... Yes, or No?"

"Okay... yes. So what?"

"So, we need to meet him. Can you speak to him and get his time... today? I will come and get you. This is urgent."

"Why? What happened?"

"Will explain when we are in the car driving to meet your friend."

"Alright."

"Is he a senior guy or a rookie?"

"Senior."

"Great. Let me know when… I will come and pick you up." Leo disconnected.

"At the least, I will come to know what the heck these drawings refer to… if not where." Leo thought to himself.

He went back to his laptop. The moment he opened it there was a notification of a new video clip on his WhatsApp.

Leo opened the app and saw that the video had come from an unknown number. But the title of the video was something that instantly attracted Leo. "Swiss bankers Atomic Shelters… Svalbard Global Seed Vault… Are we close to a Nuclear Winter?"

Leo opened the link… It was a well-made video. The commentator was American as could be seen from the accent. The video covered the Swiss Bunkers in detail… "Switzerland has a large network of underground bunkers to protect its citizens in the event of a nuclear attack, and the country is considered an international leader in bunker design and technology. Most bunkers are privately owned and located in the basements of homes and apartment buildings. There are an estimated 380,000 bunkers in Switzerland, though the exact number is a closely guarded secret."

The video then showed some of the Bunkers and the facilities therein. The video then showed the Svalbard Global Seed vault and commented: "What is the use of the seed vault if there would be no place left on earth once the nuclear winter starts?"

The last part of the video was far more interesting… it talked about how some private organizations in the US are taking over prime pieces of land and sweet water bodies across the globe and building underground shelters for themselves… with the money they have been earning from the common people and taxpayers.

And finally on the possible nuclear war, the commentator ended with a question… "Who really controls the nukes in the US? Is it the US government or some private corporations? In China it is the communist party, in Pakistan and Iran, it is the Islamic radicals, in North Korea it is Kim Jung…in Russia it is Putin… who is it really in the US?"

Leo watched the video 3-4 times. It was obvious that the video was a forward… which meant it was in circulation for a while. The video rattled Leo… coz the underground shelters reminded him of the drawings he had received and the items which were received by Jerry. "Maybe they are a part of all this," Leo said it aloud.

Momentarily, his cell phone rang. It was Jerry.

"Hey, I have received a strange video…." Jerry started telling Leo.

"Yes, I know. I just saw it." Leo cut him off.

"Oh, you already did?"

"Yes."

"Who sent you the video?"

"It came from a strange number."

"What is the number?"

Leo read out the number.

"No, mine is different… I don't know who it belongs to."

"Me neither. By the way… what happened to the engineer friend of yours?"

"Ah, yes. He said to come around 4.00. He lives in the dorm. So, you don't need to come here. Meet me at the gate of the Univ. or where we always meet during that lady's demos."

"Okay. Will meet you there at 4.00." Leo replied and cut off the call.

"At least we will be going somewhere now. Hope this pizza guy will keep on sending more intel my way." Leo thought to himself.

Langley, Virginia, US

July 30, 2024; 06.30 PM

Nash was intrigued by the complexity of the behemoth built by Cobblestone over the last several years. The more he researched, the deeper it became. Nash wondered which came first… the concept of making money or the concept of owning the world. It was one led to another, but which one… he wondered.

In any case, whichever was the primary concept, one thing was pretty clear that in the process of making money and owning the people in key positions globally… who were literally "bought" or "blackmailed," well, the word "blackmail" was not in vogue these days… instead it was "persuaded" … so, "persuaded" …. to further the agenda of Cobblestone. Now it had become a massive monster which had no fear of ever getting destroyed.

After Krish's visit, Nash had been "studying" Senator Cohen. It was a story about near-rags to riches of a Jewish boy belonging to a family of meagre means becoming a powerful senator. A complete right-wing radical, a staunch opponent of Islam and anything that was related to Islam… noticed by someone like Rumsfeld quite early on and then mentored… as also a follower of Bernard Baruch and Stephen Schwarzman… which had helped him in becoming a hawk on the Wall Street.

Wall Street and Rumsfeld got him into mainstream politics… plus marrying the daughter of a Jewish financer magnet helped him become a senator quite early on. Senator Cohen's relationship with Cobblestone had been quite old. So, C.Light's ownership question was superfluous. Nash could figure out as to why other established DEW orgs like Lockheed or Raytheon etc., were not involved in this specific "initiative" … coz C.Light was solely under the control of Cobblestone and Senator Cohen and there was no chance of anyone knowing the secret mission.

Nash was analysing his own conclusions… "Putting nukes in space would cause unnecessary attention plus it was tedious and complicated in terms of getting the nukes up there in the space. Other countries would also join soon and that was not something Cobblestone desired. They wanted it completely discrete so that they could surprise the world and then exercise their complete control… by having Laser weaponry in space."

"So, what Elon Musk's SpaceX is for NASA, Gregory Brink's C.Light is for Pentagon. And then there is Starlink too. This is Public – Private Partnership that they have been talking about. Great!!! But who controls the Red Button here?" Nash wondered.

"So, the underground project is directly related to the lasers in space. The control unit would be in a completely deserted location in the wilderness… where even the adventure tourists never ventured. Yet it would be accessible to a water body…. just in case someone as lunatic as Kim Jung of North Korea suddenly decided to drop a nuke on the US or nuke the North America itself. Being underwater would prevent them from being physically destroyed."

"But why three sites?"

Nash was unable to get that logic. "Perhaps the site at Nunalla Egg River in Caribou River Park Reserve near Hudson Bay seemed to be the most appropriate for the Control Center as well as for living underground / underwater."

The way the construction was going on at the Hudson Bay site, Nash had become certain that the underground and underwater facilities would be connected by a tunnel, and it would be seamless. The underground Control Center facility would not be visible to any "by-chance" visitor as its curved dome protruding over the ground would appear like a small grassy hillock… nothing more…. Complete with moss and everything else that would match the surrounding area.

"If this is the case, why the other two sites? What purpose do they solve? Unless…. Unless they are meant as living quarters for other folks… like the SecDef, Director of CA, Senator Cohen? Or Is there something else cooking that we don't know?" Nash wondered.

He looked at his watch; it was 6.30 PM. Nash decided to wind up and leave. He closed his laptop, got his backpack, closed the door of his room behind him as he left for the parking lot. As he approached his car, he saw someone standing near his car looking at a cell phone.

"Who the hell is that?" Nash wondered to himself.

"Oh, Hello there!!!" The voice seemed familiar

"Ah, it is you. What the heck are you doing here Sergei?" Nash had recognized the voice and now he could see Sergei's face.

"Waiting for you. What else?" Said Sergei.

"Well, you know my office," Nash said.

"This specific area is not visible to the cameras in the parking lot. I have made certain of that." Sergei said.

Nash laughed.

"Okay, so don't tell me that you left the topic of those two operations that we talked about," Sergei said.

"I am still analysing, Sergei. It is far more complicated than what you would think. So, once I know the real picture, I will certainly let you know. By the way… do you know a company called LH Raumfahrt and its… let us say "owner" Ludolf Hoffmann. Since this is your operating area, I thought you sure would know."

Sergei laughed. "You are so sleek, Nash. I came to ask you if you had any details, but here you are, desirous of knowing more details from me…"

"Yes or No?" Nash asked, ignoring Sergei's comments.

"Well, yes. But why? What has he done that pricked your interest?" Sergei asked.

"What his firm does or rather manufactures… that is of interest to me. It could be quite dangerous considering his range of expertise." Nash said.

"C' on Nash. Don't talk in riddles. Tell me in plain, simple words. My brain is still made in Russia… it is slow and old-fashioned." Sergei said with some sarcasm. "Your brain is made in India… runs faster than the roadrunner."

"Okay… tell me what you know, and I will fill you in." Nash still did not specify anything.

"In short, the guy manufactures Radars, Satellites, Solar Panels for Satellites, Missiles… apart from Green Energy and Biotech stuff."

"Jesus Christ…!!!" Nash exclaimed!!! "How the heck did I miss that critical portion? Solar Panels… of course!!!!!"

"Nash, could you be more specific?" Sergei asked.

"Sergei, All I can tell you right now is this guy can prove to be an extremely dangerous guy. Could you please for God's sake… find out what he is up to… as of now and in the coming months. Who does he collaborate with? Does he have any specific connections… to any specific organizations? Like BND or any other org. I need this intel ASAP. I know you are not my responsibility… but I need this intel all the same." Nash suddenly appeared to be quite serious.

"Oh. Woah, Woah… slowly Mr. Nash! I am entitled to know what exactly I am looking for." Sergei said.

"No Sergei… nothing at this stage. Perhaps at the next stage. I don't want to give my perceptions. I want to give you facts. You can then decide what is best for you and your family. But not now. Right now, please find out what Mr. Ludolf Hoffmann is up to. Is he building any underground shelters for him and his family? Is he manufacturing something unique? Who transports his satellites into space… The European Space Agency (ESA)? And whose satellites are they… Germany or any other European country and most importantly… who has the control of the Satellites?"

"This is a lot of information. I can't get it sitting here. I need to be on ground… and I am not going now. Perhaps early next month. I will be here for a couple of more weeks."

"If you can go early, it will be of great help."

"Help? To whom? To you?"

"To humanity… that includes you. Can't you think beyond you and I?"

"Woah. You seem to be quite serious. Nash, tell me what the truth is."

"Next time. Not now. I already told you. Please get me this intel. Now, let's go. I am sure you did not come here specifically for me." Nash opened the door of his car, threw his bag inside and sat in his car. "The quicker you are in getting the intel, the quicker

I will be in getting the facts together and getting the real picture. Bye." Nash said, closing the car door and starting the car.

Sergei made a gesture of saluting Nash and let Nash depart.

"WTF is cooking. Something serious, I guess. Alexei was supposed to meet Ludolf. But the way Nash looks at him, he seems to be quite different. Meaning he is not what he looks... then what the hell is he? If he is so dangerous, then why the heck the Chinese are courting him? Heck... there are more questions than answers. I had told the agency guys that Ludolf was courting the Chinese... all they did was to put him under a 24x7 watch. You can't find an effing pin just by keeping a 24x7 watch. You need to get "involved." I'm not sure if anyone from the agency has even attempted it. Maybe, as Nash suggested, I need to get there now before it is too late." Sergei turned and walked towards his parked car. He had decided to get back to Europe immediately. "I would have to get the paperwork in place and get a nod from the boss."

Most of the time, personal relationships helped the agency to get specific intel, avoiding ego tussles of bosses. Even though the bosses were quite aware of these dotted relationships, they could not stop or eliminate them.

Jersey City, NJ, US

August 3, 2024; 10.30 AM

The drawings were spread out on the dining table and both Jerry and Leo were going over their individual notes and making marks on the drawings.

"What I don't understand is… all the three drawings are almost identical, then why there is a difference in their structures?" Leo said, making a gesture with his hand.

"Look I don't understand even a thing. These drawings are of some goddamn underground, underwater structures…. of which we don't even know the location. Where the heck are they located? Then we don't know what their purpose is…. well, if you consider the video, then yes… in case there is a nuclear war, then you go into one of these. But man, these must be only for the rich and the famous… not for the common public like us. We live in the US and not in Switzerland… where everybody is a millionaire." Jerry sounded quite frustrated.

"Yeah. I agree. But still, what is the purpose of having three different designs of identical structures?" Leo repeated.

"They are not identical now… coz they have different designs." Jerry pointed.

"Yeah… what I meant was conceptually identical." Leo insisted on his point of view. He continued…

"So, what do we have… drawings, video, Pentagon, scuba items. That's it. Okay, the scuba items match with the underwater buildings. The Earth Pipes relates to an underground ventilation system. The video relates to underground shelters. Now, who controls the nukes in the US… I haven't got a clue. But why should we worry about who controls US nukes… coz they are not going to drop them onto us… if at all somebody else… maybe Russia, maybe China. So, why worry? We can go to Montana or Wyoming and live there. Nobody will nuke that area."

"Yes… that is the only alternative. But how do we know when they will drop the nukes? They will not give is 48 hour or even 24-hour advance intimation… would they?" Jerry said.

"So, what do we do now?" Leo asked.

"Guess we wait for more intel. Once we have enough intel, we write a book… and publish it. Somebody will get a boot on his or her or their backside. So… we wait." Jerry said.

"Who are we exposing by doing this?"

"Search me. I only know that someone is using us. We are like the pawns."

"What if we decide not to do this?"

"Maybe nothing will happen. Maybe they will screw us royally before they find someone else. Those guys must be quite powerful."

"Yup. Did you see that man in # 208 again?"

"Yeah… he is there for sure. But I have not seen him… whether he is black or white or yellow. But I bet he must be related to this…." Jerry pointed at the drawings.

"Perhaps. Hey, listen, I got to be going. When I get something new, I will let you know... if you get anything, you do the same."

"Yeah..." Jerry said with a yawn.

Mid-Atlantic

August 4, 2024

Sergei was watching the movie on his United Airlines nonstop flight from Dulles to Frankfurt. For some weird reason, Sergei could never sleep on a flight. Presently, he was watching Pierce Brosnan, Salma Hayek's movie "After the Sunset." Sergei loved Salma Hayek. For some reason, he always thought she was a Russian. "Russian women are like her," he would always say.

The movie was quite funny, he thought. "Wonder why I did not watch this earlier," Sergei said as he sipped his drink number 5. He was a true Russian. Drinks never had any effect on him.

As he finished watching the movie, suddenly, he remembered Nash's words… "Who has the control on the satellites?"

"I will be damned. That bugger is so effing clever… no wonder he is where he is today. Had I not seen this movie, I would not have understood the meaning of what the heck he had been saying." Sergei suddenly sat upright and went back to watching the last part of the movie. He watched it 3 times over.

He asked the flight attendant for a paper and pen and also a drink. When she brought them to him, he thanked her and gulped down the drink in one go. Then he took the pen and started drawing a line diagram.

"So… Ludolf manufactures satellites, solar panels, radar… Nash did not say anything about a missile, so let me keep it to these three. Satellite and solar panels are together… they go up in space. Radar is on the ground."

"Who controls the satellite… hmmm… the country which sends it? or maybe the European Space Agency? But what if… like shown in the movie…Ludolf decides to take "remote" control of the satellite and also the radar… he could… coz he has built it. He would always have components installed in the satellite platform which he could activate at will and take control. This is effing shit man… this is disastrous!!! But what a satellite can do on its own…. Unless… unless what? Think Sergei, think!!!"

Sergei was lost in his thoughts…. Then suddenly he thought of missiles. "But how can a satellite fire missile? They are on the ground. Can Satellite destroy another satellite…? God alone knows. Man!!! This is so freaking crazy. Sergei wanted to get out of the aircraft and take a walk in the fresh air!!! He started cursing himself.

"I should have asked Nash about this. But this damn thing never came to my mind. I need to get some technical dope from someone on this. What can a satellite do from space… it can't fire a missile or a nuke from space…. Unless… unless it is carrying a nuke with it. Is that even possible? I doubt it."

"Why was Nash excited… something to do with solar panels…. so what? Every satellite has solar panels… I don't understand. Again… I should have asked Nash. I am dumbass… I don't ask questions. How the heck am I supposed to get answers? I need to catch hold of some satellite expert now."

During the entire duration of the flight, Sergei kept on cursing himself for not asking the right questions to Nash. When the flight reached Frankfurt, Sergei decided to make a call from the airport itself.

"Even if Nash is sleeping, he better answer the phone." Sergei quipped.

However, after landing in Frankfurt, Sergei's efforts to get Nash on the phone were wasted as Nash did not answer the phone. Sergei cursed himself and thought for a while about whom to contact.

He then went to the mobile kiosk in the arrival area of the airport and bought two sim cards… one of Vodafone and one of Orange. He took his spare mobile, inserted the Orange card in it and called Alexei. Sergei was absolutely sure that Alexei would answer the phone… which he did. After stating all the possible questions Sergei requested Alexei to keep the answers ready. He would call in another 6 hours.

After disconnecting the phone, Sergei took out the sim card from the phone… broke it into pieces… and flushed down the pieces in the commode in the men's room. The other sim card would be used for the call later in the day. From arrivals, Sergei then took the escalator down to catch the underground S-Bahn train from Frankfurt International Airport to Frankfurt City Center. "Once in City Center, I will decide where to put up," Sergei said to himself while he bought the train ticket.

New York City, NY

August 7, 2024; 01.30 PM

It was hot and humid, but it did not bother Leo as he was almost in a trance… in a confused state of mind as he entered his favorite Mediterranean eatery. Absent-mindedly, he placed his order and later collected his tray. He had not noticed that the man standing behind him was smiling at his absent-mindedness.

Leo sat at one of the tables. Since lunchtime was almost over, the restaurant was not crowded. After sitting at his table, Leo realized that he had forgotten paper napkins and so he was about to get up and get them when a man just put some napkins in front of Leo and said, "You had forgotten them."

Leo murmured thanks and looked at the man who stood there holding his tray, smiling at him… "May I join?" The man asked, pointing at the empty chair.

"Yes, of course. Please. Nice to see you after a long time." Leo had forgotten the name. He was quickly trying to recall.

"Thanks." The man said… "Peter Parker is the name if you are trying to recall."

Leo was embarrassed. "Well… yes of course. Silly of me not to recall the name. Too many things on the mind these days." Leo said sheepishly.

"No worries. We all have similar situations from time to time. So, what's bothering you? Anything that I can be of help… just shoot it." the man said.

Leo had been desirous of sharing what was going on with someone senior or a mature person. After all, Jerry was just a kid. So, Leo decided to open up to the man and share what was going on.

While Leo was narrating the stuff, the man was listening intently and asking some probing questions. Once Leo had finished telling his tale, the man said…

"It is really a brilliant idea to write the book. The book as such will be a true story almost as big as The Watergate. I mean really, it has the potential to become NY Times #1 Bestseller. It will put you up there with the ranks of top-level journalists- authors. Overnight, you will be a sensation… money, name, fame will follow. I think you should go for it." The man said.

"Do you really think so?" Leo asked.

"Yes, absolutely. In fact, if you need some funds to sponsor the project… the book I mean, I can certainly arrange to provide the funds. You rest be assured." The man was looking at Leo's eyes… while Leo was dreaming.

"Yes. I understand. But I am not sure who is providing me with this information and why me or Jerry, for that matter? And I hope the information is authentic… if not, I will look like a buffoon." Leo said.

"Don't be so apprehensive. Why you or Jerry… I have no clue. But I think the information coming to you is authentic. As a matter of fact, going forward, you can use me as a wall to bounce the ball… I will be able to tell you if it is authentic or not. That is if you want to share." The man said.

"Yes, that is a good idea. I will keep you informed."

"Here is my phone number, I think you already have it… but still… Call me whenever you have an update." The man said.

"Yes Mr. Parker."

"It is Peter."

"Yes, Peter."

The two finished their lunch, spoke for a while, and then parted.

"There is something big brewing up. Perhaps over the next couple of weeks, we should have a major news item which can shake the country. I am on it." Peter Parker… aka Lemur, informed the person he had called immediately after Leo had left the restaurant.

Lemur was smiling from ear to ear as he started his car. "Mr. Nash, seems like your hunch about this journalist was spot on," Lemur said to himself.

Houston, Texas, US

September 7, 2024; 07.30 PM

Mehul Nandhi was visiting the US again… it was at the behest of his mentor Dam Keytruda … who was sitting opposite Mehul and narrating his plans.

"We have arranged your lecture at the University where you will address the students, basically telling them how everything is wrong with Indian Democracy. You can lash out at the current government on discrimination of Muslims, OBCs, ST/SCs… Inflation, the economy, safety and security and the violence in Kashmir valley. We will make sure that the audience is all anti-right-wingers… mostly left liberals."

Mehul nodded in full of admiration of Dam.

"Then we will be meeting Ilhan Omar, Borge Ross himself and definitely his son and other officers. We will also be meeting some of your Pakistani supports. We need to stir up everything. You see you have now almost 100 seats…it means that you have already won. See what the Chinese media had to say; the Chinese media professional Hu Xijin had commented on the diminished powers of the Indian Prime Minister …. Well, here it is…"

"Indian Prime Minister Dodi claimed victory for the third term, but it seems more like a loss. Once the Prime Minister becomes weak, Washington may assess his long-term value. The election marks a turning point for Prime Minister Dodi from strong to weak."

"You see, the Chinese had played their part and helped us succeed… it was their successful attempt even though it partly succeeded. After all, billions were spent to create an anti-India and anti-Prime Minister narrative."

"Look, the most suitable way to bring in illicit funds into India is by using the hawala route. Another effective method is donations… Donations to legitimate but unscrupulous entities in India either directly by multinational companies or via these MNCs. Okay?"

"Yes, I understand."

"These funds are and will be used to spread civil unrest, to aid terrorism, or to disrupt elections. The disturbed peace in Northeast India and Punjab in the recent past was part of this game plan. You understand?"

Mehul nodded his head. He had no interest in all these details. He just wanted the position of Prime Minister. Rest was of no use to him.

Dam continued…. "In the era of the internet, social media, and deep fakes, our going forward would be via these visible internal and invisible external forces. Also, our plan is to question the electoral institutions of India and trigger anarchy in India. We need to give a nationwide call to the public to take the streets and make the life of the current PM miserable and oust him when he would lose his credibility and support."

"Now the Delhi CM is not in the picture… In his absence, you must assume his role as anarchist, and you must start talking about how you were born in the "system" and know it inside out."

"The idea is… upon your return to India, you have to ignite yet another Shaheen Bagh-type movement on how the 2024 elections were rigged. Western Media would pick that up and destroy India's image as a democracy and declare it an electoral dictatorship. That would give all US companies a moral platform to withdraw all FDI and the Indian economy would plunge. That is when we take over and get it back on rails. That is the idea. Are you with me?" Dam asked.

Mehul said… "Yes, that sounds great. I will do what is necessary."

Dam smiled and said to himself… "You bet. You have no clue, so you will have to listen to me." Somewhere at the back of his mind, Dam could see Borge Ross praising him profusely.

"We just had the anniversary of 9/11 last Wednesday… exactly a week ago and now we have this." Abe indicated the news on the TV, which was telecasting… "Electronic pagers across Lebanon exploded simultaneously on Sept. 17, 2024, killing 12 and wounding more than 2,700. Today, another wave of explosions in the country came from detonating walkie-talkies. The attacks appeared to target members of the militant group Hezbollah."

"Guys in Mossad are capable of doing anything, anywhere, anytime, anyhow." Someone commented. Abe and his five colleagues were trying to fathom the seriousness of the issue and what it would mean to the US.

"The pagers attack involved explosives planted in the communications devices by Israeli operatives, according to US officials cited by The New York Times. Hezbollah had recently ordered a shipment of pagers, according to the report." The newsreader was in full flow.

Abe looked at the people around the table and said intently, "Secretly attacking the supply chain is not a new technique in intelligence and military operations. For example, the US National Security Agency intercepted computer hardware bound for overseas customers, inserted malware or other surveillance tools and then repackaged them for delivery to certain foreign buyers, a 2010 NSA internal document showed," Abe looked at his colleagues and continued…

"This differs from accessing a specific person's device, like when Israel's Shin Bet secretly inserted explosives into a cell phone to remotely kill a Hamas bombmaker in 1996… and now this. I mean the entire containerload of shipment of pagers is bugged with explosives… this is like taking the supply chain invasion, as I say it, to an absolutely new height."

"China supplies so many electronic items to the US… including drones… so China can do same as pagers… like toasters, cars, solar panels etc. etc. Compromised devices will pose an enormous problem to us. It is impossible to check each and every device that comes into the country from China. Again, it may not come directly from China, but what is the guarantee that any such electronic goods coming from any other country do not have parts originating in China? So, everything, including cars, can be weaponized by China."

"Then there are these DJI drones coming from China… And these ZPMC (Shanghai Zhenhua Heavy Industries Co., Ltd.) drones are used for large-scale machinery. ZPMC's UAV Inspection System provides all the data via cloud and guess what… all the data goes to China. So, what is the guarantee that all the devices that the US buys from China, the data is not going to China… which they can use against us when the time comes." Abe sounded extremely concerned.

"Well, we created that dragon… that monster. We are always in the habit of creating and fostering monsters. That is our specialty," Someone commented.

"Chinese Deep State!!!" came another snide comment.

"But we don't learn," said the other.

"Enough!" Abe roared. "We need a solution to this issue which has now opened a new frontier… a new challenge to us."

"Simple, don't buy electronic goods from China. Period. Bring back the industry here… to the US. Or, like Trump says, increase the tariff on those Chinese goods. Or ask Americans to stop buying Chinese stuff. But then how do you ensure that the stuff made in any other country does not have any Chinese element in it.?' another agent quipped.

"I don't need immediate solutions. Think properly, rationally and let us discuss this seriously." Abe said.

"Call DARPA and tell them to find one." Someone commented.

The mention of DARPA jolted Abe. He had almost forgotten about it.

"Perhaps so. But you also have that responsibility. Let us meet a week from now and discuss your solutions. Now get out." Abe ordered his team.

"DARPA, now what should I do about it?" Abe thought to himself.

Frankfurt, Germany

September 19, 2024; 08.30 PM

"We cannot get answers to your questions, Nash. LH Raumfahrt, Ludolf's company, is virtually sealed. Anyone working at the LH Raumfahrt appears to be a loyal member of The III Path or The Third Path, which is a far-right and Neo-Nazi political party in Germany."

"So?"

"So, directly or indirectly, we get the same reply… "everything is mentioned on our website." So, even if Ludolf's company does have some plans of whatever you are thinking of, we will not know… at least immediately. This will take time. Period." Sergei said.

"What if I tell you that this is quite serious?" Nash asked.

"Even then. I don't know what "serious" is to inquire anyway." Sergei said.

"Space-based, Satellite carried laser guns… powerful enough to destroy a city at the least," Nash said.

"You mean nukes."

"No. Laser guns. Laser… you understand?"

"Yes, yes, like Star Wars… but it is only Hollywood stuff."

"Not anymore," Nash said coldly.

There was silence at the other end.

"I see." Finally, Sergei broke the silence. "I will try once again… but don't depend on my answer. If it is for real, then take it for granted that Ludolf has it figured out." Sergei said.

"I see. Does he have an ambition of sorts?"

"What kind of ambition? His family background is that of Nazi. I think his grandfather was an SS officer during WWII. If that can answer your question." Sergei said.

"Got it. So, we have no clue if Ludolf already has the Laser guns placed in some existing satellites up in the orbit… in German Satellites, that is."

"So, what… in short term and long term?"

"You figure it out," Nash said and the line went dead.

Sergei shrugged his shoulders. The only thing he could do was to inform Alexei… who could take it to the President and keep him informed. "Maybe the Russians already have it… who knows. I am still unable to understand the seriousness of this issue."

Alexei's response was simple. "There are people who want to control the world by blackmailing… it would be another kind of "sanction" on any specific country… The One who controls the laser guns can control the world. Just replace the nukes with laser guns."

"You mean it is like a space-based nuke?"

"More or less… Yes. And dangerous as well. Nukes need a big space, big satellite station and to send them into space, you need a big powerful rocket to lift them off. While laser guns are extremely light weight and easy to carry and install in any satellite. You can have various kinds of laser guns… smaller ones which can destroy another satellite… enemy's satellite, military satellites... and more advanced ones which can act like nukes... destroying cities or their target areas to dust." Alexei explained.

"Do you have it?" Sergei asked, knowing well he would not get the answer.

"Bye," Alexei said and cut off the line.

Washington D.C., US

September 25, 2024; 10.30 AM

Secretary of State Bob Mayers was worried about the Presidential Elections which were just a month and a half away and it appeared that it may not be an easy win… or maybe there will not be a win. Bob shuddered at the thought. A no-win would mean loss of job, loss of power… which Bob dreaded.

Things had not gone as planned… with all the efforts and help from people like Borge Ross, Indian voters had retained their current nationalistic Prime Minister. "Even China wanted him ousted," Bob said to himself. "We would have preferred to have the dumb turtle as their Prime Minister. We could have controlled him the way we desired. At least pulled him away from BRICS."

"Neither we could remove the Prime Minister, nor could we make the two Asian giants fight with each other and destroy each other. Both have become pain in the backside… demanding, arrogant. The sanctions on Russia did not work because of these two countries… nor did the Ukraine war make any dent in the Russian economy. The Saudis and the Emiratis have ditched us royally. The Saudis have dissolved the Petro Dollar…. That is a bloody disaster. I guess all the initiatives we tried have failed to get the right results. So, we have nothing to boast about in the election." Bob seemed worried.

"People have become smarter these days." Bob muttered. His mind went back to Abe Williams… who had started poking his nose around "DARPA's" involvement with the arms lobby. "Hope the guy just backs off… any exposure of those operations would mean me permanently becoming a political outcast."

Post lunch, Bob had several meetings lined up for the rest of the day. But he was in no mood as nothing was going in the right direction.

"Deep State… heck, I am a part of it. If we lose the elections, and if the next President decides to expose the Deep State and the folks associated with it… I will be gone behind bars…. Coz I will be the scapegoat. Everyone else can escape. I knew what people like Borge Ross had been messing up with, but I did not or could not stop them … heck it is a democracy… we can do anything… including meddling in another country's internal affairs!!! Afterall, we are the United States. Every country on the planet should bow in front of us…. What the heck… why am I feeling like Napoleon today?"

Bob tried to shake off the feeling of depression but the news from Israel was not good either. It would be almost a year since Hamas had attacked Israel and till date, all the might of the US had not been successful in getting the 100-odd hostages back from the grips of Hamas. Senator Cohen had unleashed heavy salvo during one of their meetings last week and Bob literally had to escape from the meeting. Already, there was a feeling that the government was not acting in favor of Israel.

"Shit… this will also affect the elections." Bob thought and shook his head in desperation. He had a trip to Israel coming up soon. But Bob was apprehensive as there was nothing more that the government could do. Any direct action could start a war with Iran and that would prompt China to invade Taiwan…

knowing well that US forces cannot be present in 3 different areas simultaneously. And India will not get involved with our war with China… coz we have played a nasty game with them."

"Oh, well. Que Sera Sera…. What will be, will be." Bob said to himself and started gathering his papers.

Jersey City, NJ, US

September 26, 2024; 04.30 PM

For a change, Jerry had taken a bus from NY Central to Jersey City. Route 87 would take him closer to his house. The bus was crowded although Jerry had managed to get a window seat. Another man dressed in a business jacket, carrying an old-fashioned leather bag, had occupied seat next to Jerry. The man had placed the leather bag between them and had opened the WSJ and was busy reading it. Jerry thought the guy must be a Wall Street guy working for some brokerage company or a financial investment firm. Jerry had dozed off after some time.

The bus had stopped with a jerk which woke Jerry up. He noticed that the bus was almost empty now and he had almost reached his final destination. "Another stop to go," Jerry said to himself… that's when he noticed the leather bag resting against him.

Jerry looked around for the man in the business jacket… but he was not to be seen. Curiosity killed the cat… so was Jerry … overwhelmed with curiosity, he opened the bag to check the contents of the bag.

The moment he saw the part of the contents. He immediately closed the flap of the leather bag and looked around to see if anyone was looking at him. But there was no one. As soon as the bus reached its final destination, Jerry gripped the bag in his arms and almost ran. A few minutes of fast walk and Jerry was home. The moment he stepped inside the house, he closed the front door, pulled the curtains of the windows… went to the dining table and emptied the contents of the bag…

There were three engineering drawings, two maps showing locations marked in red circles, one small notebook… with some notations written on various pages… it also had some names.

"This is a bloody treasure. That guy sitting next to me seemed to know who I was… otherwise why would he leave the bag with me? I did not even see his face!!!" Jerry said it aloud. He tried to think if the man looked like the person living in house # 208.

Jerry was not sure if he should call his Columbia friend to have a look at the drawings or call Leo and share this with him.

Jerry decided to call Leo first and got his cell phone out of his pocket. As he clicked it live, he saw a WhatsApp notification coming in from an unknown number. Recalling the earlier video incident, Jerry opened the WhatsApp message. There was another video in the message this time… with a one-line message: "You should check this out immediately."

Jerry thought for a moment and decided to call Leo first. Leo answered, asking, "What's up?"

Jerry narrated the entire story… the bus ride, the bag, the video link, and asked Leo if he had also received the video link. Leo had not checked his cell phone. He asked Jerry to wait while he checked.

"Yes. I got the video. What's in it?"

"I haven't checked as yet. Thought I will inform you first. I am gonna call my buddy at Columbia and if he is there, we will go and see him if possible, today itself." Jerry was excited.

"Okay. Sounds like a great idea. Let me know the time." Leo disconnected coz he wanted to check the video.

New York City, NY, US

By the time Leo reached home after meeting Jerry's engineer friend from Columbia where both Jerry and Leo had been subjected to quite a few shocks courtesy of the drawings Jerry had found on the bus… it was just striking 8 PM. Leo was hungry and tired. He was thinking of making some quick egg sandwiches and a cup of coffee.

However, upon reaching his apartment, he found a shoe box sealed with a 3M tape lying on his doorstep. It had his name written on it. Leo was rather surprised coz he never thought that he would receive more surprises in a day.

He took the box inside his apartment and opened it quickly. Inside, there was a thick brown envelope. "Now, what the hell is this?" Leo muttered and opened the brown envelope. Inside, there were photographs of various construction sites. At the back of each photograph, there was a sticker with a typed description of the site and the location in Lat Long.

"Whoever is sending these things must be an extremely meticulous person." Leo thought to himself.

He picked up the cell phone and called Jerry. Jerry was still on the train when he picked up the phone. When Leo informed him about the photographs, Jerry wanted Leo to come to his place immediately. Leo declined, saying he would be at Jerry's place the next morning.

"The bugger will not sleep tonight. He has already gone to the seventh heaven." Leo said to himself.

Jersey City, NJ, US

September 27, 2024; 09.30 AM

As promised, Leo had reached Jerry's place at 9.30 in the morning only to find Jerry still dozing off. Apparently, Jerry had not slept the entire night and had caught a wink sometime after 5.30 in the morning.

Jerry apologized to Leo and asked him to make coffee for himself, by the time he would get ready. Leo instead got all the material ready on the dining table. Leo had made some points and had prepared a synopsis of sorts of the entire "story." There were still some missing pieces of the entire puzzle.

"Okay where do we start?" Jerry asked when he joined Leo at the table.

Well, here is what I think is the story....

1. Someone wants to build underground / underwater shelters to escape presumably from Nuclear blasts. We don't yet know… who all are going to live there in these shelters, when will they start living there and how long they will live there?"

2. These shelters are all in Canada… why there… we don't know.

3. There are 3 such sites… why 3… we don't know.

4. In one underground shelter, there seems to be an almost circular big chamber…which is connected to an underground

structure on one side and a tunnel leading to the waterbody on the other.

5. The tunnel which leads to the waterbody connects to an underwater structure… which appears to be a living quarter and with another circular chamber, almost as big as the underground one.

6. The other two underground/underwater structures seem to be normal living quarters or storage facilities.

7. The project is sponsored by, as per the details provided in the diary or the notebook, which you had found on the bus, C.Light Inc. But there is no real evidence of any sort.

8. The people associated with the project… again as per the diary… are Senator Cohen, the Secretary of Defense, the Director of the CIA, and other folks. Again, there is no concrete evidence.

9. Mention of the Pentagon involvement… again as per the diary. No concrete evidence.

10. The big circular chamber is mentioned as a possible "command control center"… but of what, we don't know.

11. There is also a sketch of a Death Star in the diary… showing a beam originating from it destroying the "Alderaan" planet. Now I as hell don't understand what that means.

"If the Laser beam is going to destroy the planet, then why the heck they are building the underground shelters… what is the big deal?" Leo commented.

"So, what is the story?" Jerry asked.

"Well, what it seems from the so-called "proofs" that we have been provided…. Some smartass politicians are building underground/underwater shelters for themselves…. Just in case there is a war… maybe a nuclear war or maybe a Star War type war with laser guns, then these politicians can go and take shelter in those bunkers. And you and I can go to hell."

"Okay. Then what about the command-and-control center that you talked about?" Jerry asked.

"Hmmm… maybe… oh yeah… I forgot the satellite part. So, maybe they will control the satellites… sitting underground and that way, they will know where the nuclear or laser attack is going to be." Leo said.

"Does not make sense. I guess… at least in my opinion…. It would be the other way round…. That sitting underground, they will direct where the attack should be." Jerry said.

"Possible. But then, why sit underground?" Leo queried.

"What if other guys are first to strike… they have satellites too… then there will be some time before the rockets, missiles hit us… so during that time, these folks can direct their attack sitting underground," Jerry said.

"Makes sense."

So… what is the story now?" Jerry asked.

"Well, the story remains the same with an addition… of Laser wars. Like Star Wars. But if we publish such a story… we will be making a fool of ourselves." Leo said.

"Maybe we need more evidence and more information. Will they provide us?" Jerry asked.

"I have no clue. But I am just thinking loud… maybe they would want me specifically to do some investigation myself coz I call myself an investigative journalist." Leo said sheepishly.

"So, go and investigate…. Who stopped you?"

"From where I should begin… that is the biggest question."

"Maybe who funded the project… if it is C.Light Inc.; then there must be some evidence. Find it. Alternatively, find out how the Pentagon is involved in this. Or what is the significance of underwater and maybe hydroponics? Or perhaps what is the significance of waterbodies in this… coz 3 sites are near water."

"I don't know. The question is who we are fighting against… Russia? China? North Korea? Iran? Or who is going to attack us with nukes… or whatever… Laser beams? If yes, then why make only three prototype shelters that too in Canadian wilderness… if you look at the Lat Longs they have provided? I mean it will end up as a wild goose chase and I will become a laughingstock if I write a book on such fantasy." Leo seemed frustrated.

"Look, I know or understand as much as you do. Your questions are valid…. But I have no answers. Maybe the three underground shelters are for specific uses we don't know about. I have no clue. Just thinking aloud. Maybe they already have their Death Star up in space, or they may be planning to send it there…. which can be controlled from earth…. from that command-and-control center which is there in that design."

"That is a possibility. Let us check what that C.Light does. Let us Google it. You do as well as I and then compare notes. Coz the project they said is funded by C.light Inc., right?"

"Yup."

After searching the net for an hour, both concluded that C.Light manufactures DEW weapons… and yes, Directed Energy Weapons (DEWs) are used in space to damage or destroy enemy systems and platforms. DEWs are electromagnetic systems that convert energy into radiated energy and focus it on a target.

They can take the form of lasers, particle beams, or high-powered microwaves.

Leo said, "Okay… so there is the source of the Death Star. Now listen to this article… it is written by military personnel… he says…

"If we have an Intelligence, Surveillance and Reconnaissance (ISR) satellite that we're using to observe airfields, ships, missiles, or ground troops – all things that the joint force and the national command authority need to build intelligence assessments – and there's a directed energy weapon with a laser dazzler or other type of emitter that's engaging and cooking that satellite, the sensors on that bird are fried, If we can't see our targets on the ground, then we can't get that intel to the warfighter, the commander, or the President. It's a significant threat if adversaries can go from satellite to satellite, pinpointing and targeting our ISR birds. The more weight you put on a satellite, the more expensive it becomes to launch, maintain, and keep in orbit, There's a lot of considerations we have to account for as we're designing a satellite and before we launch it."

"What this military guy says here makes sense. The C.Light must have designed a satellite with the Death Star Laser gun that can pinpoint at any enemy target on Earth or in space and destroy that from space. This also means that C.Light or maybe the Pentagon does not want the enemy to know where the Death Star is controlled from and also that it exists. Hence, the location of command-and-control center in the Canadian wilderness… that too underground / underwater. Make sense. But then why whoever it is… is asking us to expose these guys and this project? Why?"

"I don't know. Who owns C.Light anyways?" Jerry quipped.

"There are two names that keep cropping up... Senator Cohen and Cobblestone. I know who Senator Cohen is... he is a Jew and supports any cause of Israel and hates Islamic states... including Saudi or UAE. If he listens to your girl, he will have her for breakfast, lunch, dinner.... Tear her apart."

"She is not "my girl." She is OOC now."

"What is OOC?"

"Out of Control... She is supported and funded by the likes of Borge Ross. So, you can imagine where that can take her."

"Where?"

"To US Congress someday in future. She is a good orator... that is what is necessary for that role." Jerry said with despise.

"Let's get back to this... So, we can't say confidently that Senator Cohen has sponsored this project so to say. It must be Cobblestone coz they have the power of money. Right?"

"That is basic 101, I should think. Coz if it was known to the government, why would anybody "select" us to publish this and bring it into the open.? Do these guys at Cobblestone... do they have any enemies? Maybe some of their enemies want to expose them."

"Yes, possibly. But let us understand the gravity and importance of this project. Is this the privatization of the Star Wars concept... that is it now sort of sub-contracted to private enterprises by the government... or is it done without government's knowledge?" So, I guess it is being done without government's knowledge... privately."

"Why?"

"I don't know... may be to blackmail someone... I have no clue."

"Look, during the Trump administration in December 2019, US has already established USSF… US Space Force. So, the government is already into this… Star Wars thing. China and Russia are also into this thing. So, why Cobblestone?"

"I don't know… maybe that is the missing link."

"During my search on the net, I found this…. Fiber Laser…Fiber-coupled Diodes. There are quite a few companies manufacturing these Fiber Laser … wherein it says here…The laser light is both generated and delivered by an inherently flexible medium, which allows easier delivery to the focusing location and target."

"Okay, so what…it does not prove anything…. Does not prove the intention."

"True… I am just giving some details… there might be some connection."

"We need to ask an expert or search ourselves what this means to Cobblestone… if they are sponsoring the project… which is what we are assuming. We could be completely wrong."

"Listen, I will go to the library and spend some time there and do some searching on this subject. I will spend the afternoon there. Will call you tomorrow. Okay?" Leo shut his laptop, shoved it in his backpack, collected his papers and walked out of the house. The weather had turned cold… indicating the arrival of fall.

New York City, NY, US

September 27, 2024; 05.00 PM

Leo had finished his "research" at the library and was at the exit of the Public Parking on the 46th street, trying to take a right turn towards 5th Avenue. The 46th street had heavy traffic, and Leo was waiting to find a gap. Suddenly, Leo noticed someone waving at him.

"What the hell is he doing here?" Leo noticed Peter Parker / Lemur waving at him.

Leo lowered the window glass and said, "What are you doing here, Mr. Parker?"

"Oh, I had come to meet someone and was walking back to my car, I noticed you."

"Are you parked here?"

"No… I can't afford to park here. I have parked at 41st and 10th."

"Oh… do you want me to drop you there?"

"No. Thank you. I will walk over there. Would you like to have coffee… it is on me. It is cold and I am dying for one myself." Lemur asked.

"Well, yes. Why not? Just hop on in and we will go." Leo asked Lemur to get into the car.

"There is Starbucks on 43rd and 9th. We can go there. It will be closer to my parking place."

"For sure," Leo said. He was also in the mood for coffee. His research was quite fruitful. He had found out how the Laser units work in the satellite. How the mirrors work and also how the cameras work. The load of the satellite has to be reduced in order to carry it in space… and make it agile. The solar panels were also important. Overall, the effectiveness of the Laser beam (minimum beam divergence) was a critical parameter and was achieved by the Fiber Laser. Solar power could be quite effective in generating the heat that is required to destroy anything on the earth. So, basically… a solar-powered or augmented Laser unit placed in a satellite in space could be a deadly weapon. It can practically destroy anything on the earth… like an ICBM or a missile or an ammunition factory or a huge area of land.

But what Leo did not find in his research was the motive for Cobblestone to sponsor the project.

"So, what were you researching at the library?" Lemur was asking.

"Well, I will tell you once we grab the coffee," Leo replied.

"Oki Doki." Lemur said.

Once they were at Starbucks and settled over their coffee, Leo started doing his data dump to Lemur who was listening intently. Finally, when Leo finished saying… "yet to find the motive," Lemur opened his trap…

"This is freaking super exciting. You must write a book. It will sell like hot cake. Really. If you want funds to get this off the ground, I can arrange to provide some funds. Seriously."

"Yeah… thanks. But I am yet to find the motive."

"Well, maybe Cobblestone guys want total control over the globe given the money they have and also the global assets they own. So, to safeguard those assets, they may be thinking of creating a security network or cover via satellites equipped with Laser weapons."

"Without the government knowing about it?" Leo quipped.

"Who cares about the government? It is likely that Cobblestone has the entire congress in their pocket... also the judiciary. I am just saying it as an example. Who knows, the government may outsource the security to Cobblestone. Or... Cobblestone wants to be on their own... private entity like Brinks."

"Yeah. Possible. But who owns C.Light? We are not sure... Is it Senator Cohen or Cobblestone?" Leo asked.

"How does it matter... Cohen cannot do it on his own. If the Pentagon is involved, it means, the Secretary of Defense is involved, some Generals must be involved... CIA cannot be far behind. I don't know, Leo. I don't understand any of this. All I know is your book can be a NY Times #1 best seller. Go for it."

"Yes, once I get the motive established... I will go for it. I will let you know. Thanks for the coffee though. I really needed it." Leo said.

After Lemur left, Leo thought about the various motives narrated by Lemur. "Maybe one of these should be the prime one. I will have to think."

Arlington, Virginia, US

September 28, 2024; 06.30 PM

It was eerily quiet in the National Cemetery. Sergei had chosen the location for meeting Nash where hardly anyone ventured at this hour of the day.

The very first question Nash shot at Sergei was… "How on earth could you think of such a weird meeting place?"

"Well, this is the place we all are finally destined to reach. So why not try it out?" Sergei replied.

"No… thank you. I will be cremated." Nash replied.

"Well, if you die of natural causes… if not, you will be toasted…. Or should I say Laser toasted."

"Meaning what?" Nash asked.

"Well, you had asked me to get some intel… you were the one who had sent me on an errand…. So, I went and got some intel for you."

"Okay… cool. Shoot it." Nash looked at his watch.

"Have you heard of Sonnenuhr?" Sergei asked.

"Nope… it is a German word for Sun Dial," Nash replied.

"You bet. But do you know what Operation Sun Dial or Betrieb Sonnenuhr is?"

"You tell me. You are the expert on continental Europe."

"That being the only thing I could get out from someone who had worked for LH Raumfahrt…. Ludolf's company."

"Yeah… okay but what does that mean?" Nash demanded.

"This being the only project where Ludolf was personally involved from conception to finish…. and was extremely confidential or secretive about. Well, I did some digging and found that the idea of a Sun Gun was conceived by Hermann Oberth in 1923. He was a rocket scientist, not a military man, and he originally wanted to use it for the purposes of capturing energy and heat transfer. He called his concept the "space mirror", and it was envisioned - well, exactly as it sounded: a giant mirror in space. It could have been part of a satellite. However, during WWII, the Nazis liked this idea and made plans to turn it into a weapon using a sodium mirror. The Nazis had updated Oberth's proposals and begun looking into the possibility of the Third Reich building a mirror weapon in orbit 22,236 miles above the earth."

"Go on," Nash said

"By the time the Allies learned of the Sun Gun plan, Nazi Germany was in ruins and the US and Soviet Union were in a mad dash to acquire Germany's so-called "wonder weapons.""

"Now both the primary and secondary mirrors of Hubble are made of a high-silicon, Ultra-Low Expansion Glass developed by Corning Glass Works. Not sure about sodium mirror though except that the Sodium has a high reflecting power."

"I am confused. What are we exactly taking about Sergei … coz you are mixing up the things?"

"Well, Sun Gun … Operation Sundial is the revised or revived concept of 3rd Reisch… revived by Ludolf and believed to be perfected by extensive research. The mirror which forms a critical part of the satellite-based Sun Gun, I am not sure what it is made up of … Sodium which has a high reflecting power or something like Hubble's mirror… light in weight, smaller in size and extremely effective. The whole assembly is manufactured by LH Raumfahrt. And yes, it can be Ghost-controlled by Ludolf."

"Okay. I get it."

"And these concepts are also known to US and Russia. So, no nukes in space… but something more dangerous is lurking in space pointed at you… which can get you cremated on ground in as-is condition."

"Are you saying it is already up in the space?"

"Possibly. I have no clue. The project has been going on for the last few years… so I am sure given the German engineering, they would have already achieved the feat. And yes, Ludolf can Ghost-control the satellite… if he decides to."

"Son of a gun."

"No… he has the Sun Gun." Sergei laughed.

"Stop joking, Sergei… this is serious stuff." Nash rebuked.

"Tell me something… can you stop this nonsense? Do you have the capacity? What will you do… write a book, publish it and expose everybody? Then what?"

"I don't know."

"Are you trying to expose some few people before the elections? So that it impacts the elections.?"

"I have not given a thought to that," Nash said. "But that is a nice thought though."

"Then why are you chasing the wild goose? Ludolf may use it to help the Neo-Nazis and ultimately grab power and rule the country and make it a nation of "purified" people. The same may be true here as well. Ultimately, in principle, everybody is a dictator… some are wearing a garb of "Democracy."

"I don't know. I just want to understand what is going on." Nash said firmly.

"No. You want to expose such people… but you are not sure how to do it."

Nash ignored the remark, so Sergei said… "Use their own methods… Create a narrative and run the narrative through or via their own media… saying it is a brilliant idea. The cat will be immediately out of the bag, and you will be able to screw the desired person."

"Thanks for the advice… and also getting the intel… albeit it is half cooked," Nash said.

"Something better than nothing," Sergei said.

"I have suggestion for you Sergei."

"Shoot."

"Why don't you tell your findings to your boss? He will get mighty impressed."

"Are you serious?"

"Absolutely."

"Seriously Nash, why do you want me to tell this to my boss…. Are you trying to smoke out the snakes?"

"Look… it is my job. If I were to become the POTUS, I would first get rid of all rouge bureaucrats. Then I would clean out the corrupt agents in National Security and clean up our intelligence apparatus. I would also clean out the agencies which have been weaponized with undue powers. I would declassify all the documents that show Deep State Spying, censorship, and corruption."

"Is that all?"

"No… I would make sure that our intelligence agencies are not spying on our citizens or on opposition party members. And stop the bloody disinformation campaign."

Sergei clapped and said… "And you would have gotten rid of the so-called Deep State. Right? Deep State is like a poison Ivy. As long as people like Borge Ross, are alive, the Deep State will continue to operate. It is there in every country… even in Europe… in a different form though. Have you seen the news… there was this big rally in Chicago… the hometown of our ex-POTUS… demanding that the help to Israel must be stopped immediately and the illegal migrants should be allowed to get absorbed into the society? Did you ever notice that all these illegal immigrants have been sort of relocated or made to settle only where there is a Democratic government…not Republicans? They are creating vote banks, Nash. People like Borge Ross are creating a false narrative to implode the US… or for that matter any other country… be it be Bangladesh or even India for that matter. The modus operandi is the same. You can't get rid of them… never."

"Thanks for the encouraging lecture. Would you mind telling your boss what I told you to tell?"

"Yes. That I will do. But if you are trying to do what you say you would do… then be careful and watch your back. Remember, you have a family."

"Okay… I am going home now. Thanks for the intel. Great job." Nash said.

"That's it? I thought you would at least treat me to a nice dinner in some Michelin Star Restaurant."

"Next week in New York. Remind me." Nash said, turned and started walking back to his car parked outside the cemetery gate.

Sergei smiled and kept looking at departing Nash…. "I know you want to expose those guys… but they are like Amoeba… cut their limb off and they will grow it again."

What Sergei had not mentioned to Nash was that based on the technical inputs given by Alexei, Sergei was able to dig in more and had been able to get precise information about the status of the so-called Sun Gun. He had promptly passed it on to Alexei who surprisingly did not seem perturbed.

"Okay. I will pass it on. But that is not like the nukes." Alexei had said, "Yes, it can destroy communication satellites for sure. Let us see. Spasibo (Good Night)!!!"

"Even that guy had said only Thank you… no appreciation of hard work. What the world has come to."

It was the first time Lemur was seeing the old man Borge Ross in flesh and blood. Till now, he had only heard of him and his power that controlled half the world.

Lemur had always dealt with Ross's son, Jeffery Ross. It had been several years since Lemur had been associated with Ross…. First indirectly, then directly. It was way better than working for the FBI. Money was good… steady source. Private Detective was only a façade.

Data dump was given by Lemur this time to the old man Borge Ross… who listened intently.

"This is great information. Tell me how you came to know this guy… Leo… you never mentioned it." Borge Ross spoke up for the first time.

Lemur was about to mention Nash but thought otherwise coz involving Nash would mean that Lemur had to go into the past and mention how he had come to know Nash and how Nash had saved his backside. Instead, Lemur thought it better to keep Nash out of this and make up a story.

"Well, I was running a personal errand and had been to the Columbia campus. There was this demonstration going on…. on the Palestine issue. I saw Leo standing there and taking some pictures and making a video. My curiosity got the better of me, and I sort of decided to follow that character. Rest, I have already mentioned." Lemur replied without blinking his eyes and without halting.

Borge Ross kept looking at Lemur… not knowing if Lemur was telling the complete truth or hiding something. Presently, he said…

"Now, I will ask you to run one errand. We will provide you with some documents as "proof" … fictitious as they may be… or partially true… which you need to hand it over to this journalist guy as also some handsome amount of money. My suggestion will be to use your car-breaking skills and plant the documents and money inside his car.… where he should find it immediately. Once that is done, the rest will fall in place. We then watch the fun." Ross turned to his son and said…

"Get our regular media guys and brief them on what needs to be published or put in the social media. Set a proper narrative… which should look authentic. Brief them on "How" to spread the news. Start doing the media releases." Ross looked at his son for confirmation.

"Got it. Will be done." Jeffery Ross assured his father. "First thing tomorrow morning."

Borge Ross was happy coz this was indeed great news to prick Cobblestone and Cohen who Borge Ross hated. "After all, I have pumped in a lot of funds into this election… I want to make sure that I get benefited."

"Even though being a Jew himself, how can he hate his own clan?" Lemur wondered. "Anyway, what the heck, I will get paid a handsome amount… why bother? I will run my last errand and be done with this stupid thing." Lemur said to himself.

There were specific reasons why Ross was happy with whatever Lemur had briefed him on. Riverly with Gregory Brink went back quite a few years. Even before Brink had become famous and powerful, it was Ross who had even China in his grips.

Borge Ross and the Chinese premier spy agency Ministry of State Security (MSS) had worked hand in glove in the 1980s, where Ross had provided substantial funding to MSS through the Economic System Reform Institute (ESRI) and China International Culture Exchange Center (CICEC).

It was just that Ross was playing a 'double game' by pursuing Western interests to infiltrate China while at the same time forging a close partnership with the Chinese intelligence network and top bosses of the Chinese Communist Party. The apparent reason was the opportunity that Ross had seen to benefit him from China's economic growth in the 1980s. But this partnership fell apart with the change in the Chinese regime after 1989.

Ross's China Fund and MSS started making overtures to China in the 1980s. He first identified and handpicked Liang Heng, a bestselling author in 1984 to set up his shop in China. Heng had become famous after publishing his memoir 'Son of the Revolution' that was a personal account of how China was opening to the West and the purges carried out at regular intervals by the Chinese Communist Party. Liang had introduced Ross to quite a few important people in the Chinese establishment. The façade kept for this whole initiative was that Ross wanted to help China to carry out reforms.

By that time, Ross had already set up 'Free Society Establishment', a funding arm actually known for instigating coups, political upheavals, and chaos in various countries through a web of well-funded Non-Governmental organizations (NGOs).

But given the fact that bets were very high in China, Ross had decided to set up a separate entity which would work only in China.

In 1986, Ross had set up 'China Fund' with a $1 million endowment. Through Liang's network, the China Fund initially partnered with a Chinese think tank, Economic System Reform Institute (ESRI). In October 1986, Ross had opened the China Fund formally in a signing ceremony at Beijing's Diaoyutai State Guesthouse. This was his first trip to China.

Ross struck gold by roping ESRI as it was considered to be close to the premier Zhao Ziyang, who had become the party's general secretary the very next year. Zhao's personal secretary, Bao Tong, was also known for helping the China Fund-ESRI joint venture whenever they needed to get through the Chinese bureaucracy. Behind the façade of helping China to shape reformist economic policies, the China Fund started spreading its tentacles very fast.

Within a year of its establishment, it set up an artists' club in Beijing and an academic unit at Nankai University in Tianjin. Within the first two years of arriving in China, Ross' s China Fund gave hefty grants for at least 200 proposals. However, as the Fund started pushing the envelope too far by funding research on sensitive topics like the notorious 'Cultural Revolution' that had resulted in the torture and deaths of millions of Chinese in 1960s, alarm bells started ringing in Chinese official circles and Zhao Ziyang had to step in despite his support for Ross and China Fund.

Zhao then had agreed to sever ties between the ESRI and the China Fund, bringing in the China International Culture Exchange Center (CICEC), a group under the Ministry of Culture, as its new partner institution.

Ross had traveled to China in February 1988 to sign a revised agreement with Yu Enguang, a Chinese spy master who was a high-ranking official of the MSS. CICEC itself was a front for the MSS. It would have been too naïve to accept that Ross didn't know about this 'open secret' though he tried to defend himself later by pleading ignorance about this fact. Ross got along well with Yu Enguang at a personal level.

The latter secured Ross a rare meeting with the top leadership of CCP in Beijing. Ross then reconfirmed his commitment to bankroll joint operations of China Fund and CICEC. MSS was using Ross's money to fund its operations under the garb of cultural exchange programs carried out by CICEC. Ross and the China Fund talked about their focus on 'cultural exchange programs,' which was a common phrase used frequently by the Chinese intelligence agencies to give legitimacy to their spy operations.

Chinese authorities suspected that the China Fund played an active role in fueling demonstrations at Tiananmen square that ended in a massacre of thousands of people by Chinese authorities. After the arrest of Zhao as well as his secretary Bao Tong, both of whom backed Ross and his China Fund, the Chinese authorities began their crackdown.

Ross had immediately shut the shop leaving many of his Chinese associates in the lurch and at the mercy of Chinese authorities. MSS, in its updates to the top party bosses, days before even the Tiananmen massacre happened, had given details about the role of China Fund as a CIA front in fueling these demonstrations. According to The Tiananmen Papers, a huge cache of internal CCP reports related to the massacre, which was leaked later, the MSS had told the party bosses, "Our investigations have revealed that Liang Heng, the personal representative of the

(China Fund) chairman Borge Ross, was a suspected US (CIA) spy."

It was clear that Ross had co-chaired the China Fund-CICEC partnership with a top-level Chinese spy master Yu Enguang (also known as Yu Fang). The MSS used the funds provided by Ross's China Fund to finance many of its operations.

While it was projected that Ross was thrown out unceremoniously from China, it might not have been so. Chinese Premier Xi has always been an enigma. Both he and Ross were (still) believed to be just putting up a show of discord. Before Ross changed his tracts and became a sudden detractor of Xi, he was invited to the annual Boao Forum for Asia conference on Hainan Island, on the southern tip of mainland China, in the spring of 2013. This was just a few months after Xi first took over the reins of China that year.

The common area of agreement was their stand on India. India's enemy would always be China's friend. Ross had been backed by China in his game to attack India's Adani Group. Adani's growing muscle to finance and execute critical infrastructure projects such as ports and airports in countries like Sri Lanka, Israel, Myanmar, and potentially Greece, big-ticket coal mining projects in Australia, various infrastructure undertakings in the African region, had started hurting China's interest.

China sponsored, Ross-backed well-timed attack by Hindenburg Research on India's Gautam Adani in January, ahead of the group's mega (over \$3 billion) follow-on public offer, was the revenge Xi and Ross had planned. Ross had then boldly confessed publicly that "Hindenburg attack on Adani will weaken Prime Minister Dodi's hold on India and lead to the revival of democracy" – referring, probably, to his own version of democracy that he'd like to apply to rapidly emerging countries outside the US.

An NGO called the Organized Crime and Corruption Reporting Project (OCCRP), funded by Ross-backed Free Society Establishment, Rockefeller Fund, and erstwhile CIA-backed Ford Foundation, had then launched the Hindenburg 2.0 attack on the Adani Group.

The NGOs funded by Ross often pick up fights with states or governments to expose their weakness or by "manufacturing" perceptions that could weaken investor confidence in the economy. This enables creating the right kind of opportunity for the billionaires like Ross (so-called philanthropist) and his elite cronies like the Rockefeller's and Rothschild's of the world, to use fully to their advantage by speculating on a given country's misfortune. The bigger the misfortunes, the bigger the generation of large profits, be it the toppling of a central bank or submerging countries in a deep currency crisis.

However, while Ross's influence in the Chinese sphere had been diminishing, the influence of Cobblestone in the Chinese market had been increasing steadily. That had been hurting Ross's ego for a while now.

Cobblestone had issued a report recommending that investors should triple their allocations in Chinese assets. Cobblestone's argument was that China, the world's second-largest economy, should no longer be considered an emerging market. Over time, Cobblestone started believing in an increased allocation to China will boost returns and provide diversification benefits that compensate investors for heightened uncertainty today.

Some conservative investors theorized that China's regulatory clampdown could signal the end of the country's economic miracle. A leading proponent of that theory had been Borge Ross as well. What Ross wrote for the Financial Times, read... "Investors in Xi's China Face a rude awakening." Ross had argued that Xi did not understand how markets operated and that the crackdown by the Chinese government was real.

Ross had also postulated that many pension fund managers allocated assets to their target markets, so they were closely aligned with their benchmarks. As an example, he had cited that one-third of Cobblestone's ESG Aware Emerging Market Fund represented investments in Chinese companies. Ross had concluded that the US Congress should pass a bipartisan bill requiring asset managers to invest only in companies where actual governance structures are transparent and aligned with stakeholders. The US Congress House of Representatives- Select Committee of the Chinese Communist Party, had then sent to Gregory Brink of Cobblestone…requesting information about Cobblestone's facilitation of American capital flows to Chinese companies that have been blacklisted by the US government.

Ross had been always on the lookout for an opportunity to grind an axe against Cobblestone. Now, with whatever Lemur had narrated, he had found an excellent opportunity to tarnish Cobblestone.

Lemur could see the happiness in Borge Ross's eyes. Lemur knew Ross's antisemitic views and stand… which he always wondered … but this glee in Ross's eyes was quite different.

Washington D.C., US

September 29, 2024; 08.30 PM

Spring Valley in DC is considered as the epitome of affluence. A beautiful two-story bungalow with Corinthian architecture showing off in the front and a walled compound with a video camera installed at the gate, stood in the autumn dark. There were a few non-descript cars standing in front of the bungalow.

The scenario unfolding inside was after Sergei had whispered about Ludolf's possible SunGun in the ears of his boss. The news had immediately reached the corner offices in various sections of the government and the congregation of VIPs was now inside the bungalow.

Russ Pankrats, Director of CIA, Graham Hick, SecDef, Secretary of State Bob Mayers, Senator Cohen and Gregory Brink were sitting around the massive dinner table. The dinner was over, and they were all sitting with their glasses of Rémy Martin Louis XIII Magnum Cognac.

With the servers gone and doors closed, Gregory cleared his throat and looked at Russ and said… "The floor is all yours Russ."

Russ took a sip of his brandy and said… "Well, I am not sure how to put this… but there seems to be a leak somewhere in our system. Coz just today, I have learned from my source that our Operation Taranis has already been either accomplished or is in the verge of getting accomplished in Germany. There is a company, LH Raumfahrt in Germany, belonging to one Ludolf Hoffmann, which seems to have accomplished this feat. I am trying to find out as to how our intel was leaked out to Germany."

Secretary of Defense Graham Hicks laughed and retorted… "Don't sweat, Russ. Little knowledge is always a dangerous thing. The principle of Operation Taranis is based on a Sun Gun concept which was conceived by one Herr Hermann Oberth in 1923. He was a rocket scientist, not a military man, and he originally wanted to use it for the purposes of capturing energy and heat transfer. During WWII, the Nazi's liked this idea, and made plans to turn it into a weapon, using a sodium mirror. The Nazis had updated Oberth's proposals and begun looking into the possibility of the Third Reich building a mirror weapon in orbit 22,236 miles above the earth." Graham paused.

"Go on." Gregory said

"By the time the Allies learned of the Sun Gun plan, Nazi Germany was in ruins and the US and Soviet Union were in a mad dash to acquire Germany's so-called "wonder weapons. We had now brought it out of the cold and started working on it. So, Germany has not stolen it from us, it is the other way round. They already had the concept… it is just that your boys had been sleeping and making merry with the European street girls… and so, they were late to get the intel." Graham stopped.

"Can you not stage a sabotage this German company… what was the name?" Gregory asked.

"LH Raumfahrt. And No, we will not be able to coz we ourselves buy some of our critical components from them for our satellite and radar systems." Graham answered.

"So, where does this leave us? Do we have options?" Gregory asked.

"I think we should proceed with our plan coz no one knows our plans. So, if the Germans or Europeans have it… the Sun Gun, we can have it too and it would be a surprise to everybody. We can assume that Even the Russians have it. The Chinese may not know but even if they do… it will take some time for them to catch up." Graham said.

"I agree." Bob Myers opened his mouth for the first time.

"Guys, do you even know who this Ludolf Hoffmann is? Let me enlighten you." Senator Cohen seemed angry. "Ludolf's grandfather was an SS officer during WWII. He ran away to Argentina. We were never able to catch hold of him. He was quite close to Hitler. His son turned out to be a sissy, but the old man mentored Ludolf extremely well and so, Ludolf strictly believes in the "Aryan" philosophy of the Third Reich. So, if his company has already developed the so-called Sun Gun and deployed it in space via Euro-space, then we need to know. Coz it can cause severe damage to Israel."

"Senator, these are all speculations based on some story told by Russ's boys. How much of it is true, we don't even know. So, there is no point in fretting and fuming over this issue. It is in fact a non-issue." Graham said.

"We will find out who all are associated with Ludolf and what is the real situation quickly," Russ said.

"No need. Don't bother. Graham, I agree with you. Let us continue with our project and get it up quickly. I need to see the progress ASAP." Gregory retorted.

"Understood. Thank you." Graham quickly acknowledged.

"I hope there are no other issues… Russ?" Gregory asked… "Hopefully, there is no leak or leaks."

"Well, no." Russ was highly embarrassed. "Had I known the historical perspective, I would not have called for this meeting," Russ said sheepishly.

"What about the underground and underwater constructions at the three sites?" Gregory asked.

"The work is progressing as planned. The command control center will be completed first. The one for the Seedbank will be the next and the one for the health… hospital and pharma dev center will be the last. The second and third will be completed almost neck to neck." Graham replied.

"Alright. If there is nothing more, then we can call it a day." Gregrory said, finishing his remaining drink in one gulp and getting up from his chair.

"I made an ass of myself." Russ thought to himself as he walked towards his car. "Clearly, Graham took the opportunity to score a few points today. Not sure why the heck they involved that jackass, Bob Myers. He has no role to play. Oh… how I hate these scums." Russ was furious and he could not express his anger… which frustrated him even more.

New York City, NY

October 1, 2024; 08.30 AM

Lemur was sitting in his car keeping an eye on Leo's parked car in front of his apartment complex. Eventually at 8.30 AM Lemur saw Leo walking towards his car. Momentarily he opened his car door and got into the car.

Unknown to Lemur, there was someone else who had been keeping an eye on Lemur ever since Lemur had arrived there. Lemur had arrived at 3.30 AM and proceeded to break open Leo's car. It was an age-old Toyota Camry with no alarm system. While Lemur was busy opening the car and carrying out his task, there was someone lurking in the shadows… wondering what Lemur was doing there. That person had come there to carry out the exact same task… but with a different motive.

Observing Lemur carrying out his task, the man slowly withdrew in shadows and had gone back to his car parked nearby. Lemur had never seen or suspected that he was being caught in his actions.

Presently, Lemur could observe Leo's reaction when Leo found the brown envelope stuck under his steeling wheel. Leo looked around from the windshield to check if anyone was observing him. The he opened the envelope and saw the contents. Lemur could see the excitement on Leo's face. Leo seemed to count the money multiple times… coz he could not believe having so much cash. Lemur had put $10,000 along with the proof which Borge Ross had provided him.

Lemur observed Leo took out his cell phone and was about to dial a number, when he changed his mind and kept the cell phone away. Leo then started the car and waited for another couple of minutes before driving it. Once he was on the road, Lemur started following it. The man in the other car also started following Lemur.

Lemur realized that Leo had not changed his routine. He was heading for the Public Parking lot on 46th street. He was certain that Leo would go to the library and spend a couple of hours there before heading to his next destination. Lemur managed to find a spot to just about squeeze in his car and wait till Leo's return to the parking lot.

However, this time instead of going to the library Leo proceeded to 42nd street to Bank of America. He went to the ATM. There were already a few people in the line. Leo waited. He wanted to deposit $5000 in his account. The rest of the amount he would deposit the next day. However, while standing there in the line, Leo thought about the implications of putting $5000 in the bank… coz he had thus far never deposited more than few hundred dollars. Finally, after debating with himself he decided not to put the money in the bank, and he came out of the line.

He called Jerry and informed him about the brown envelope containing significantly important papers being placed under the steering wheel… and that he wanted to drive down to Jerry's place to discuss the matter. Leo, however, did not inform Jerry about the money that he had received.

Jerry agreed to meet him and so Leo went back to the public car park on 46th Street and got his car out. Since Lemur was certain that Leo would be back after 2 hours, he was busy browsing his cell phone and did not notice Leo leaving the parking lot.

While Lemur was busy browsing his cell phone, the man in the other car was paying attention on Lemur as well as on the exit of the parking lot. Momentarily he saw Leo leaving the parking lot, the man did not follow Leo. He had a hunch about Leo's next destination. He wanted to check where Lemur was heading.

After two hours Lemur had become impatient coz, he had not seen Leo leaving the parking lot. Without waiting anymore, Lemur decided to abandon the chase and go back to Jeffery Ross's office to inform him that he had accomplished the task. Jeffery did not like speaking on the phone coz he was of the firm opinion that someone might be recording the cell phone conversation.

Lemur parked his car a block away from Jeffery's office which was on West 57th Street and decided to walk. Lemur was so preoccupied with his thoughts that he failed to notice that he was being followed. When Lemur finally entered the building, the man chasing him was extremely surprised…

"That is the office of the Free Society Establishment!!!" The man muttered. It was a rude shock to him…. "I can't believe this." He said to himself, turned back and went quickly back to his car.

"I guess, we have a potential problem at hand." He again muttered to himself.

Jersey City, NJ, US

October 1, 2024; 10.30 AM

"Okay, what have you got this time?" Jerry asked as soon as he let Leo inside his house.

"Oh, wait till you hear this." Leo said "Someone broke into my car and put this brown envelope under my steering wheel. The guy used sticking tape to hold the envelope in place. And then he locked the car door again. Can you believe this?"

"Yeah… this means the guy we are dealing with is a professional. When he was sitting next to me in the bus, I could not suspect him…!!!"

"Yeah… I know. Well, here are the so-called proof… Most of them are photographs. Here is the Secretary of Defense abord his Yacht with his family on the shores of Florida… It is a 100 feet long big Yacht worth $ 7 Million. This was gifted to him by Cobblestone's Brink. There is no mention of this Yacht in SecDef's assets."

"Here is another photograph where the SecDef is seen with Gregory Brink of Cobblestone on another Yacht, which belongs to Brink. Both are with their respective families."

"Here are some copies of the documents showing SecDef, Cohen and CIA chief, Secretary of State etc… all big names owing Cobblestone stocks."

"Leo… please stop. This is not the evidence. They don't prove nothing. I mean nothing related to the underground / underwater stuff. Someone is trying to fool you, fool us. We need some proof that shows the direct involvement of Pentagon in the underground / underwater and the Star War whatever, project or operation. And we don't have it. These are all garbage stuff. Seriously."

"Well, I just shared what I got." Leo said… "Why would they pay me $10000 for such garbage stuff? Am I missing something?" Leo thought to himself.

"Perhaps we need to wait for some more concrete evidence … who knows… they may send us…or they may not. I don't know. But seriously, if that someone wants you to write the book, it is not going to get written overnight… nor it is going to get published overnight… and certainly not before the elections if someone is trying to screw somebody." Jerry said.

"Makes sense." Leo said, picking up all the photographs and copies of the documents and shoving them in his backpack. "We will wait."

Money had reminded Leo of Lemur aka Peter Parker… coz he was the one who was excited about the book and had told Leo that he would fund him if necessary. "If Peter Parker is the guy, then why the heck did he break into my car and left the money there. He could have paid me in person. Or… is Peter Parker is not what he says he is… and possibly working for somebody…. using me as a scapegoat." Leo was suddenly frightened. "Shit. Good that I have not deposited the money in my bank account"

Openly Leo just said… "I will call you in case I get something." and collecting his backpack he went out of the door.

There was hardly any customer in the Barnes and Nobel located on the M St NW in DC. In the far corner two elderly men were sitting back-to-back engrossed in reading. There was a pile of books in front of them.

The lady at the counter had recognized one of them as their regular customer. She had not seen the other guy… but apparently, they were not connected as the unknown man had come first and was more interested in the history section… while the known face had come a little later and had gone to the autobiographies section. They were sitting with their backs to each other… so the lady figured that they were two different customers.

"This is unbelievable" Nash said…. His lips hardly moved.

"Yes. I also could not believe myself." The other man whispered… He was Doug Walter, commonly known as Meercat in his professional circle. His face somewhat resembled a Meercat, and someone had christened him as Meercat. Meercat had officially retired from the CIA a few years back and had started his own Private Investigation Firm. At CIA he was in the National Clandestine Service in the counterintelligence center…. and was tasked with keeping an eye on some of the key federal officials…. Including FBI and CIA as well.

Nash and Doug had one thing in common… both were die-hard nationalistic in nature. Their paths often crossed, and they soon had become friends. After Doug's retirement Nash had been using Doug's services whenever he wanted absolute care.

Doug, aka Meercat had been put on the trail of Leo and Jerry even though Nash had asked Lemur to follow them. Nash always believed in perfection and trust. He definitely had more trust in Doug. And now it had been proven again.

"I could have never imagined this Nash. Never." Meercat said under his breath.

"Well, don't be surprised if you find 75% of this government's employees are puppets of Ross. He is the one who runs the government from behind the curtain. Well, I am sure there are others too like him."

"That is frightening." Meercat said.

"Some of the Dem's ex-Presidents may probably be on Ross's role. I won't be surprised. The one in Chicago seems to be definitely under his wings." Nash whispered.

"Heard that Ross guy is Jewish, and he is also antisemitic. He is the one supporting all these Palestine demos." Meercat whispered.

"Yes. But let that be. Now this is what I think… Ross may create conditions which would put Leo's and Jerry's life in danger. So, I think you need to protect them… well Leo in particular. Jerry may not be under their radar yet. So, keep a hawk's eye on Leo and try to protect him if required." Nash whispered.

"Understood. Meeting here was a good idea. I kind of liked it." Meercat said.

"You first, or should I?" Nash asked.

"You go first. I will keep your back." Meercat replied.

"Great job. Thanks." Nash whispered. Got up, chose one book from the pile of books, and went to the counter to pay. It was close to 6.45 PM. Nash looked at the closing hours written on the glass door.

"Another 15 minutes and the shop would close." He thought to himself. He pulled up his great coat collar and walked out in the bitter cold.

Meercat soon followed the suit.

New York City, NY, US

October 15, 2024; 02.30 PM

Jeffery Ross was listening to the ideas thrown at him by media people he had invited to his office. He had explained them the situation and wanted them to come up with a few good ideas to publicize the matter… faster and to wider audience. The lady who was in charge of the Media Management at Free Society Establishment was also present with her two assistants who were taking notes.

"The best way is via social media" a smartly dressed blonde said as soon as Jeffery had completed his narration.

"Dumb blonde" Jeffery thought to himself. "It is basic 101, even a third grader would tell that." But he said nothing.

After many ideas and hot debate, it was finally decided that the best way to publicize fast and to many was via a video… which would go viral quickly.

- The title should be extremely catchy, and it should not be too big and too verbose.

- Putting it on social media… like WhatsApp or TikTok or Instagram would be the fastest way to reach many across the country.

- It should be released by lunch time coz people will be able to check it out immediately here on the east coast and since it would be morning time on the West coast, people would be able to check it out too.

"When can we have the proof?" The lady Media Manager asked.

"We will need at least two weeks to get it out to social media. So, proof should be ready in 7-10 days."

"No. Give us a date and time." Jeffery demanded.

"October 22nd. And final video on October 25th towards end of the day That is the best we can do."

"Okay. October 22nd it is" Said the lady Media Manager.

Jeffery got up and left the conference room.

Leo was sitting at the dining table taking the sip of the coffee made by Jerry. They had decided to go over the complete chronology of events, put the facts together and edit the "story" written by Leo.

Leo had spent better part of last week in "writing" the story. He wanted Jerry to read it and together they would edit.

"Let us make a file folder to keep all the documents and let the folder remain at your place Jerry. It is better that way. In any case, you are the one who is going to publish it.... whenever the time comes."

"Hope so." Jerry smirked.

Leo took out all the material out from his backpack that he had received thus far, laid it on the table. Then he took out almost 30-40 odd A4 size pages from his backpack and dumped them on the table.

"Now, what the heck is that?" Jerry asked.

"Oh, that is the story that I have written." Leo replied.

"Written… I thought you would have typed… you have a laptop… don't you?"

"Yes. But it is easy for me to correct the text or the diction on paper… plus I can put some notes in the margin area for my reference… and I have no fear that I would lose anything if my laptop crashes… unexpectedly."

"Man… what a pessimistic guy you are." Jerry laughed.

"Pragmatic… not pessimistic.".

"Alright, where do we start?" Jerry inquired.

"You start reading the story…if there needs to be a correction, we can do that immediately. Then we can give reference numbers to the documentary evidence that we have. That way we are clear. When we receive new evidence, we can include that at the appropriate place."

"Okay sounds good…. But what kind of evidence are we expecting now.?"

"Well, like what the other two underground constructions meant for. Or In what way Pentagon is directly associated with the projects funded by Cobblestone."

"Are they?"

"Maybe. I don't have evidence."

"Okay… let us start. And yes, keep the entire file in some safe place."

"Like where?"

"I don't know…. may be under the vegetables in the vegetable tray in your refrigerator. No one will possibly check he fridge"

"Who you think would want to check? FBI?"

"I don't know. I am just saying be careful."

"Okay." Jerry shrugged his shoulders. "Should we?"

Over the next two hours both Jerry and Leo went over what Leo had written. They made some corrections, wrote down the evidence numbers and referenced them to page numbers of the script.

Finally, around 1.00 PM, they finished the proper filing of the papers….a book that would be born in the future.

That done, both decided that it is time for lunch and even a burger from McD would be a reward.

Langley, Virginia, US

October 28, 2024; 12.30 PM

Russ Pankrats looked at the watch… it was 12.30 PM. "Another half an hour!!!" He cribbed. Russ had missed his breakfast as he had an early morning meeting. The war in the Middle East had made his life miserable.

Momentarily, his cell phone rang. It was his wife. He wanted to disconnect the phone but thought otherwise and answered.

"Yes honey."

"Hey, have you seen the video, I just shared with you on WhatsApp. It was forwarded to me by my friend. It mentions the Agency and hence I forwarded it to you. Are you guys working on some Sun Gun like in Star Wars? Cool… you never said anything about it to me…. Blah blah blah…."

Russ had practically stopped hearing anything after he had heard the Sun Gun. He was practically frozen. "A viral video on Sun Gun… this is a bloody disaster." The first thought that came to Russ's mind.

He opened WhatsApp and checked the video sent by his wife. After watching the video Russ wanted to find a hole big enough for him to hide. Their entire plan… rather plans "Operation Castellon and Operation Taranis" were lying in the open. Russ's mouth went dry. He had forgotten about his lunch.

The phone on his table suddenly came alive and Russ jumped with a jolt. He picked up the phone. It was secure line… "1400 Hours, Spring."The man at the other end whispered and the line went dead.

Russ was completely frozen… as if someone had removed all the blood from his body. He wanted to die…. Rather than getting prosecuted for treason. "How the f**k this has happened? Where is the bloody leak? Who leaked out the entire information…. Who?" Russ was furious as well as shit scared.

He took his jacket, long coat and went out of his cabin closing the door behind him. While walking towards the car parking he realized that he had almost lost all the energy from his body. His legs seemed to weigh a ton each.

He somehow drove the car to Spring Valley. The camera installed at the gate saw his car and did face recognition process and then opened the gate. There were already 4 cars in the parking lot.

When Russ entered the dining room, he saw Graham Hick, SecDef, Secretary of State Bob Mayers, Senator Cohen sitting around the table waiting for Gregory Brink. Russ took a seat. No one said a word or uttered any greetings to Russ.

Exactly at 2.00 PM Gregory entered the room and took his seat.

He immediately turned to Russ and said one word…. "Explain."

Russ was dumbfounded. He could not utter even a single word. He felt as though he had lost his voice. With great efforts he said….

"I don't know anything about this. I have no clue who leaked it or how this got leaked out."

"Okay. Any suggestions for damage control?" Brink asked.

No one replied.

"Let us just forget that anything has happened at all. If there are any reporters or any media personnel… just laugh it out saying it is absurd. This is just a Hollywood story spun by some idiot. Also, blame it on Russia. Mention… Russia might be thinking of putting nukes in the space and hence they are trying to divert the attention. Be pleasant. Be cheerful… Make jokes. Perhaps organize some big party and let the booze flow. People should think that someone had done a Halloween joke. Yes… that is it… Halloween joke." Gregory paused.

"Now coming to this guy Leo or whoever he is… catch him and eliminate him. Get hold of the so-called proof or evidence he has collected. That is a must. That is a must and needs to be done within 24 hours. Let him not escape out of the country. Russ… hopefully you can get at least this thing done. If not, tell me now. I can make arrangements." Gregory said. His tone was quite harsh and cold.

"In any case I will make my own plans" Gregory thought to himself as he did not want to trust Russ.

"Yes. I will get it done." Somehow Russ managed to say.

"Within 24 hours." Gregory said in a rough tone. He got up from his chair and left the room. No one said anything and left the room one by one.

After coming back to the office, Russ got hold of his team and told them to get all the intel on this Leo guy… where he lives, his car, his wife, kids, anything, and everything and eliminate him immediately.

"Sir, this is the territory of FBI… not ours." Someone reminded him.

"I don't give a shit. Don't teach me. Just get it done" Russ shouted. "Set up a small command center … ops room and first locate him. You have 2 hours. Get out."

After the team went Russ collapsed in his chair.… Holding his head in his palms. He wanted to cry. He had no clue how the heck this had happened.

However, Gregory Brink was quite calm. He had understood who would have played such a mischief. He had understood his adversary quite well.

He dialled a number and asked the person to meet him in half an hour. Gregory knew what he wanted to do. "I am capable of returning the favors with interest." He said to himself.… And got busy with his own work. He had forgotten about the video. He was confident that his man would get the job done.

Langley, Virginia, US

October 28, 2024; 03.30 PM

Norman Timken was quite perplexed at the irrational behavior of Russ. He had never seen Russ in such a panic mode and foul mood. Something terrible must have happened…. But why was Russ perturbed about a guy named Leo. Norman did not even have any specific details like… last name, location, address etc….. without which it was like searching for a needle in a haystack.

The face of Leo which was flashed on the video seemed like a distant shot and was out of focus. The ops room was being set up. It would require another half an hour to get started. The only way Norman thought he could get hold of Leo is via his cell phone. He would concentrate on Leo's cell phone… which of course Norman did not have but was positive that someone may call out the name Leo and that would trigger the next step of getting the specific cell number.

Leo was a very uncommon name… most people would go by Leonard… not Leo. So, it would be easy to catch. But there were over 8 Million people in NY city alone. That is what Norman was afraid of… as Leo name would get lost in the chatter of 8 million people.

"No harm in trying. If we get lucky… fair enough." Norman thought to himself. He had alerted his street teams as well. They would be ready to move and close in within minutes.

418

Leo was visiting Rockefeller Plaza while on his way home. He wanted to buy a new jacket for a while and had been saving some money. But now he had $10,000 and he thought he could definitely afford to buy a good sturdy jacket for winter. The shopping mall was crowded. Halloween was nearing, and he could see shops with display of Halloween costumes. Leo was still busy doing window shopping and had not decided on a specific place to buy the jacket.

Momentarily his cell phone buzzed. It was Jerry. He was in a panic mode.

"Where the heck are you. I have trying to get you for a while." Jerry sounded as if something terrible had happened.

"Why… what happened?"

"There is a video which has gone viral, it has leaked out all the information that we have received, and it showed your photograph and said you are the one who got all this sensitive information out of Pentagon. Now you will be the most wanted person. You must run and hide someplace for a while." Jerry was speaking fast.

Leo suddenly went blank… "What the hell Jerry was talking about… what video. How come I did not get it… who the hell knew all the information that I had… suddenly Perter Parker's face came to Leo's mind. "Oh my god… that guy. He is the only one whom I narrated everything. He must have taken my photo either while leaving the restaurant or while entering. Jeez…" Leo was thinking fast.

"Leo… Leo… are you there?" Jerry was asking…

"Yes. Thank you, Jerry. Bye" Leo immediately disconnected the phone and started to go back to the parking lot where he had parked his car.

While he was moving someone bumped into him… apologized and started walking. Leo momentarily lost his balance. But he managed and started to walk. His cell phone rang… thinking it was Jerry; Leo answered the phone.

"Throw your cell phone in the next garbage bin. You are being followed by 3 agency men… either FBI or CIA. Just throw your cell phone. You will find 2 cell phones in your jacket's right pocket. I will call you on one of them. Right now, just throw your cell phone into the garbage bin… it is right in front of you on your left." The phone went dead.

Leo thought for a second and threw his phone into the garbage bin. He must have walked 5 steps when a phone rang in his pocket. He picked up the one which was ringing…

"Listen, go to the shop which is on your right-hand side… pick up a Halloween costume with a witch hat. Wear it. Throw this cell phone in the garbage bin. Keep the other phone with you. Wearing the outfit, go to the Starbucks… there you will find an empty coffee jar on top of the trash can. There is a piece of paper inside with an address. Get the paper. Go out of the mall, get into the yellow cab, and go to the address. Get down one block before the address and walk the remaining distance. The key to the apartment is below the door mat. Collect it and go inside. Wait for my phone. Now throw this phone off. Be quick. There are 3 guys coming on to you." The phone went dead.

Leo did what he was told to do. He threw the phone, went to the shop, bought the Halloween costume. Wore it, came out, went to the Starbucks shop, found the empty coffee cup, got the address, went out and got into the yellow cab.

The cab driver was Hispanic. Hardly spoke any English. He was playing loud music. Leo tried to concentrate. "How the hell did they know I was there. Who was the man guiding me. How did the phones come into my pocket… Ahhh… when the guy bumped into me. Why is he helping me? Is he the one who gave me all the leads… and the money? I thought it was that Peter guy. He was a sweet talker… F**k… I should not have told anything to him. He must have been working for FBI or CIA or whatever."

The phone in Leo's pocket rang. Leo answered. "You, okay?"

"Yes."

"Throw the phone from the car window on the grass knoll on next turn."

"Okay."

The phone went dead.

Leo did exactly what he was asked to do. Now he had no cell phone. He felt even more insecure.

Leo gathered that he was nearing the destination. He told the driver to stop and drop him before the destination. The driver did not care. He got his money and went away. Leo walked the remaining distance to the apartment. He found the key under the door mat. He opened the door, went inside, and collapsed on the only sofa in the living room.

He was so tired. "How the hell did they track me?" he had that question pricking him. "Cell Phone… but of course… Peter had my cell phone… OMG. No wonder the guy was telling me to throw my cell phone into the garbage bin. But why 2 -3 different phones? May be they were following my voice or my face via cameras in the mall? Yes… that is the reason the guy asked me to wear the hat. Clever…. Which means the guy must also be working in either CIA or FBI. Now what?" Leo thought to himself. His heart was still pounding hard. His throat had become dry.

He removed his Halloween garb and started to explore the apartment. It was a one-bedroom apartment with a small sofa, one small dining table and one bed. There was a fridge and a microwave and an electric plate to heat up the things.

Inside the fridge Leo found some fresh bread, Margarine, eggs, and some lettuce leaves. Leo now became aware of his hunger… but decided to pass it. There were some water bottles in the fridge. Leo took one and came back to the living room.

It was almost 6.00 PM… Leo sat down. The sofa was quite comfortable. He was so tired that he dozed off while sitting.

Langley, Virginia, US

October 28, 2024; 06.00 PM

"How the f**k could you lose him. How many years have you all been working… damn it. You can't even catch one simple civilian."

"We did not know his last name, no address, no phone number… yet we could get him. Out of the phone chatter of 8 million people in the city, we could zero onto him in just half an hour. But the mall is so crowded… plus it is Halloween time… too many kids running around. My 3 agents were on him in just under 3 minutes. But…" Norman paused.

"But what? Russ shouted.

"But I think he acted like a pro."

"What?"

"Yes… either he is a pro, or he was helped by a pro."

"Elaborate"

"He switched cell phone one after another. This means he had the phone with him earlier on… or there was somebody that gave him the phones. Coz there are areas which are not covered by Mall cameras. Only a pro could figure that out. We checked all the videos… He throws one phone then disappears, then we see him on another phone, then he disappears… then he never appeared… he was gone. This meant… either he was a pro, or he was helped by a pro. But if he was helped by a pro… he himself would not know the angles of the Mall cameras. He would appear lost. But that was not the case. So, I think we are dealing with a pro."

"Go on"

"There were other 3 guys chasing him. They were not ours. They looked like hired killers…. We have their pics… and from their appearance, they looked to be carrying what I think …. a Mauser each. They moved very swiftly… but when that guy Leo disappeared, they also disappeared. So, I am not sure if they were his would-be assassins or his accomplice. Either way Leo name could be German or Russian too. So, it is not that we are dealing with some simple civilian. We might be dealing with a pro or a team of pro." Norman stopped.

Russ was sitting in his chair lost in his thoughts. He felt like someone had checkmated him in one simple move.

"What if he reappears… can you find him?"

"No. coz now he will not be in the same shape size and tone. Not a chance. But… we can try something else."

"What?"

"The way we got hold of him was there was someone calling him and he repeated… Leo, Leo are you there? The voice seemed to be of a young person… perhaps in his 20s. We have his phone number. We can catch hold of him and get the details of this guy Leo."

"Do it…. But not today. Remember, Leo has discarded his phone. I am sure your guys must have recovered that phone. Check it out completely and then approach the young guy. Perhaps tomorrow morning. Find out his whereabouts first. Don't rush. I don't want any hassles with the media. The elections are round the corner. I don't want last minute f**k up of any kind." Russ said.

"Bad news again. We could not get his discarded phones. By the time our guys went, the phones were gone."

"What the f**K… I mean how come your guys are so slow? Can't they move fast? Anybody could have picked up the phone. All one has to do is to throw out the sim card and use the phone again. It is that simple. Anybody could have picked up the phone."

"Or may be his assassins or accomplices… they could have picked up too. Unfortunately, we can't see the trash cans via cameras." Norman said.

"Go after that young guy, first thing in the morning." Russ said. He wanted to puke. He was feeling sick. He felt defeated.

Gregory Brink had already got the message that Leo had vanished. Gregory understood as to who would be helping Leo. But he remained calm. Nothing disturbed him.

New York City, NY

October 28, 2024; 11.00 PM

Leo was still sleeping in the sitting position with his mouth wide open. Momentarily, Leo stirred and that is when it dawned on him that he was still sitting on the sofa holding the bottle of water in his hand. He also became aware of a person sitting on a chair near the opposite wall. His face was under shadow which Leo could not see properly.

"Are you feeling, okay?" the man asked. "You look exhausted."

"Yes. But who are you… Are you the one who helped me escape?"

"Perhaps." The man replied. "You must be hungry. I have brought burger, fries, and a coffee for you. It is on the table. Go and eat while it is warm. We can talk later."

Leo nodded his head and went to the dining table. He sat at the table and started eating. He was famished. Suddenly he remembered that he had not asked the man sitting in the shadows if he had eaten or not.

"How about you. Have you eaten?" Leo asked.

"Maybe. But let us not worry about me. You finish your dinner." The man said.

"Can I know your name?" Leo asked.

"What will you do by knowing my name? Publish it in your book?" The man asked.

Leo was taken aback. He must be the man who must have sent me the pizza boxes and other stuff. He thought to himself.

"You will find the trash can in the kitchen" The man said.

When Leo came back to the sofa, the man said… are you okay to talk?"

"Yes" Leo replied.

"Okay. Now you are finished here in the US. Your buddy has burned you… your identity."

"My buddy?"

"Yes, the one who always followed you, told you about becoming # 1 NYT bestseller. Remember him?"

"Peter Parker?"

"Is that his real name?" the man asked.

"I don't know. That is what he told me."

"So, your Mr. Spider-Man… Peter Parker happens to be an informant of Mr. Borge Ross. I am sure you know who Borge Ross is?" The man asked.

Leo felt like someone has given him a kick in his guts. "What? He… Mr. Borge Ross's employee?"

"Yes. And it was he who gave you the last consignment of papers and whatever after breaking open your car…."

"Money. $10,000. I still have the money. I haven't spent."

"Keep it. You will need them. Ross wanted to use you for their selfish benefit. You are just a pawn. No more. Your death will mean nothing to anyone. But by making a video on the basis of what you told Mr. parker, and putting your name, picture alongside, Ross made a bait to the powers… Pentagon, CIA NSA etc."

"So, he tried to kill multiple birds in one stone. It is the show of power. You are nobody. A dispensable item no more."

"Now what?"

"Now nothing. You need to find a new name, new identity, new country to live in and survive. Find a country where there is no extradition treaty with US. Anyway, the US will forget you after a few years. Then you can return. Till that time, you need to run away…. Go to Mexico… Haiti, Honduras. You have the money. Use them. We can manage to take you to Mexico and leave you there. If you are okay with it."

"What happens to Jerry?"

"We don't know. It is because of you he has come on to the radar or the agency. I don't know what they will do to him or about him."

"What do I do now?"

"Nothing for next 7 days… till the elections are over… nothing. Just sit here and relax. There is no internet here. So, don't open your laptop. Any electronic associated with you can get you in trouble…. like emails."

"Then?"

"After the elections, we will make arrangements to change your identity and ship you across the border. After that you are on your own Mr. Investigative journalist. And BTW… here is your cell phone… but without sim card. Naturally." Said the man

"Thank you."

"You will be able to use it after going to Mexico, okay?"

"Yes."

"I have kept some fruits and salads in the fridge. You will be receiving pizza and burgers at your doorstep for next seven to ten days. Please do not venture out at all. We will get you some clothes. Don't worry. If you venture out and get caught/ killed, it is your responsibility. Not ours."

"Who are We?"

"Nobody… as far as you are concerned. Period." The man's tone had changed. "Now you can go to the bedroom and sleep"

"Okay. Thank you for saving my life."

"By the way where have you both kept all the material that you received. Coz the people who came after you will be looking for that stuff and if it is with that boy…. Only God can save his life." The man said.

"It is in the vegetable tray in his fridge. It is a n file folder." Leo said.

"Hope they don't find it. Otherwise, your friend Jerry… right… will be gone. Trust me. They don't care about you or I. Good night."

"Good night" Leo said and went to the bedroom carrying his backpack with him. After about fifteen minutes Leo came back to the living room only to find that it was empty. The man sitting in the shadows had vanished.

"I am screwed because of Peter Parker." Leo thought to himself.

New York City, NY, US

October 29, 2024; 09.30 AM

Jerry had tried to call Leo several times, but his phone had been turned off. Jerry was afraid that something might have happened to Leo after the video went viral with his picture and name. Jerry wondered if Leo had given this information to anyone else… coz the information used in the video matched their own information. In addition, Leo's name was mentioned in the video.

"Or is it that Leo sold the information to somebody… but in such a case why they would use Leo's name? Also, the video maker did not have any evidence. All the documents are with me." Jerry thought to himself.

Suddenly Jerry remembered Prof. Matthew. He was excited and thought that he would go and meet Prof. Matthew and get his guidance on this matter. With that thought, Jerry quickly got dressed up and left his house for Columbia. Before going out Jerry opened his fridge and saw that the file folder was still in the vegetable tray. Satisfied, he left for Columbia.

When he reached Columbia, the activity was as usual. He found Prof. Matthew in his room.

"Hello Prof. Matthew. Good morning."

"Morning Jerry. What brings you here? I don't think you have any class today." Prof. Matthew replied.

"No Prof. Matthew. I came here to meet you and get your advice" Jerry said.

"Oh. On what?"

Jerry narrated he entire story till the disappearance of Leo to Prof. Matthew.

"Jerry, do you recall that I had once told you to stay miles away from the Deep State elements. Yes?"

"Yes Prof. Matthew."

"But then you completely ignored my advice and got yourself involved with the Deep State elements. You could have chosen to ignore their advances… but in your own wisdom, you went ahead and go entangled in their net."

"But where is the Deep Sate in this Prof. Matthew?"

"What you have been describing so far are and will always be a part of the Deep State… the National Security Apparatus, Various Federal Departments, their Bureaucrats, the Lobbies that we had spoken about, people like Ross and Cobblestone, the government machinery. Did we talk about them or not?"

"Yes, we did… but how was I supposed to understand that this belongs to Deep State.?"

"Jerry basic 101… Anything clandestine such as what you described, will it happen without the knowledge of the governments? The answer is No. So, there is something big which has been taking place outside the purview of common men… so, definitely the Deep State elements are at work. You can't get rid of them Jerry. Government creates departments just to siphon out money so that they can use that money for clandestine purposes. Those departments are never audited and never supervised by anyone except the POTUS. Here in your case too, the Deep Sate elements are at work, and I am not sure how you can escape their clutches. Your friend Leo, he must have been a pawn too or maybe he was implanted by them. Cathy Dexter is one of them. I told you to stay away from her as well. Now I don't know what or how I can help you. Sorry Jerry, you have already crossed the bridge. You may have to manage on your own. All I can do is wish you a good luck."

Jerry was crestfallen. He did not know what to do. He thanked Prof. Matthew and with heavy feet and a heavy head he left the campus. He had no idea how he reached home. He was mentally and physically tired. He wanted to sleep.

When Jerry reached home, he was in for a surprise. His entire home was ransacked. Everything lay on the floor… including the stuff from the fridge. Jerry could see that all the veggies were lying on the floor.

"So, these guys came here for getting the papers… Prof. Matthew was right. I should have listened to him." Jerry said to himself. That was the last thought in his mind. Something heavy struck on his head from behind and Jerry collapsed on the floor with thud.

Langley, Virginia, US

October 29, 2024; 03.30 PM

"What did you do with the kid?" Russ asked

"Kid? Oh, he was about 22-23. We sort of banged him on his head from behind. He was gone alright. We checked, didn't we?" the man answered.

"And what are these?" Russ showed the file folder and the papers which were on his table.

"Ah those… the papers Sir. You wanted."The man smiled and replied.

"You can take them to clean your backside. This is trash. This is of no use. These are not the papers that we wanted. You idiots. Get lost… Get out." Russ shouted.

Russ knew that his game was over. The papers were either with Leo or with Jerry who must have kept them in some safe place….and they may suddenly surface at some time in future. But in any case, he, Russ, would be gone.

SecDef had addressed the press and the media. He laughed it out as a big prank. "Such things like Sun Gun never existed, nor will they ever exist except perhaps in Hollywood." He had laughed it out and had gone on to suggest that perhaps Russia might be putting the Sun Gun in the space…. If they do it, we will do it, then perhaps Chinese will do it, then India will do it, then perhaps Germany will do it… So, you see we all will have

Laser guns… ha ha ha ha… He had laughed aloud. "Yes, but one day very soon Russia may put the nukes in space…. That is something we will not tolerate."

He had ended the press briefing on an extremely high note. He had, however, ensured that Operation Castellon and Operation Taranis were still on and would be completed as scheduled.

Langley, Virginia, US

Nash was sitting in front of the fireplace and was burning the papers from a file folder. For the past one hour he had read through the handwritten document… which he thought was quite impressive given the context and the material. The main objective was to expose the shenanigans of the Deep State elements… but it was only half achieved.

"Another 7 days to go and we will know the results of the elections. If the Reps come to power, maybe… just maybe… these behind the curtain activities may get curtailed if not stop." Nash thought to himself.

Meercat had left Leo at midnight and had gone to Jerry's place. Jerry was fast asleep. Meercat had entered Jerry's house, retrieved the file folder… replaced it with some garbage literature and had gone without making a sound. Jerry was still sleeping like a baby. Meercat then walked across the street… to his temporary home… to # 208.

Meercat had then delivered the file folder to Nash at 8.00 AM. If anyone had searched #208, they would have found nothing…. No fingerprints… no evidence of any kind.

Nash had learned about Jerry late in the evening. He felt extremely sorry for the kid, but he could not have saved him.

"Had he not called Leo while he was in the Mall, Jerry would be safe." Nash thought.

Nash had also learned about Sergei the same evening. Apparently, Sergei had just disappeared from his place in Vienna, Austria. Grapevine was that he had defected to Russia. "Yeah… perhaps he might be building something under the Lake Baikal to live there." Nash smiled and thought to himself… "Now that the cat is out of the bag, soon we will have quite a few "Private Death Stars" roaming around the earth… The American, the German, the Russian and perhaps the Chinese."

"The entire purpose of the Deep Sate is to get undisputed ownership of the Space, Land and Water and control everybody living on the planet. Whichever party comes to power, the Deep Sate will always thrive." Nash thought to himself.